THE HISTORY OF TELEVISION

THE HISTORY OF TELEVISION

RICK MARSCHALL

GALLERY BOOKS
An imprint of W.H. Smith Publishers Inc.
112 Madison Avenue
New York, New York 10016

A Bison Book

Published by Gallery Books
A Division of W H Smith Publishers Inc.
112 Madison Avenue
New York, New York 10016

Produced by
Bison Books Corp.
17 Sherwood Place
Greenwich, CT 06830

Copyright © 1986 Bison Books Corp.

ISBN 0-8317-4218-6

Printed in Hong Kong

1 2 3 4 5 6 7 8 9 10

CONTENTS

THE BEGINNINGS

Previous spread: The first mass-produced RCA black and white television set — 1946.

In commercial terms, television fairly well burst on the scene in 1948. To the children of the 1980s, a backwards glance at entertainment history would include the Age of Radio before TV, sound movies before radio's Golden Age and, way back, silent movies. (What in the world did people do with their time before that?)

But in fact television was frequently discussed and conspicuously experimented with for two decades before 1948. It was often a matter of speculation even before that; many cartoons looked forward to the day when pictures and sounds could travel through the ether. Fiction, too—and not always science-fiction—considered the possibilities. Edward Bellamy's *Looking Backward* (1888) predicted the transmission of 'music and sermons' for the masses on 'musical telephones.' Later, an uncanny vision of the future was presented in Charlie Chaplin's *Modern Times* (1936): Charlie is discovered smoking in the washroom by his boss via TV monitor.

In a sense all the predictions were not startlingly prescient. The inevitable march toward television was plain to see in both communication and technology. Literature and art—the combination of story and image—had been on converging courses for centuries. The precursors were cave paintings that told stories; medieval tapestries that recounted whole battles; Renaissance triptychs that portrayed the Passion story; the morality cartoons of Hogarth and Gillray and the picture-stories of Rodolphe Töpffer and Wilhelm Busch. At the end of the 19th century—all within ten years of each other—this narrative/visual synthesis found its apogee in three separate but related forms: the motion picture, the comic strip and the animated cartoon.

The technological imperative was no less inexorable. To add to Franklin and Faraday's experiments with electricity, there were Volta's battery; the theories of Ohm, Ampere, and Henry, whose work all ran in currents; Morse's telegraph; Caselli's 'photo-telegrams' that reproduced the sender's handwriting; Herr Professor Nipkow's disc-scanner, a crude but prototypical television of 1884; Bell's telephone and scores of Edison's discoveries, including the talking machine, the motion picture, the electric light and the rectifier.

To join these honored scientists, inventors and tinkerers, came a corps of Electronic-Age geniuses bent on using the very air (or ether, that theoretical substance that transports pulsating 'waves') for communication—messages, signals, even entertainment. Hertz discovered waves; Marconi sent messages over them; De Forest developed oscillators; Zworykin received patents for the iconoscope and kinescope, which enabled the capturing and transmission of television images, and, in England, John L Baird organized a regular system of television broadcasting.

In Dr Baird's time (he introduced wireless television in 1925) there were concurrent experiments elsewhere in the world. In America there were public demonstrations of television by AT&T in 1922 and General Electric in 1928. On 7 April, 1927, Dr Herbert Ives of Bell Laboratories watched an image in his office of a tap-dancer, televised from the sunlit skyscraper roof above. He soon was able to display a moving image of Herbert Hoover (then Secretary of Commerce) to an audience in New York—a 'live' transmission from Hoover's office in Washington, DC. In 1928 General Electric's experimental television station, W2XCW in Schenechtady, New York, began thrice-weekly half-hour broadcasts simultaneous with programs over its radio station WGY. The same year the station broadcast television's first live drama, *The Queen's Messenger*, with separate cameras focused on every actor as well as on a prop table for close-ups other than faces! And, in England, daily television transmissions on the BBC began.

For all the activity, these experiments were

Below: Samuel F B Morse, the inventor of the telegraph. On the table is his telegraph key.

still just that—experiments, often crude and usually impractical. It is fascinating to consider that just at the moment when the novelty of sound was added to pictures ('all-talking, all-singing' movies), pictures were being added to sound (that is, radio was receiving its visual missing half via television). Yet silent movies were obsolete relics by 1930, and television was a full two decades away from wide-spread acceptance and utility. Why?

Just as the answer lay in a multitude of obstacles, mostly technical and commercial, so did television's advent rely on a new group—not of ideas, which had converged through the centuries in a seemingly inevitable rendezvous; and not of scientists, although they were still essential path-finders. The new group consisted of entrepreneurs. Businessmen saw the commercial possibilities in television, sniffed the value of patents and dreamed of the manufacturing bonanzas. So while in England and on the continent, state-subsidized television assured its measured growth and support, in America, TV's Bronze Age is filled with fits and starts, wild improvisations and a gambler's style of mid-wifery.

There were also ridiculous predictions; now that television seemed to be closer than ever, the

Above: *An elderly Thomas Alva Edison speaking into his dictaphone machine.*

Left: *Thomas Alva Edison at age 31, with an early model of his phonograph.*

anticipation was, in some quarters, breathless. In July of 1930 a Schenectady theater installed a temporary, five-foot screen for television images – ironically as part of its vaudeville, not movie, portion of the show – and the *Theatre Guild* magazine reported the occasion thusly: 'With this successful experiment, the technical arrangements are virtually complete for projecting on normal-size motion picture screens . . . television will be a regular feature in the large RKO theaters before the New Year.'

David Sarnoff was no less a publicist, but he was an official of RCA, the Radio Corporation of America, and the National Broadcasting Company. He was also frequently given a platform in *The New York Times's* science pages, where he wrote on 13 July, 1930 that 'television would be a theater in every house,' with benefits for children, and would provide 'cultural education.' He even nobly foresaw the television as a vehicle for 'home art galleries.' Sarnoff also looked to the day when 'color as well as shadow' could be transmitted.

A year earlier Dr Vladimir Zworykin, his expertise and his patents, joined RCA. Sarnoff fully expected RCA to be the leading manufacturer and seller of the television sets that his visions of culture and art would need to enter the home. Nevertheless his own background was vitally

Above: *Professor John Logie Baird with his first television apparatus, built in January 1927.*
Right: *Lee De Forest, the inventor of the three-element audion tube.*
Opposite top: *The young Marchese Guglielmo Marconi, photographed with his 'black box' — the first apparatus for wireless telegraphy — when he arrived in England in February 1896.*
Opposite bottom: *David Sarnoff, RCA executive and visionary of home entertainment.*

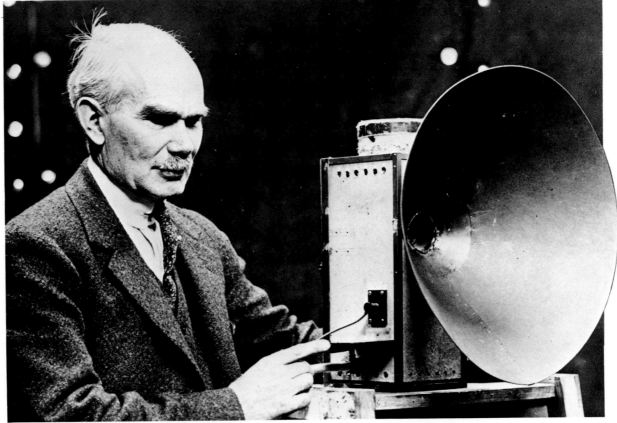

involved with new forms of communication. Sarnoff was a youthful wireless operator in 1912 when he received the first news of the *Titanic's* disastrous collison with an iceberg. He remained at his post for 72 hours and from this came his belief in wireless impulses as essential modes of communication; he also, as he moved up the corporate ladder of the American Marconi Company and its successor, RCA, foresaw entertainment as well as communication and commerce.

'I have in mind [he wrote in a 1916 memo to his superiors] a plan of development which would make radio a household utility. The idea is to bring music into the home by wireless. The

Below: *Felix the Cat (and later Mickey Mouse) was a pioneering 'performer' on television in the United States. During the late 1920s, Felix and Mickey whirled for hours on a phonograph turntable in front of television 'eyes' while RCA and NBC engineers in the field made reception tests.*

receiver can be designed in the form of a simple "radio music box" and arranged for several different wave lengths . . . events of national importance can be simultaneously announced and received. Baseball scores can be transmitted in the air. This proposition would be especially interesting to farmers and others living in outlying districts.'

What now seems so mundane was revolutionary when the young Sarnoff proposed it, and he brought the same long-range vision to the nascent technology of television.

First there were problems to be overcome, however. Radio waves could be picked up on crystal sets, even without electricity. But tele-

vision necessitated masses of wires and tubes, sophisticated cameras and broadcast arrangements, and troublesome receivers. To the nightmarish financial hurdles for broadcasters and consumers was added the fact that television, unlike radio, could transmit to an effective radius of only approximately 45 miles. Hardly dismayed, Sarnoff and his fellow competitors — William S Paley of Columbia Broadcasting, Allen DuMont of DuMont Labs, Philo Farnsworth of Philco and others — merely gritted their teeth and pursued their goals.

Their progress can adorn the textbooks of American enterprise and ingenuity, but some of their techniques were odd. The first television

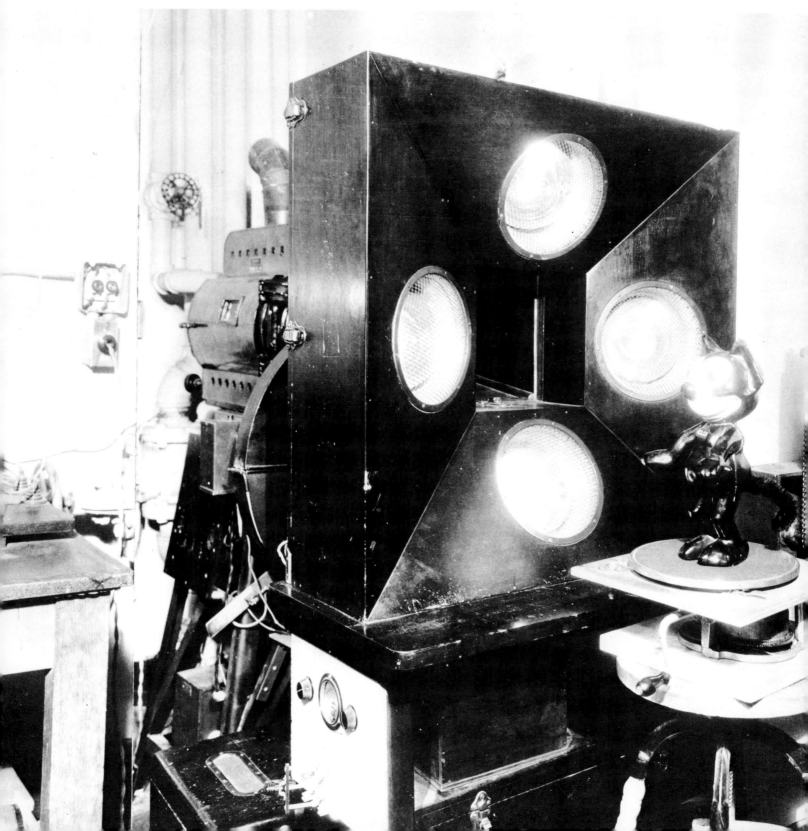

star was not a person but a doll — Felix the Cat. To constantly monitor factors of definition and transmission, a small replica of Otto Meesmer's classic cartoon creation was placed on a rotating phonographic turntable. Under bright lights and before test-pattern backgrounds, Felix spun for a dizzying decade as technicians checked, adjusted and improved their equipment. Besides the fact that the doll worked cheaper than actors, his advantage was a solid black figure, his staying power, and his impervious nonchalance under the lights; early television studios required exceptionally bright lights for contrast and definition in figures. Crew members wore pith helmets to avoid the technological age's indoor equivalent of the sunstroke. (*The New York Times*, by the way, in reporting Felix's contributions to increasing the number of lines on the TV screen — thereby sharpening the image — characteristically mis-identified the lowly cartoon figure as Mickey Mouse.)

Schenectady may have experimented with five-foot screens, but most of the sets in use displayed images on smaller screens. In 1933, in a demonstration of cathode-rays, a 200-line screen (3 × 4 inches!) achieved sharp definition. Televisions progressed from indistinct 60-line scans to 120, 180, 240, 343, and 441 lines.

In 1936 RCA showed off its advances in technology and larger-screen sets. It had begun field

Below: A televised image of Felix the Cat as he appeared in the early television experiments of the late 1920s.

Above: A 1935 demonstration of a televised program of a horse show from the Crystal Palace Grounds in London, using the Baird Intermediate Film High Definition process.

tests to 'iron out the kinks' on 29 June, when a ten-watt transmitter was installed atop the Empire State Building; on 7 July the Company staged a show for its invited licensees. The show's program: speeches by three RCA executives; 20 lively Walter Lily Dancers; a film of a locomotive; a Bonwit Teller fashion show; actor Henry Hull offering a monologue from his role in *Tobacco Road*; Graham McNamee and Ed Wynn doing comedy bits and a film of army maneuvers.

The 225 licensees, and a limited number of public eavesdroppers, huddled around small flickering screens in a semi-darkened lab room. They were told by David Sarnoff that outside the labs, three sets were in operation in the New York area, the furthest being in Harrison, New Jersey. He added that there were no plans for RCA to design commercial television sets that year.

On 6 November RCA repeated the event, this time for the press. Three hundred guests beheld 20 TV sets in a row, some 6× 8-inch mirror-tops and the rest 8 × 10-inch front-facing screens. These were prototypes of commercial sets, and a reporter for the New York *Herald-Tribune* recalled the early novelty days of nickelodeons as reporters gathered around the 'greenish-white' images that were 'less flickering than home movies.' Betty Goodwin, who was to be the RCA/NBC announcer at these early events for years to come, welcomed the guests to the broadcast.

On this day the broadcast consisted of a newsreel of Franklin Roosevelt; footage of a storm in Greenland and the Italian army at maneuvers; music by the Ink Spots (singing 'Mama Don't 'Low No Piano Playin' in Here') and Hildegarde; a Robert Benchley comedy monologue and a newsreel explanation of the television studio's procedures.

Significantly, there was still more of an audience in the control room than there was in the entire metropolitan area. Sarnoff announced at this occasion that there were now 50 sets around New York — most of them in the homes of RCA technicians, who could check reception.

Amid this activity, D.H. Munro, television chief of the BBC, visited New York. Although by this time the British were broadcasting with more regularity than the Americans, his reflections were more aesthetic than commercial; he was 'terrified,' he reported, that small screens and their attendant technical problems, the inevitability of close-ups and small casts of players, would 'limit the scope of productions.' At the time the BBC was telecasting daily experimental programs from Alexandra Palace. Events like the Derby and Wimbledon were seen in over 3000 home sets in use around London.

EMI was developing television receivers in England, and in France experiments were being conducted from atop the Eiffel Tower. There were active laboratories in Holland (working on 405-line screens, the most advanced to that point),

Above: *Columbia Broadcasting System executives checking their television plans in 1930. Left to right: E K Cohan, William S Paley, H V Akerberg and G Stanley McAllister.*

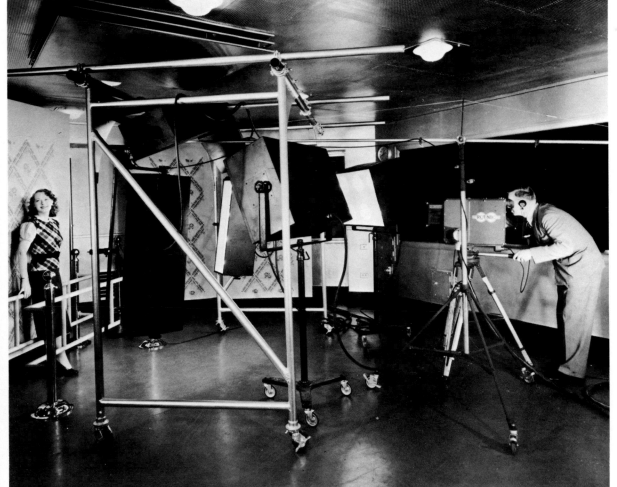

Left: *A 1938 New York television studio. Betty Goodwin, NBC's first television announcer, is before the camera and is being televised over the experimental station W2XBS in New York.*

15

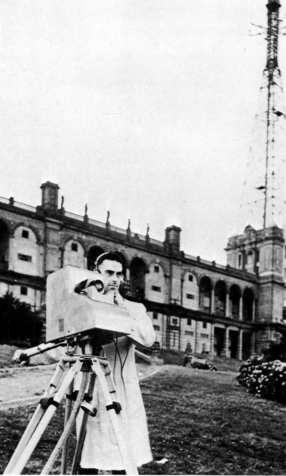

Above: *The British Broadcasting Corporation televised the Derby from Epsom for the first time on 1 June 1931.*

Right: *The Marconi-EMI Instantaneous television camera stands in front of the Alexandra Palace television station in London.*

Opposite: *The Berlin Olympic Games of 1936 were televised.*

and in Germany television was reaching sophisticated levels. There was widespread television coverage of the Olympic Games at Berlin in 1936; events were filmed by a movie camera, developed in two minutes, and broadcast.

Nineteen thirty-six was also a watershed year in the progress toward network and widespread broadcasting in the US. On 1 December Bell Laboratories tested the coaxial cable, an innovation that allowed simultaneous carrying of many telephonic transmissions. But already its significance for the infant industry of television was recognized; the coaxial cable was instantly nicknamed 'the TV Pipe', and Dr Frank Jewett stated that 'this is not a television circuit . . . but it is a necessary step toward television.' The test line was between New York and Philadelphia.

In Philadelphia, at the Franklin Institute, David Sarnoff demonstrated that commercial foresight is not synonymous with wisdom: 'Unlike a play on a stage or a motion picture, which may run for a year,' he ventured, 'the television program, once it has been shown to a national audience, is on the scrap heap; it is finished.' Possibly with premonitions of *I Love Lucy* dancing in their heads, the Academy of Motion Pictures Arts and Sciences in 1936 empowered a Research Council Scientific Commitee to investigate this new electronic mystery, which was on everyone's mind, and ascertain the threat

to the movie industry. In a formal report the committee foresaw a more orderly reaction than the 'hurried, disorderly, and costly' conversion to sound by Hollywood; after all, television had been discussed for so long. But they also looked forward to the 'technical and commercial complexity' that would continue to impede the popular acceptance of TV – at least until 1937 'or more probably in 1938!' Further, they added, 'it should be noted that its scope, as far as we can prevision it, is limited to home entertainment purposes in urban areas.' It is interesting to note that *Variety*, the show-business daily, for years harbored an animus toward television. This changed when program schedules filled up, when performers switched from stage and radio, and when television companies started buying ad space.

Slowly the technical advances were chipping away at the logistical problems in bringing the TV set into millions of American homes. In 1937, *Life* magazine surveyed the progress but yet had to conclude that 'television is a scientific success but a commercial headache.' In that year David Sarnoff and William Paley traveled together to Europe and were impressed by mechanical and broadcast innovations. They were also impressed by the funding available to the BBC which, in addition to straight government sub-

sidies, received three-fourths of the 'use tax' levied on television set owners. Whether their motives were primarily an acceptance of the American situation or a determined pursuit of advertising revenues – or a combination of both – they returned with a statement looking to 'the American capitalist free-enterprise system' and 'advertisers to support the fledgling television industry.' Massive infusions of capital, they noted, were needed to develop technology and produce shows.

Paley entered broadcasting when his family's Congress Cigar Company of Philadelphia, of which he was advertising manager, doubled their sales because of commercials over the Columbia Radio Network. The Paleys bought controlling interest and in 1928, William, a graduate of the Ohio State University, became president. Columbia eventually achieved radio leadership over NBC and Paley set his own sights on television's future role.

So the course seemed set: develop programming to the point where stage conditions were receptive to the new form; inaugurate (at a loss, of course) a schedule of shows to assure the public of entertainment viability; keep the scientists working to lower costs, increase efficiency and make larger, more attractive home sets; and keep the stream of public-relations chatter flowing – Public relations: the public must be convinced of TV's inevitability and the affordability of sets. Advertisers must be recruited to the new medium. And investors must come – straight-out financiers, as well as licensees, potential appliance-store representatives, parts manufacturers, etc.

Consequently the few pioneer television companies started to produce regular program schedules starting around 1937. By then consumers could buy custom-made sets for less than $500, and a dozen hours of programs a week was their reward. But the companies produced the shows routinely, for publicity value (the schedules were printed in newspapers) and to continue their own refinement process (when technological adjustments had to be made on sets, the manufacturers would send servicemen to homes to effect the synchronization). Many chat and information programs were uniformly mundane, but there was also a constant effort to employ 'name' talent. A typical sampling of early NBC fare in 1937 included Walter Damrosch giving a piano recital; Hildegarde again (she was under contract to NBC and had appeared, incidentally, on television in England and Germany – the first international TV star); fashion shows; the Madison Square Garden six-day bicycle races; Betty Green discussing childrens' fashions; and Pinky Lee, comedian.

There were two notable dramatic presentations in these early days of television. In 1937 Louis Hector starred as Sherlock Holmes in *The Three Garridebs*. The New York *Herald-Tribune* noted that the production would offer 'no serious

Below: *Fontaine Fox, in his cartoon panel, 'Toonerville Folks,' in 1939, poked fun at the impending effects of television.*

PROBLEM OF TELEVISION

"GEE WHIZ! MOM! HOW ELSE AM I GONNA SEE ENNYTHING!"

F.Fox

(© 1939, by Fontaine Fox)

Left: *A 1939 RCA Victor television receiver with its five-inch screen. It had a built-in radio and carried 24 tubes for the television set and eight for the radio.*

Above: *A see-through television receiver with an 8 × 10-inch screen attracted a lot of attention at the 1939 New York World's Fair.*

challenge to the contemporary stage or screen,' but called it 'an interesting welding of film with studio production.' The teleplay combined filmed exterior shots with live interior action much in the way today's contemporary video productions on PBS and the BBC mix film and video. On 7 June, 1938, Gertrude Lawrence starred in an act from her stage success *Susan and God.* It was not, however, for all the publicity it excited, a full-blown event. It was not the whole play, there was little movement, and there were an inordinate number of close-ups, tailored to the small-screen requirements. The actors complained of the 'fearful heat' and the bizarre make-up of oranges, reds and browns (television did not reflect reds at the time). Also in 1938 the first

feature-length movie was presented on television when NBC broadcast *The Scarlet Pimpernel.*

Yet in 1938 there were, reportedly, still but a hundred sets in the United States. And six synchronization adjustments had to be made over 12 months on each of them. The companies continued to produce shows, and NBC inaugurated a tour of its facilities for 50 cents. RCA signed an agreement to broadcast from the New York World's Fair (constructing a Hall of Television in its RCA Pavilion), and CBS hired Gilbert Seldes as its Experimental Television Program Director. He was the network's entertainment counterpart to the brilliant Dr Peter C Goldmark, who was even then developing color television.

The Milennium was always being preached.

RCA announced the marketing of home video sets for 1939. DuMont Labs of Passaic, New Jersey, announced plans to market their sets for $150–$200, and to broadcast Paramount movies (the studio had bought an interest in DuMont), and it began the first assembly-line production of television sets. As TVs went on sale at New York's Bloomingdale's, Abraham & Strauss, and Davega, NBC announced a permanent broadcast schedule of five hours (minimum) a week: still pictures and charts every Tuesday, Wednesday and Thursday from 3 to 4 PM, and live talent or films every Tuesday and Thursday between 8 and 9 PM. New York – no, the United States – appeared ready to break the 100-set mark.

In 1939 a milestone that will be noted with mixed emotions was reached – the first commercial sponsorship of a television program. George Ross's *Show-Biz Interviews* was sponsored by Andrew Geller's shoe store. Nor was sports untainted. Later that year Red Barber switched for a day from WOR/Mutual radio to broadcast a Dodgers-Reds baseball game on NBC. The sponsors were Proctor and Gamble soap products, Wheaties breakfast cereal and Socony oil. Contemporary reports indicate that the images were extremely weak but that the audio, including sponsor notices, was clear as a bell.

Other highlights of the 1939 'season' were live performances of Gilbert and Sullivan's *Cox and Box* and *H M S Pinafore* (with a young Ray Heatherton, later a children's-TV pioneer as 'The Merry Mailman'); location coverage of the premiere of *Gone With the Wind* and Noel Coward's *Hay Fever*. At this time the Federal Communications Commission began to ease its restrictions

Above: *The first opera telecast in the United States incorporated scenes from Pagliacci – 10 March 1940. In the cast were (left to right): Hilda Burke as Nedda, Allesio de Paolis as Beppe, Richard Bonelli as Tonio and Armand Tokatyan as Canio.*
Opposite top: *NBC telecast a Columbia University baseball game in 1939.*
Opposite bottom: *A young Red Barber talking with Dodger manager Leo Durocher before the first professional baseball game ever telecast – Dodgers vs Reds, August 1939.*

and policy strictures, which had heretofore been blamed on fears of 'letdowns' among consumers. It appeared evident that the persuasive arguments of the young television lobby, somehow paralleling its financial strength, were slowly overtaking the traditional industry interests. Moreover, the radio and film industries – in addition to those companies already involved in TV production and manufacturing – were casting hungry eyes on this growth industry.

Even so, Europe was still far ahead of America in certain areas. The New York *Herald-Tribune* reported in 1939 that the 'BBC with its schedule of two or more telecasts every day as contrasted with the present American average [two to five hours a week] is the measure between a smooth-running, relatively intensive program schedule and a schedule hardly out of the engineering demonstration class.' The article noted the advantages of government support and didn't mention, but could have, the vast geographical obstacles to national service in the United States. 'What is very popular in England and unknown over here,' the article continued,' is the 90-minute play . . . The British have turned over television to trained program showmen; the Americans are not as advanced in that regard.'

The article also notes the trend of major New York stores and restaurants featuring TVs as 'crowd-catchers.' One location was 'so congested that nothing short of a stench bomb seems capable of making people leave the building so that other people can gain admittance.'

Another European comparison was noted by T H Hutchinson, Television Program Director for RCA/NBC, who visited Germany shortly before the War. He reported 'frank amazement' at the strides in European television programming and technology. Returning to the US, he spoke of 'pictorially perfect stages' and sets with 20 to 26-inch diameters, as well as 12×14-foot screens. He examined a dozen models available to consumers, and – observing studio-production sets – noted a routine use of six cameras on each stage, and the widespread use of a coaxial cable. Back home, America was catching up. In 1941 full approval was granted by the FCC for commercial TV operation. A Dodgers-Pirates baseball game was broadcast from Ebbets Field in Brooklyn, and a Bulova clock was displayed to announce the time – for a commercial fee of nine dollars.

During the War, television – which had just seemed to be gaining its long-awaited impetus –

Left: *Harry Lillis 'Bing' Crosby was an early television star whose relaxed demeanor gained him even more fans.*

Opposite top: *'Buffalo Bob' Smith playing his ukelele for the kids in the 'Peanut Gallery.' Entrance to the Peanut Gallery was something special and had to be booked months in advance. Some mothers threatened to kill for tickets for their moppets.*
Opposite bottom: *Buffalo Bob and his upstaging marionette – Howdy Doody.*

was curtailed severely. CBS offered a nightly newsreel, and presented *The Gillette Cavalcade of Sports*, consisting mostly of boxing and wrestling matches easy to present over television – static platforms, well-lit, with minimal production demands. Very occasional sports programs afforded the only daytime programming through the War Years.

In 1945 The American Broadcasting Company tentatively went on the air with chat and variety programs. ABC was a re-formed branch of NBC that had been required under an anti-monopoly edict to be divested. In its early years it rented studio facilities from its rivals, and only became a network in 1948 when WCAU in Philadelphia signed on as an affiliate. ABC's first stars were

Henry Morgan and Bing Crosby, while DuMont had Ed and Pegeen Fitzgerald hosting a variety program, and Ted Mack bringing his famous *Amateur Hour* over from radio. NBC discovered it had one of television's first 'personalities' when John Cameron Swayze, slick-voiced and with trademark boutonniere, became the popular host of the *Camel News Hour*. Dennis James, later a ubiquitous game-show host, was a football announcer for DuMont and Mel Allen, later the voice of the New York Yankees and probably the most famous 'voice' in American sports broadcasting, inaugurated his television career as host of *College Football* on CBS.

In 1947 baseball's World Series was very conveniently played between two New York teams

(the Yankees and the Dodgers) and was televised. Coaxial cables were being laid as fast as they could be, but there was as yet no national network; there were two regional networks in the East and the Midwest, but there was finally real numbers in the category of private TV-set ownership – 170,000 sets. President Harry S Truman's State of the Union message was televised. He was not yet reaching a vast video audience, but it was at least a significant audience. Soon thereafter that audience was reached by NBC's *Puppet Television Theater*, starring Buffalo Bob Smith and Howdy Doody. Foreshadowing President Reagan's 'Star Wars' offer to the Russians, RCA in 1947 offered to share its technology with rival manufacturers in order to speed up the sale of television sets.

Also in 1947 an interesting event occurred. E F McDonald Jr, the president of Zenith Radio Corporation, postulated that advertising revenues alone could not pay for television's expansion and production costs. To support the future of TV, he declared, the public would have to pay for programs the same as it did for magazines, newspapers, and movies.

The interesting event? Nobody listened.

The Television Age had finally come, and no one was prepared to let any more delays — whether due to technical difficulties or theoretical interruptions — stop the show.

THE
FORTIES AND
FIFTIES

By 1948 television had arrived. After all the years of rumors, all the articles concerning its imminent arrival, all the promotion about its inevitability, all the tantalizing peeks under the tent-flap, it had come to America. Many homes had it – thousands by the week ordering them – and those that didn't knew that it was merely a matter of time. The collective public mind had crossed the imaginary Rubicon: TV was no longer thought of as a fantasy, a curiosity, or even a luxury. It was being thought of as a necessity.

TV was in the position of the struggling singer who makes the big time with a hit after a career of disappointing records. Television was, in 1948, a 20-year overnight success.

Perhaps the clearest view of the country's new love affair was offered by a foreign visitor. Alistair

Cooke – a transplanted Englishman who eventually became a fixture on American TV screens via hosting *Omnibus* and *Masterpiece Theatre* – offering the following observations in an essay titled 'The Television Craze in America' for the BBC in 1949.

'. . . Television is going to be part of our world. And people who try to ignore it, or preach against it, or keep their children away from it, are soon going to show up as "nutty" people, exercising their virtue in a vacuum, like old gentlemen who brandish sticks at motor-cars . . . We are doomed – or privileged, according to your point of view – to be the television generation.

'[The promoters and radio stars] are not worried, because they know the technical possibilities. They have watched the great rush for television sets before any great news event, and *after* the discovery of only one great television comedian – Milton Berle.'

Cooke observed that Berle 'did very nicely in night clubs and none too well in radio, but his swift pantomime and absolute mastery of a forgotten library of vaudeville gags and situations has brought the intimate nonsense of vaudeville back with a bang. The radio comedians, more than any other radio stars, appear ready to accept the fate they fear: the end of mass radio. Thereby they can help it come true. "All I know about television," said Bob Hope lately – and he spoke for legions in the radio and the movies – "is, I want to get into it as soon as possible."

'It may all lead to galloping arthritis of the lower limbs. But Americans have put up with more chronic nagging ailments – radio advertising, for instance. If they can take radio commercials in sight *and* sound, and they are taking it gamely, they can put up with anything.'

Apart from his comments on Americans' indiscriminate cultural masochism, Cooke touched the surface of truth with his views of vaudeville on TV. In the first dozen years of the Television Era – a period that most will concede to be the Golden Age of Television – television did best what it *could* do best. That is, it could have immediately turned to two-dimensional comedies, hackneyed quiz shows, and formula dramas. Instead, it postponed those creative turns and thought very hard about the limitations as well as the special potentialities of the form.

Whether such celebrations actually occurred or whether TV's first generation was merely astonishingly adaptable and gifted, we have little record. But the outstanding accomplishments of television's first dozen years were mostly in the fields perfectly suited for the small screen:

Slapstick comedy, built on unsophisticated premises and stage settings, and relying on visual humor.

Live drama of the intimate, not the grand, sort, actually involving the viewer more than he had ever been throughout the history of drama.

Previous spread: Desi Arnaz Jr (left), Sr (center) and Lucille Ball in I Love Lucy. **Opposite:** *Milton Berle, 'Mr Television,' in typical burlesque costume – baggy pants, loud jacket and all – carrying a baseball bat.* **Below:** *In 1945, Berle began his long career on television, for CBS, starring in a show called 'Let Yourself Go.'*

News. Television, in public-affairs events (not the instant sort of news, which would only be captured by TV in the days of portable cameras) was able to both inform and propagandize in ways that newspapers and newsreels and radio news could never do.

The medium Bob Hope yearned to enter in 1948 consisted of four networks — already the lexicon of a new technology was accepted without quotation marks or asterisks — totalling only 37 stations in but 22 East-coast cities. No matter: stars and advertisers alike were as certain of continental coverage as the man on Main Street was of his having a set by Christmas.

One advertiser with absolutely no hesitation was Texaco. The oil company had an established hit radio with the *Star Theater*, and wanted to switch to the video tube; further, so sure was the company of the new medium and its nature that it designed a makeover from a drama-and-variety format to a comedy showcase. At the time of these determinations, Milton Berle was a guest host on the *Texaco Radio Star Theater*; he was tried on the TV entry. Then, as part of a planned audition — a kind of on-the-job tryout of refreshing honesty — he was followed by Henny Youngman, Morey Amsterdam, George Price, Jack Carter, Peter Donald, Harry Richman, and then Berle again, twice. Bingo! The chemicals mixed just right — overwhelming favorable reaction from critics and viewers convinced Texaco, and NBC, that Milton Berle was perfect for the job.

More, he was perfect for television, itself, at least in 1948. The humor was visual (and outrageous) — perfect for the small screen. The stage settings were basic, straight-on, theater-like — perfect for the limited technology. The pace was frenetic, and the guests came and went with dizzying abandon — perfect for grabbing viewers' attention. There was even a symbolic rightness to it all: the show was clearly an uninhibited throwback to the vaudeville stage, and as such represented the prototypical aura of it all. Performers knew that they, as well as Berle, were pioneers in a new medium. Before 'Uncle Miltie' there were television hits — *Ted Mack's Amateur Hour* and *Howdy Doody* were certifiable Vid Presences — but it was all still a competition with radio.

The *Texaco Star Theater*, with Berle seemingly present every moment as host and sketch-participant, usually in bizarre burlesque costumes, was not at all as slap-dash as the frenetic pace might have suggested. It had a relatively big budget for productions and guests, and was managed tightly; even the ad-libs, so much a trademark of the sketches, were neatly timed, if not actually planned. After a few months, store managers and restaurateurs and movie theater managers noticed something on Tuesday nights: their trade was down. People stayed home to watch Uncle Miltie; bought TVs to watch Uncle Miltie. The final triumph — really so swift once

the battle lines were drawn — of TV over radio entertainment was complete and symbolic. People used to stay home, too, for radio's *Amos and Andy*; theater owners used to interrupt their fare and place a radio tuned to the comedy on stage, so patrons would not foresake the movies. Uncle Miltie was also Mr Television, but he might also have been dubbed Uncle Moses. Via the *Texaco Star Theater's* videogenic atmosphere, Milton Berle delivered the Promised Land.

Berle's formal debut on the new show was 8 June 1948. Less than two weeks later another institution was born: *The Toast of the Town*. If Berle was born-again vaudeville and burlesque, then Ed Sullivan revived the traditions of legit variety. Sullivan, a former sports reporter for

Ed Sullivan, the inexperienced gossip columnist who hosted the very first variety show for CBS and went on to rule the Sunday night airwaves for more than 20 years, featured acts from around the globe.

impressionists (led by Will Jordan; in a sense all the others were doing Jordan doing Sullivan) also seized on Sullivan's catch-phrase 'Really big show' when listing his acts. The host occasionally became a performer, but usually only as straight-man to a puppet, Topo Gigio — and even at that he never overcame his awkwardness. Usually Americans want their favorites to be larger than life and better than themselves (forever creating ersatz royalty out of politicians and movie stars), but sometimes they take to someone as humble as themselves; Ed Sullivan was an unlikely early superstar who greatly defined television's flavor and role for a generation.

Later in 1948, CBS introduced a show that was to be another pathfinder: *Studio One*. Live drama, so tentative in TV's early days, staked its claim in the new territory with a production of *The Storm*, starring two actors who remained as constant figures on the screen through the years, Dean Jagger (in addition to many guest roles, he would play the principal on *Mr Novak*) and John Forsythe (later of *Bachelor Father* and, of course, *Dynasty*).

Before the significant year of 1948 closed, another personality came to television, a man who seemingly charted the middle course between Berle's humor and Sullivan's everyman appeal. Arthur Godfrey brought his CBS radio *Talent Scouts* to the screen — simultaneously broadcasting on TV and radio — and was a hit as much for his relaxed folksiness as for hosting the acts he introduced. Although most of the performers were eminently forgettable, he did 'discover' a wealth of certifiable talent, including the McGuire Sisters, Julius LaRosa (whom he later fired — on the air — for 'lacking humility'), and Patsy Cline, whose first appearance made her an overnight star and occasioned a hurried demand performance the following week. Red-haired, freckle-faced Godfrey would chuckle and purr, chat about his sponsor's products instead of pitch them, and sing little ukelele songs when the spirit moved him. He was so popular that he had a concurrent show, *Arthur Godfrey and Friends* (LaRosa was one) on the nightly schedule, and a four-day-a-week morning show, *Arthur Godfrey Time*.

In 1949 the daytime schedule was opening up beyond the variety formats of the Arthur Godfreys. Housewives were identified as the target audience and, appropriately, household items were advertised. One of radio's last bastions, the serial drama, was raided, and when detergent products underpinned their sponsorship the shows were christened as they had been in radio, 'Soap Operas.' DuMont's *Faraway Hills* and NBC's *These Are My Children* were the first of their ilk.

Other teletraditions were established before the 1940s ended. John Cameron Swayze became the first 'news personality' when the *Camel News Caravan* found success. Since then television has

the racy *New York Graphic* in the 1920s and thereafter a Broadway columnist for the New York *Daily News* (that paper's answer to Walter Winchell), introduced acts and then withdrew to let them do whatever they did that justified their invitation. Sullivan thereby gave television a true showcase of variety — in an incredible 23-year run, there was everything from embarrassingly corny trained-dog routines to Russian ballet; TV debuts of Elvis Presley and the Beatles; acts of such unpredictability that scores of impressionists (who found a gold mine in Sullivan's perpetual awkwardness, strange posture, and inevitable malapropisms) would announce: 'Right here, tonight on our stage, the entire Boer War! C'mon — let's hear it!' The

Above: *Al Hodge, as* Captain Video, *tests a new zapgun.*
Above right: *A very young Tony Randall got his start on* Captain Video, *went on to* Mr Peepers *and finally hit pay dirt with* The Odd Couple.
Opposite: *William Boyd, a washed-up Hollywood romantic leading man, made a comeback by playing Hopalong Cassidy in the movies and later became a millionaire because he owned his own* Hopalong Cassidy *television show.*

been replete with news personalities (as opposed to journalists, a distinction usually lost on the viewing public and always ignored by the news personality), and he was to continue his career with intermingled stints as quiz-show host, commercial pitchman, and even actor. *Ripley's Believe It Or Not* debuted on NBC's Tuesday schedule — hosted by Robert Ripley himself, believe it or not — and spawned the tradition of viewer-participation anthology pastiches like *You Asked For It*, and another generation's *Believe It Or Not*. Inspired by the DuMont network's popular broadcasts of wrestling, ABC introduced *Roller Derby*, and both sports were perfect for the television screen. Their violence was only outdone by their phoniness, and the bizarre personalities and names of the athletic actors — played with ferocious seriousness — proved that TV could be a theater of the absurd too. Jon Gnagy turned a generation of American youngsters into aspiring artists. With his trademark flannel shirt and goatee (in the 1940s? This guy has *gotta* be an artist!), he endlessly drew spheres, cones and vanishing points and pitched art supplies for Art Brown, Inc.

In June of 1949 two more genres made their bow. William Boyd brought his hundred-odd (and some were very odd) *Hopalong Cassidy* feature films to Sunday afternoons, and the TV Western was established; virtually absent today, at one time it overwhelmed all other forms of TV programming. And DuMont introduced an incredible package of five-day-a-week low-budget hokum, *Captain Video*. First played by Richard Coogan and then Al Hodge, Captain Video proved — and it was possibly the first major proof of a truth that has since gained the force of one of Nature's Laws — that production values and quality writing had virtually no relationship to audience acceptance. The show was perched at just such a ladder rung in the business that many starving actors in their salad days — including Jack Klugman, Tony Randall, and Ernest Borgnine — got their video starts in its spacey scripts.

As the schedules needed filling, a thematic virtuosity asserted itself. Many shows failed, but many displayed staying power. *The Lone Ranger* — he of masked mysteriousness and veteran's status of Fran Striker's novels, a comic strip, movie serials, and a radio show — became one of the fledgling ABC's first hits. He was played by Clayton Moore, with his faithful Indian sidekick Tonto played by Jay Silverheels. *The Life of Riley* pioneered the now-standard video stereotype of the American father as Fool. The blue-collar comedy ran for a while on NBC, with Rosemary DeCamp and a seemingly uncomfortable Jackie Gleason as Chester A Riley; it seems, in retrospect, that he was waiting for Ralph Kramden to materialize, but another factor added to the melancholic mood of the show — it had no laugh track and was not filmed before a live audience. Despite all the insulting idiocies perpetrated in the name of TV comedy, Gleason's *Life of Riley* (and early episodes of *M*A*S*H* later on) proved that the small screen

Opposite top: *Sid Caesar and Imogene Coca were the toast of Saturday night with their comedy on the hour-and-a-half* Your Show of Shows.

Below: *The Lone Ranger (Clayton Moore) and Tonto (Jay Silverheels) discover dirty work at the crossroads.*

needed the communal ambiance of the theater to 'feel right.' In 1953 a more appropriate William Bendix, with Marjorie Reynolds, Tom D'Andrea, Gloria Blondell, Martin Milner, Sterling Holloway, and Henry Kulky — and the laugh-track — proved a success; the new *Life of Riley* ran on NBC five years. Bendix's catch-line, 'What a revoltin' development *this* turned out to be!' became the first of many phrases to be spawned by television and to become part of the national vocabulary.

And, finally, the game show reared its head to claim its place in TV's artificial sun. Diverting to the audience (sometimes even challenging to their minds), always varied in content if not form, and deliciously cheap to stage and pro-

duce, the game show had been a feature of radio and TV from its earliest moments. But a prime-time entry, *What's My Line?*, convinced everyone that quizzes and games had their major place in the scheme of things. John Daly, a self-consciously distinguished news reader from ABC, was borrowed by CBS for the games. A regular panel (consisting through the years of celebrities like Bennett Cerf, Dorothy Kilgallen, and Arlene Francis) had to guess the professions of eccentric nobodies and — through their blindfolds — mystery somebodies. It was genuine fun, and the long-running daytime and weeknight game proved to be the flagship for the gameshow factory of Mark Goodson and Bill Todman.

As the new decade dawned, so did a new

type of television. On 25 February 1950, *Your Show of Shows* debuted on NBC. Headlined by Sid Caesar, but really lorded over by producer Max Liebman, new heights of comedic virtuosity and brilliant writing were scaled.

Imogene Coca was Caesar's comic sidekick; the pair had been matched with Liebman on TV's *Admiral Broadway Revue*, but for only 17 weeks. It seems that the show was so popular that *Admiral* could not keep pace with the sales demand it generated, and therefore cancelled its advertising vehicle. Nevertheless Liebman carried the magical chemistry of Caesar and Coca to the new show, and added Carl Reiner and Howard Morris to the repertory company. It was indeed a troupe: improvisational in its

Right: *William Bendix and Marjorie Reynolds played Chester A Riley and his wife, Peg, on the NBC version of* The Life of Riley *from 1953 to 1958. Previously, Riley had been played by Jackie Gleason, with Peg played by Rosemary DeCamp, in the Dumont version in the 1949–50 season.*

creative process, the crew was meticulously professional in its presentation, although a madcap ambiance cleverly camouflaged that fact. Caesar was a man of a thousand accents and lightning-quick response; Coca was a virtuoso comedienne in the daffy extreme; Reiner and Morris were perfect foils as straight-men or bit-players for any occasion. Big-name guests clamored to be on *Your Show of Shows*, and the stars created a wealth of zany characters week after week – Prof von Wolfgang, Doris and Charlie Hickenlooper, Somerset Winterset, *et al.*

But just as important as the players were the writers, and here is what set *Your Show of Shows* apart from other ensembles. There has possibly never been a comedic crew assembled like Reiner, Mel Brooks, Neil Simon, Woody Allen, Larry Gelbart, and Selma Diamond, the writers who put the words in Caesar's clever mouth and the premises under his capable feet.

If Berle could prove that TV was a receptive vehicle for stage comedy, then Caesar proved that TV could initiate its own form of consistent ensemble humor. After its all-too-brief five-year run, *Your Show of Shows* left television with a legacy that was occasionally matched but could hardly be surpassed.

Besides thematic improvisation, TV was proving itself capable of format experimentation, not really that surprising in pioneer days. But a late-night variety show proposal was met with scepticism, gloomy predictions – and finally audience acceptance. The brainchild of NBC's Pat Weaver, the genre had a few antecedents but was untested on network insomiacs. Weaver had a vision, however, and even a tip-of-the-tongue instinct for the perfect host. Jan Murray was invited but declined. Creesh Hornsby contracted a fatal disease and died the weekend before the show's debut. Tex McCrary and Jinx Falkenburg – an unlikely husband-and-wife team (he an adman, she a former Miss America) – proved too laconic for the tube; they later secured employment on radio. Wally Cox was too withdrawn, and Martin & Lewis, predictably, were too brash, especially after Jerry Lewis succeeded in smashing a sponsor's 'unbreakable' glass. Weaver's patient but determined search was over, however, when he settled on Jerry Lester.

Lester was a relatively obscure baggy-pants comedian who oftentimes could make Milton Berle look distinguished. But once again the chemistry – unpredictable, crazy antics all compressed on the tiny screen – was right. Part of Lester's ensemble was the chesty Dagmar, confirming the vaudeville prescription with the outlandish costumes and exaggerated mugging. The show was christened *Broadway Open House*, and it was a hit. It ran three nights a week on NBC, with Morey Amsterdam filling the time slot the other two. Sparklingly funny himself, the comic cellist seemed unfortunately pale in

comparison to the manic Lester. Wayne Howell was the announcer and Milton deLugg the musical director; when the program was eventually transformed into *The Tonight Show*, their roles were inherited by Ed McMahon and Doc Severinson, respectively.

Another unlikely smash was *Kukla, Fran, and Ollie*. The Chicago program went national in early 1949 and was a nightly 15 or 30 minutes on NBC, switching to ABC in the fall of 1954. The show was the first of TV's cherished and small group of pixilated programs ostensibly for children but understood by adults (*Rocky and His Friends* and *Soupy Sales* are of this lineage as well).

Burr Tillstrom was the puppeteer, so only his hand-puppets and voice were in evidence, along with the wholesome, unpretentious straight-line presence of Fran Allison between viewer and stage. Kukla was the program's Pogo, honest and earnest; Ollie was the counterpart of Albert the Alligator, a one-toothed dragon of bombast, schemes, and inevitable deflation. (The comic strip *Pogo* and the TV show *Kukla, Fran, and Ollie* were happy affinities whose development was precisely concurrent: there was no 'borrowing' of characters or themes.) Others of the Kuklapolitan players, all engaging in preposterous pursuits and absurd preoccupations, were Fletcher Rabbit, Beulah Witch, Madame Oglepuss, and Colonel Crackie. The delightful intellectual masterpiece that was *Kukla, Fran, and Ollie* survived in different show-cases into the 1970s, where it expired on somewhat appropriately, Educational Television.

The brilliant and insightful Lawrence Spivak

Above: The incomparable Burr Tillstrom was the mastermind of the Kukla *(left),* Fran and Ollie *(right) show that emanated from WBKB in Chicago. Tillstrom also supplied the voices of all the puppets – Kukla, Ollie, Beulah Witch, Fletcher Rabbit, Madame Oglepuss, Colonel Crackie,* et al.

brought his no-nonsense *Meet the Press* from radio to television, and it remains – as it intones today – 'television's longest-running public-affairs program.' It gained nothing intrinsic from the switch, except, possibly, a more willing reservoir of newsmakers to be interviewed in the telegenic era. Through the years the country's most important print journalists asked the questions (it was significant that only gradually did television newsmen join the panels). CBS followed with *Face the Nation* and ABC with *Issues and Answers*. Another radio transplant – this one more logical – was Allen Funt's *Candid Microphone*, which became *Candid Camera* on CBS. The show has lived to this day on network, syndication and re-run, elaborately staging set-ups for unsuspecting citizens. This writer was in the sixth grade of the Village School, in Closter, New Jersey, when *Candid Camera* set up its ill-concealed lens in the gymnasium. I felt clever when I watched the lens following boys in their struggling chin-ups, and ventured a guess (not at all that clever) that *Candid Camera* was filming us. I had mixed emotions when the segment aired, because many of us mugged; our reactions were not honest. But an older and wiser television sage now realizes that such was probably the frequent intention of the staff in the first place.

Musical programs proliferated on early TV, and it was a natural environment. Interestingly, among the first was a pioneer on other forums: Paul Whiteman, who brought jazz to the concert hall and music to radio. The portly, aging bandleader was host of the *Goodyear Review* Sundays on ABC, and, improbably, also hosted

Above: *Eleanor Roosevelt, producer Ted Ayres and Senator Margaret Chase Smith before the 4 November 1956 broadcast of* Face the Nation, *a news program that premiered on 7 December 1954 and still is being broadcast on CBS.*
Right: *Allen Funt brought his* Candid Microphone *radio show to television with* Candid Camera.

a program called *The TV Teen Club*. Whiteman was also ABC's vice president for musical affairs.

Other musical programs included radio stalwarts who were not to be lost in the stampede of the airwaves: Morton Downey; Fred Waring and His Pennsylvanians; Kate Smith (whose theme was 'When the Moon Comes Over the Mountain' before it was eclipsed by 'God Bless America'); *Kay Kyser's College of Musical Knowledge*; Horace Heidt; Bob Crosby; Spike Jones (whose visual antics made radio fans realize they were missing fully half of the musical atrocities); and Ray Anthony. Meredith Wilson, brilliant composer and wit, scored with a Sunday night show on NBC years before his classic Broadway hit *The Music Man*. And Nat King Cole, urbane, smooth, and a genius whose velvety vocals unfortunately overshadowed his jazz-piano talents, ran one season on NBC before a reported lack of sponsorship ended the stint (Cole was black and encountered opposition in some markets in the 1950s).

Two shows that were to have healthy tenures were decidedly *not* mere transfers from radio. Mike Stokey's *Pantomime Quiz* — basically the game of charades, but played by some of Hollywood's most intelligent personalities through the years — could hardly have been done on radio. Likewise *Arthur Murray's Dance Party* was purely visual and resolutely durable,

Far right: *Roy Rogers and Dale Evans in a less-than-serious moment.*
Below: *The incomparable Kate Smith was a radio star singing 'When the Moon Comes Over the Mountain' beginning in the early 1930s, and also was a hit on television.*

as the graying Arthur and Kathryn waltzed right into the rock 'n' roll era.

A pair of mother figures appeared on the scene at the same time but from two very different backgrounds; their concurrent popularity illustrated an unheralded but undeniable democratizing role of television. Both were ethnic and both were somewhat melancholy light comedies about families and life. *Mama* was based on Kathryn Forbes's writings and the adapted stage play *I Remember Mama*. The television program about Norwegian immigrants in 1910 San Francisco starred Peggy Wood as Mama; Rosemary Rice as daughter Katrin, whose nostalgic leafing through family albums opened each episode; and a youthful Dick Van Patten as son Nels (Van Patten was later to be a video parent himself in *Eight Is Enough*).

'Yoo-hoo! Mrs Bloom!' These words opened each episode of *The Goldbergs*, weekly glimpses

his *persona*, which had been camouflaged by radio since Ziegfeld Follies days; on radio, listeners had only his voice and his assurance to know that he was The Perfect Fool. On TV they could see his wonderfully comic face, his silly costumes, and, best of all, his tentative and bumbling manner. One of television's great moments was his dramatic debut a few years later in Rod Serling's *Requiem for a Heavyweight*; and one of television's great stories is the account by Serling and Keenan Wynn how the legendary veteran Ed Wynn fretted to distraction about doing live drama.

Garry Moore brought a variety program to the air; he eventually clicked with one of TV's great ensembles, including Durwood Kirby and Carol Burnett. The crewcut-topped Moore always seemed less talented than his regulars and guests, but had unerring instincts, and was diminished enough so that his stars could shine. Gene Autry, and then Gabby Hayes, and then Roy Rogers, were early entrants in TV's genre of children's Westerns. Autry and Rogers, of course, parlayed their already considerable empires via TV exposure. Gene had his horse Champion and his sidekick Pat Buttram at his side when he signed off with 'Back in the Saddle Again.' Roy had Dale Evans (he, by the way, was 'King of the Cowboys' and she was 'Queen of the West') as well as Trigger the Wonder Horse and Gabby Hayes, recalled from his weekend Western-anthology series. Roy's theme, of course, was 'Happy Trails to You.'

Joining Hoppy, Gene, Roy, and the Lone Ranger in the days before the Adult Western were *The Cisco Kid*; *Annie Oakley*; *Action in the Afternoon* (a Western filmed in Philadelphia's back lots); *Range Rider*; *Wild Bill Hicock*; *Kit Carson*; *Brave Eagle*; *26 Men*; *Judge Roy Bean*; *Buffalo Bill, Jr*; *Tales of the Texas Rangers* and the anthology episodes broadcast on *Death Valley Days*, first hosted by Stanley Andrews and then Ronald Reagan, Robert Taylor, and Dale Robertson.

Perry Como's somnambular style ironically seemed perfect for the TV screen (a Wednesday night slot in 1950 began a long television career, continuing today via annual specials), but Frank Sinatra's flashier appeal somehow was not. Two variety shows of his failed, although one was slated Kamikaze-fashion against the invincible Caesar and his legions. Country music was more congenial to the tube — or at least more adaptable — and DuMont's *Country Style* was the first of many programs, the most prominent being *The Grand Ole Opry*, broadcast from Nashville with all the legendary stars of the day, and Red Foley's *Ozark Jubilee*, from Springfield, Missouri, where many future legends got their start. Each was telecast on ABC.

Three veteran stars of other media were more wary than Sinatra when approaching television. Groucho Marx, still appearing in movies (sometimes without his brothers) but knowing that

into an urban Jewish family's everyday affairs. Its warmth and charm were the direct result of tight creative control of its star, creator, and chief writer, Gertrude Berg; she had managed a solid radio success for the program before switching to the tube. Eli Mintz as Uncle David and Larry Robinson as Sammy were also notable in the cast.

Another character gently brimming with motherly counsel was the black maid Beulah. Less intrusive than a later TV maid, Hazel, and in fact less stereotypical as a maid and as a black than her reputation suggests, *Beulah* was a fine program derogated by civil-rights groups. Before it left the air, however, a trio of talented actresses played the lead: Ethel Waters, Hattie McDaniel and Louise Beavers.

The exodus from radio continued through the early 1950s. Ed Wynn tried a Thursday night show on CBS and was grateful for the return of

those days were numbered, had established himself as a radio host of the quiz show *You Bet Your Life*. Since 1947 it had been a hit, and his entry into videoland was not haphazard. A full staff of writers, audience testing, and tightly controlled scripts (hardly a word was ad-libbed on the seemingly informal show) went into the preparation. The result was satisfactory: Groucho's show was a solid hit and still runs in syndicated replays. His double-entendre remarks were quoted each week, as were the lines 'Say the secret woid and you win a hundred dollahs; something you find around the house,' and 'Tell 'em Groucho sent you.' (What *were* retailers supposed to do upon hearing that news?)

Another veteran was cautiously planning his television move. Jack Benny was as careful as if he were counting pennies into a charity coffer at Christmastime. Wary of making an ill-considered career move, he spent a couple of seasons hosting comedy and variety specials. When he and TV were comfortable with each other – and with public and advertisers clamoring for his presence – he assuredly constructed one of the classic comedy programs of all time.

Left: *Groucho Marx and his announcer, George Fenniman, pose before a telecast of* You Bet Your Life.

Below: *Buddy Hackett appeared in a revived syndicated version of* You Bet Your Life *in the 1980s. It flopped.*

Honed in vaudeville, movies and radio, the Benny *persona* was as well-defined as any in American comic history. At one time his character was that of an egotistical scold, but he had modified it into a personality who received no respect from friends, associates and strangers; whose daily life was full of deflating surprises; whose egotism had mellowed to smugness and excessive cheapness. Likewise his delivery — timing, pacing, inflections and, on television, his expressions — received the precision-craftsmanship of a fine watch. Benny, on television, was one of the few comedians who could make a career of being insulted at every turn; it is surprising that hardly anyone else, save Rodney Dangerfield, adopted the device.

But Benny played his set-upon act against other players, not just in monologues. A brilliant cast of supporting players followed him from the movies and radio: his wife, Mary Livingstone, who played his girl friend on TV; his valet, Eddie 'Rochester' Anderson; twitty singer Dennis Day, always pleading for more air time; pesky announcer Don Wilson, always angling for himself and his nitwit blimp of a son,

Harlow; Frank Nelson ('Yessssssss?'), who was the impertinent clerk wherever Benny shopped and Mel Blanc, who played several roles. Blanc was Prof LeBlanc, defeated violin teacher to the confident Benny; he was the off-stage 'sound' of Benny's barely serviceable Maxwell auto and he was the monosyllabic Mexican. ('What's your name?' 'Sy.' 'Sy?' 'Si.' 'And your sister?' 'Sue.' 'What does she do?' 'Sew.' 'Sew?' 'Si.')

Jack Benny attracted the biggest celebrities as guests and continued his comedy into the 1970s. His personality and delivery drew the viewer toward the set, and contributed to his reputation as the greatest TV comedian of them all.

His friend George Burns was the third veteran who made the transition not only from radio but from turn-of-the-century vaudeville. His *Burns and Allen* Show, with madcap wife Gracie, had been a staple of radio, but the comedy duo sensed they were right for television. Bringing their excellent writers with them, Burns also personalized the medium in a slightly different way than Jack Benny did: he maintained frequent eye contact with the viewer, to whom he directed both asides and whole soliloquies.

Above: *Jack Benny often had guests on his* Jack Benny Show. *Here he is with the Smothers Brothers, Tom (center) and Dick (right).*

39

Even 'The Groaner' — Bing Crosby — might show up on The Jack Benny Show.

The stage's audience was too dispersed to do this, and in movies it would ruin the cinematic illusion; on radio, of course, it could not be done at all. Burns felt that the new medium was a personal one, and played his knowing glances to the hilt. Other than that, there was little change in the characters of George and Gracie: he was little more than a straight man for her harebrained chatter. Harry von Zell played George's hapless announcer (Burns played a show-biz figure in the show) and the neighbors were portrayed by haughty Larry Keating (later Fred Clark) and flighty Bea Benedaret. A delicious surrealistic touch toward the end of the series (which ran from 1950–59) was George's own television set. It enabled him to see whatever action was transpiring in the plot, above the crowd, as it were, and to be shared with us. How this could be was never explained – nor how it could not quite empower him in time to prevent Gracie's mistakes from turning into disasters.

Memorable shows continued to establish themselves: *Mr Wizard*, the perennial children's science show hosted by Don Herbert; a pioneer daytime quiz show, *Strike It Rich* ('The Show With a Heart'), over from radio; two more soap operas, destined to have long runs in the

afternoon, *Search for Tomorrow* and *Love of Life*; a classic kid's program, *Rootzie Kazootie* (starring Todd Russell's puppets Rootie, Polka Dottie, and El Squeako) and several religious programs.

Homilies had been a part of TV from the start, and many stations signed off with Sermonettes ('Perhaps they made people Christianettes,' television evangelist Jimmy Swaggart once joked), and the day of the religious superstars arrived in the early 1950s. ABC's *Old Fashioned Revival Hour*, succeeded by *The Hour of Decision with Billy Graham*, were the first to break out of the Sunday morning and afternoon ghetto; they appeared at 10 PM on Sundays. Bishop Fulton J Sheen (*Life Is Worth Living*) was placed by DuMont opposite Milton Berle on Tuesday nights and often drew healthy ratings. In 1952 Sheen edged out Berle and others as The Outstanding Television Personality of the Year ('That's all right,' quipped the Texaco star; 'we both work for Sky Chief'). Norman Vincent Peale began his success-cum-religion pep talks to enthusiastic response, and Oral Roberts began his enormous television ministry via syndicated films of his sweaty tent crusades and miracle healing services. A series of long-running dramatic and anthology religious series were begun by the major denominations: *Lamp Unto My Feet*; *Look Up and Live*; *Frontiers of Faith*; *This Is The Life* and *Crossroads*. The Lutheran Church in America was to produce an award-winning children's stop-action puppet-animation series, *Davy and Goliath*.

A new type of interview show was spawned by television's special qualities in the early 1950s. Certain radio interviewers were able (and willing) to intrude on their subjects, but could only do so to a point. Via the TV camera, the interviewer could be as much a star as the subject; lighting and set design could set the mood for the entire interview and editorial direction could make a newsmaker trivial and a nonentity newsworthy. Mike Wallace was an entertainer who pioneered these techniques. Jumping around the networks, he created a brand of interviewing, if not journalism, that many have copied. In 1951 he and his wife Buffy Cobb debuted with *Two Sleepy People* mornings on CBS (it was an early CBS experiment in color broadcasting); later it became the *Mike and Buffy Show* in the afternoons. For DuMont he conducted *Nightbeat*, and later had a 10 PM Sunday slot on ABC with *Mike Wallace Interviews*, and the syndicated documentary series *Biography*. He acted (on *Studio One* and *The Seven Lively Arts*), hosted quiz shows (*The $100,000 Big Surprise* and *Who Pays?*) and finally became a news reader at CBS, hosting the network's final move to a half-hour news format. Ultimately, of course, he went on to his greatest fame as one of the correspondents on *60 Minutes* – doing what he did at the start, making his interview subject squirm with 'incisive' and 'penetrating' questions. If Wallace

has an equal in the field of creating news as well as reporting it, it is Barbara Walters, another entertainer-turned-news-personality. To her can go the credit of prodding Sadat and Begin to make peace, and asking starlets what kinds of trees they would be if they could.

A rather more sophisticated form of TV newsmaking came in the person of Edward R Murrow, who is virtually an icon in the television news business. His *See It Now* (produced by Fred Friendly, a molder of the *persona* that was Murrow) set new standards that TV newsmen have forever emulated; and it truly defined a new language in American communications.

See It Now was an interview program operated on the Gestalt Theory: the whole was greater than the sum of its parts. Meticulous research preceded the sessions, and superb production values – background shots, camera angles, artful lighting techniques – were always present. And yet there was something more, an added factor that TV provided. By inflections of the voice, by raised eyebrows on Murrow's concerned brow, by the very choice of subjects week after week, *See It Now* was able to be an editorial as much as news, commentary as well as reporting. The brilliant productions, in sum, form a document of the times, but it is not an impartial document. It is of the world as seen by

Murrow, dreamed of by Murrow, or that has let Murrow down. Seen thus, the television set is revealed as an astoundingly effective propaganda device, and Americans have felt reassured that they have been comfortable with personalities bringing them their information. Murrow was packaged by Friendly as masterfully as advertisers primp a product – a straight news interview, presumably, does not need to rely on close-ups of the concerned interviewer's face, shirtsleeves and open ties – but in the course of the program, invaluable visits were paid to Dr Albert Schweitzer, Dr Jonas Salk, and Carl Sandburg. There were also many tributes to General George Marshall, many criticisms of Senator Joseph McCarthy, and profiles of Southern towns – the type of handling that an early generation might have done, but labeled as 'editorials,' and a later generation has done under the label 'advocacy journalism.' Murrow is a Saint to this tradition, a true giant of television techniques.

In 1953 he added *Person to Person* to his credits. It was an interview show, too, and its gimmick was to 'enter' the homes of the subjects. Murrow would stare at a screen, seeming to make eye contact with his guests, though of course this was not possible (it is visually implied today, but does not happen, on sets such as those used by *Nightline*). His list of subjects included the great celebrities of the day; Murrow elicited wonderful and candid comments, and provided viewers with tours of the celebrities' homes.

Probably the crowning factor in this period's claim to being the Golden Age was the live drama. As scripts and kinescopes are resurrected critics do well to stand in awe of the dramatic achievements of the 1950s. Of course there were poorly written plays and badly acted performances – distance lends enchantment – but it should be noted that the majority of work produced in any discipline is usually junk. This is true in painting, music, comics and movies, but even viewed by this sober yardstick, television drama of the 1950s does not cover an altogether vast multitude of sins. The most vital creative period for most forms is at the beginning, and television was twice blessed to have playwrights as gifted and adaptable as Paddy Chayefsky and Rod Serling there as the foot-soldiers of live drama.

The dramas were live for several reasons. They were conceived in the tradition of legitimate theater, and to record them seemed somehow dishonest. Tape was not sophisticated enough to use. Radio plays, a close relation, were always performed live. There was a commercial attraction in the live performance, denoting respect for the viewer.

In any event, the dramas were live and they were taken seriously by the industry, by the acting community, by the viewers – and by the sponsors' advertising agencies, many of whom established creative departments involved in

Below: Playhouse 90 *was one of the outstanding live drama shows on television. Here, Richard Basehart (left) and Trevor Howard, as handcuffed prisoners of a neurotic German, play chess in 'The Hiding Place,' in a 1960 broadcast. James Mason played the jailer.*

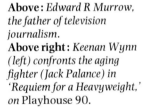

Above: *Edward R Murrow, the father of television journalism.*
Above right: *Keenan Wynn (left) confronts the aging fighter (Jack Palance) in 'Requiem for a Heavyweight,' on* Playhouse 90.

casting, story editing and actual production. A listing of some of the programs is more than a nostalgic trip: it forms the honor roll of an under-appreciated portion of American letters and dramatic history – *Philco Playhouse*; *Hallmark Hall of Fame*; *Armstrong Circle Theater*; *Lux Video Theater*; *Robert Montgomery Presents*; *Goodyear Playhouse*; *Schlitz Playhouse of Stars*; *Celanese Theatre* and *Studio 57*.

Among their triumphs were these: *Studio One* presented 'Twelve Angry Men,' starring Robert Cummings, Franchot Tone and Norman Fell; The *US Steel Hour* presented 'No Time for Sergeants,' starring Andy Griffith; the *Bell Telephone Hour* presented 'The Mikado' with Groucho Marx; the *Kraft Television Theater* presented Shakespeare's 'Comedy of Errors' with James Daly (father of Tyne Daly); *Four-Star Playhouse* offered a rotating group of four actors playing various roles (at one time consisting of David Niven, Charles Boyer, Ida Lupino, and Dick Powell; Niven and Boyer were coincidentally teamed later in an ensemble series, *The Rogues*, with Gig Young); and *Playhouse 90* presented the monumental TV drama 'Requiem for a Heavyweight,' with Ed and Keenan Wynn and Jack Palance superbly cast as the punchy, gullible fighter.

Standout individual productions during the

1950s included Paddy Chayefsky's classic 'Marty,' starring Ernest Borgnine as the reticent and sensitive butcher and Nancy Marchand as his date; 'Amahl and the Night Visitors,' Giancarlo Menotti's Christmas operetta composed for television; 'Burlesque,' a sardonic drama with Art Carney; the legendary television production of 'Peter Pan,' with Mary Martin in the title role; 'The Caine Mutiny Court-Martial;' 'Patterns;' 'The Petrified Forest,' with Humphrey Bogart, Lauren Bacall and Henry Fonda; 'Cyrano,' starring Jose Ferrer; 'The Miracle Worker;' 'The Green Pastures;' 'Days of Wine and Roses;' 'What Makes Sammy Run?;' 'The Moon and Sixpence;' 'Our Town,' starring Paul Newman, Eva Marie Saint and Frank Sinatra; 'A Christmas Carol,' starring Frederic March; 'The Man Who Came to Dinner,' with Monty Woolley (of course!), Buster Keaton, Bert Lahr and Joan Bennett; 'Arsenic and Old Lace,' starring Helen Hayes, Boris Karloff and Peter Lorre; and 'The Great Sebastians,' starring Alfred Lunt and Lynn Fontanne.

Television had already proven – finally – that it was commercially viable. It had also demonstrated its catholic appeal, its capacity for innovation, its clear entertainment value and its talent for providing information and persuasion. With the live drama, television asserted its maturity as well.

It also continued to display diversity. All of the characteristics enumerated above – except, perhaps, for commercial viability – were concentrated in the unorthodox creative genius known as Ernie Kovacs, a perfect television-talent. He was commercial enough to have steadily worked in TV: he started *Ernie in Kovacsland* as a nightly half-hour in 1951, then *Kovacs on the Corner*, a daily NBC morning

Above: *Ernie Kovacs, the most unusual television comic, adjusts his puppet show on* The Ernie Kovacs Show.

comedians and newsmen — to be iconoclasts of content, Kovacs was an iconoclast of the very form and its parameters. He created a cast of characters that will live in dementia; Percy Dovetonsils, the myopic poet; Pierre Ragout; Wolfgang von Sauerbraten; Irving Wong; and the bizarre Nairobi Trio, a group of musical, mechanical-looking monkeys, one of whom periodically smashed another on the head with neither missing a beat. Kovacs's reliance on Kurt Weill cabaret music invoked some of the intellectual dissolution of the Weimar Days, and some visual bits were reminiscent of Chuck Jones and Tex Avery cartoons. To use the terms innovative, surreal and zany seems only to put a limit on his essence. Television viewers were privileged to visit the mind of Ernie Kovacs for the time he was with us. He died in 1962, at age 42, in a tragic auto crash.

Possibly the closest talent to Kovacs — although more conventional and therefore decidedly more commercial — was Steve Allen, who emerged at the same time. Born to vaudevillian parents, Allen did his early work in radio comedy of the improvisational sort — on-the-spot, off-the-cuff humor, and interplay with audiences. He graduated to guest spots on network quiz shows (witticisms and literal humor, ever his trademarks, served him well) and hosted a game show, *Songs for Sale*. He graduated to a nightly hour on the CBS network in early 1951, and then moved to a noontime daily show. Finally he took the late-night spot vacated by the demise of *Broadway Open House*. It was broadcast at first only on NBC's New York station, but Allen had ownership and creative control.

What happened? Comedic hell broke loose. A certified genius, Allen did not rely on the slapstick of his predecessor Jerry Lester; but his humor was no less physical. He did character and costume bits. He picked phone numbers at random and, with the audience listening, carried on nonsensical conversations with the dazed party. He took his cameras onto the street and accosted passersby in bizarre ways — or he secretly focused his cameras on the street and provided voices to the unknowing pedestrians. He literally rolled on the floor over pieces of silliness, whether his own or his guests'. He attached a thousand teabags to his body and was dunked by a crane in a vat of water. His speech was peppered with non-sequiturs like 'Schmock! Schmock!' and 'How's your sister Shirley?' and his desk overflowed with crazy props and noisemakers.

The cerebral side of Steve Allen has seen him write several books and engage in left-of-center political advocacy. He is a consummate musician and improvises as well on the jazz keyboard as on the verbal up-take. 'This Could Be the Start of Something Big' and 'Gravy Train Waltz' are among the thousands of songs he has written.

In the comedy/variety realm, Steve Allen

program. *The Ernie Kovacs Show* was a live prime-time hour on Tuesday nights, after which he hosted the *Tonight Show* two nights a week in 1955. For NBC he went back to a morning show, and again back to a prime-time hour in 1956. Thereafter he produced a number of specials, and, at the time of his untimely death in 1962 at the age of 42, he was producing half-hour lunacies. Such bouncing around does not indicate that something was wrong with Ernie Kovacs, but that something was right. Certainly he was hard to categorize, and to many he may have been an acquired taste.

He was, in a sense, the perfect television comic (and he was more: a comedian, a humorist, a satirist, a parodist, a commentator, an ironist) because he used the plastic medium of TV as no one did until computer graphics and MTV a generation later. Kovacs blithely ignored the limitations of the medium and explored the potentialities. One of his half-hour shows contained absolutely no dialogue, and another concentrated on visual illusions (water pouring sideways, etc.), exploiting the false reality that only television can create. He used stop-action video tape as cleverly as the most avant-garde animator. While TV was allowing others —

Left: *A reunion of two all-time greats of television – Arlene Francis and Steve Allen – who appeared together many times on* What's My Line?
Below: *Steve Allen performs during an 'Eyewitless News' segment of* The Steve Allen Comedy Hour *on NBC.*

retired from *The Tonight Show* to concentrate on challenging Ed Sullivan on Sunday evenings. Starting in 1956 – and providing respectable competition – Allen produced a unique and classic cast of regular characters who complemented his own multifaceted comedy and performing talents. Among the ensemble were Bill Dana (Jose Jimenez); Dayton Allen ('Why not?'); Pat Harrington Jr; Louis Nye (the suave jerk who always said, 'Hi-ho Steverino'); Don Knotts (the perennially nervous man on the street); Tom Poston (absent-minded to the point of forgetting his name); and Gabe Dell. Comedy mixed with sketches and music, mostly provided by jazzman Allen and his bandleader Skitch Henderson. One of the writers on the show was portly Allen Sherman, who later achieved fame with parodies of traditional songs.

Allan also discovered Steve Lawrence and Eydie Gorme (before they were married). Since he left the show in 1960, Allen's multitudinous activities have included much TV: a weekly comedy hour for ABC; a *Tonight*-style late-night syndicated show for Westinghouse (if possible, more manic than ever); the hosting of *I've Got a Secret* for several seasons; an innovative program for Public Broadcasting (*Meeting of the Minds*, where actors playing historical figures from disparate times compare notes in character); hosting a Robin Leach anthology series, *Start of Something Big*.

Two more members of the Enchanted Circle became active in television at this time: Bob and Ray. Although Bob Elliott and Ray Goulding came from radio, fashioned most of their routines as radio-serial spoofs, and returned to radio, they were stellar lights of the small screen and still occasionally appear. Debuting in 1952 and sharing a nightly half-hour with *Kukla, Fran, and Ollie*, Bob and Ray immediately confirmed their status as first-class comics and supreme parodists. Their various characters, whether playing soap opera roles or in any number of interview situations, employed literalisms, irony and nonsense to the *n*th degree. To their cast of thousands (Wally Ballou, ace reporter; Mary Backstayge, Noble Wife; Biff Burns, sportscaster; Elmer W Litsinger, Spy; Kent Lyle Birdley, announcer, *et al.*) came the assistance of a female sidekick on their TV show, first Audrey Meadows and then Cloris Leachman, as Linda Lovely, Weathergirl.

Back in the real world more hits kept America's TV sets on for longer periods each week (the A C Neilsen Company was now rating shows' popularity for the advertisers). *Amos 'n' Andy* was another immigrant from radioland, but experienced some significant transformations. On radio the characters had been played by whites, Freeman Gosden and Charles Correll. In the 1950s a new sense of realism was abroad in the television industry; besides, blackface

was definitely dead. So recruitment began among black character actors to translate this valuable property to the video airwaves, and by luck or hard work one of the most brilliant comedic ensembles in television history was assembled. Amos and Andy were played respectively by Alvin Childress (appropriately modest, honest and straightforward) and Spenser Williams Jr (rotund, lazy, and gullible). Inspired casting occurred when Tim Moore played the scheming blowhard George 'Kingfish' Stevens; Moore was a virtual encyclopedia of expressions and reactions. The players cast as Sapphire (the Kingfish's wife), Lightnin' the janitor, lawyer Algonquin J Calhoun, and others were comedians of the first order. The plots were pure sitcom formula — foiled schemes, lies found out, petty financial shenanigans — but, as later series *I Love Lucy* and *The Honeymooners* were to prove, routine screenplays could be serviceable vehicles for quality lines and character work.

Unfortunately the growing civil-rights movement objected, with more and more pressure, to the depiction of blacks in *Amos 'n' Andy*. Never mind that whites were often similarly caricatured; the argument ran that there were no corresponding characters of dignity and authority on TV, as whites surely had. The point was valid, but the pressure groups sadly found it easier to

demand subtraction than addition. *Amos 'n' Andy* was cancelled and even withdrawn from syndication, depriving America — black and white alike — of some genuinely inspired comedic moments.

Other sitcoms established their own audiences, many with memorable casts. *My Little Margie* gave Gale Storm a taste of success, and paired her with Charles Farrell, once a silent-screen hero of the Great Profile variety. (After the show's demise Farrell was the distinguished mayor of Palm Springs, California.) They played father and daughter, Vern Albright and Margie, who always got into predicaments. Each episode would begin with separate monologues of father and daughter mulling over their problems ('Believe me . . . I've got a problem') and close with framed portraits of each coming to life with comic 'morals' for the viewers. Oddly, *My Little Margie* spun off as a radio show, running concurrently with the TV show — different scripts, same players.

I Married Joan starred Joan Davis (billed as America's Queen of Comedy) and Jim Backus as a scatterbrained housewife and her husband, Bradley Stevens, a domestic court judge. Davis was definitely of the physical school of humor, regularly practicing routines like being showered with vegetables, seasoning and water as she

Above: *Tim Moore, as the Kingfish, being watched by Spencer Williams, as Andy and Alvin Childress, as Amos, in 'The Piggy Bank' episode on the* Amos 'n' Andy *series.*
Opposite: *Spencer Williams (Andy), Tim Moore (George 'Kingfish' Stevens) and Alvin Childress (Amos) starred in* Amos 'n' Andy.

attempted to swipe a recipe from a chef obviously cooking for multitudes. The NBC show lasted three years in the early 1950s before Davis' terminal illness caused its demise.

Ozzie and Harriet became a TV classic of long staying-power (14 years, in addition to eight previous years on the radio). The principals were Ozzie Nelson, a bumbling middle-class husband and father; and Harriet, his wife (in real life Ozzie had been a big-bandleader and Harriet Hillyard his vocalist); their children, in real life and on the show, were David and Ricky. All the plots revolved around the boys' problems and Ozzie's wimpy predicaments; Don DeFore and Lyle Talbot played two neighbors. During the course of the show David grew up and married, and Rick became a rock 'n' roll star of major proportions (many episodes would end with him singing a song with full back-up in a house-party situation – with no plot tie-in to the scene. Nevertheless it promoted his records).

Our Miss Brooks was another radio switch, with virtually the entire cast making the move. Eve Arden, former screen star, played Constance Brooks, high school teacher. Blustery Gale Gordon was cast as the overbearing principal Osgood Conklin; Richard Crenna as crack-voiced Walter Denton (his later credits included *The Real McCoys*, *Slattery's People*, and *It Takes Two*); Robert Rockwell as heartthrob teacher Mr Boynton, and Jane Morgan as Connie's landlady Mrs Davis.

Ann Sothern scored a success as Susie McNamara in the sitcom *Private Secretary*. The platinum movie veteran was constantly getting her boss Peter Sands – played by Don Porter, later of *Gidget* – in and out of scrapes. Porter's rival was played by longtime character actor Jesse White.

But in truth all the family shows, all the sitcoms, all the bright comediennes, of the era were pretenders to the throne. Lucille Ball, once a Goldwyn Girl, once 'straight-man' to the Marx Brothers (in *Room Service*), once popular radio star (of *My Favorite Husband*), transferred her radio success to television after assuring herself and her husband, Cuban bandleader and crooner Desi Arnaz, creative control. In remarkable bits of prescience, Lucy and Desi owned the production company (Desilu), performed before a live audience (the first sitcom to do so), and filmed the episodes prior to airing (over CBS's objections). The premise was stone-cold simple: Ricky Ricardo, bandleader, and his wife Lucy live in New York; their friends and landlords are Fred and Ethel Mertz (William Frawley and Vivian Vance). Impulsive Lucy gets into funny predicaments.

After that, *I Love Lucy* is a textbook example of what inspired comedic talent and quality writing can do. Lucy's slapstick was seldom done to a better turn by male or female (images come to mind: Lucy in the candy factory, unable to wrap the chocolates fast enough; Lucy with blacked-out teeth; Lucy as Harpo Marx), but it was basically her personality that made the show. Lucy was not stupid or essentially incompetent; but she was childlike. She took childlike delight in scheming an innocent

Above: Ann Sothern was the star of Private Secretary, *and later became the voice of an automobile in* My Mother the Car.
Above left: Gale Storm was Margie Albright and Charles Farrell was her father, Vern, in My Little Margie, *which featured her inimitible way of delivering her lines and using a short gasp after every sentence.*
Opposite: Lucy loves Desi.
Following spread: The Mertzes and the Ricardos in I Love Lucy – *Vivian Vance, William Frawley, Desi Arnaz, Lucille Ball.*

trick. She pleaded with Ricky to meet a celebrity as a child would plead. When foiled, she would react in childlike innocence and instant contrition. Not only was hers a totally honest character, it was necessarily appealing, almost compelling. There is a fine line in comedy between childlike and childish, and Lucille Ball – like Laurel and Hardy before her – had the magic touch.

When Lucy's eyes lit up, Ethel Mertz was turned from a respectable housewife to a co-conspirator in nonsense. There was a similar spell cast on viewers, too. *I Love Lucy* is the most popular comedy show in television history, and it continues to be shown around the world today, in some cities as much as seven times daily. It is no longer a TV show; it is a phenomenon.

In the mornings a Pat Weaver creation, *Today*, set a new tone in television. Hosted by Dave Garroway, urbane and laconic, *Today* allowed Americans to arise to news, weather, and nonsense, especially after the chimp J Fred Muggs stole the show. Jack Lescoulie and Frank Blair were the human sidekicks.

Below: *The great comedian Red Skelton, who prefers to be known as a clown, as Freddie the Freeloader.*

On Sunday evenings Red Skelton graced the NBC landscape. If other TV comics were satirists and parodists, Skelton was a clown, and proud of it. He created memorable characters in Clem Kadiddlehopper, and the Mean Widdle Kid, and the seagulls Gertrude and Heathcliff. More than others of his genre his humor and his personality seemed to totally lack cynicism. His send-off line, 'God Bless,' was warm and sincere, the very opposite of bathos after his hour of silliness. Dinah Shore came to television (a big kiss – 'Mweeeah!' – was *her* send-off line) in a musical-variety format; she was later to host a long-running syndicated talk show, reflecting her charm and vaunted Southern hospitality.

Liberace was another personality who possibly drew as many detractors as fans – but it all adds up in the ratings count. It couldn't have been his schmaltzy piano playing; the nation's musical taste was still reasonably intact, and Liberace's boatload of gimmicks – candelabras, bizarre dress, etc. – were obviously there to camouflage the other deficiencies. In television, especially among cult followings, the word 'music' covers a multitude of sins.

'The story you are about to see is true. The names have been changed to protect the innocent.' *Dragnet* came to TV, and a remarkable program it was. On the surface it seemed to be cops-and-robbers stuff clad in a straitjacket of wooden acting. But producer and star Jack Webb (Sergeant Joe Friday) set a mood and pacing that was perfect for television. The stories were intimate and compact, narrated by Webb *à la* Philip Marlowe. But this was pure police-procedural drama, almost documentary, and Webb's limited assortment of monosyllables and monotones were somehow appropriate. Such no-frills drama would have been boring in the movies, but was tailor-made for half-hours on TV. 'Just the facts, Ma'am,' as Sergeant Friday used to say.

A different sort of sitcom was *Mr Peepers*, starring Wally Cox. Peepers was withdrawn and shy, what a later generation might call wimpy. Yet the junior high-school science teacher was clever enough to come out on top of every situation, and even eventually marry his plain-jane sweetheart in the series, Nancy Remington (Patricia Benoit). Brash Harvey Weskit was played by Tony Randall; delightful character actress Marion Lorne was also in the cast. The whimsical *Mr Peepers* had the rare gift of being both madcap and sensitive, cut from special cloth.

In the summer of 1952 a personality invaded network television, and the landscape has never been the same since. Actually, Jackie Gleason was already a veteran of network TV; his hour-long comedy–variety program had been airing weekly on DuMont since 1949, and he was the star of *The Life of Riley* for a season. Before that, Gleason was a seasoned veteran of night clubs,

Below: *Jackie Gleason (right) and Frank Fontaine rehearse a 'Joe the Bartender' sketch for* The Jackie Gleason Show. *Gleason was Joe and Fontaine played the oaf with the beautiful singing voice, Crazy Googenheim.*

theater and movies, where he specialized in a pop-eyed, bumbling-hero *persona*. And later The Great One was to prove himself a superb dramatic actor and accomplished popular music composer and conductor. It was his Saturday night show on CBS that formed his most memorable moments and major contributions to television comedy. Besides hosting the usual television array of celebrities in skits, and guest stars of all stripes, Gleason formed an ensemble of comedy players — about half of them himself under different character roles. There was The Poor Soul, TV's pantomimic answer to the comics' Caspar Milquetoast; Joe the Bartender, who sang and played straight man in comedy routines; Charley Bracken, the loudmouth; and Reginald Van Gleason III, outlandishly foppish and always inebriated. Of his real-life players, Gleason was blessed with the talents of Art Carney (likewise to become a respected dramatic actor, with an Oscar in his future), Audrey Meadows (late of the *Bob and Ray* TV show) and Joyce Randolph, among others.

This group came together in the *Honeymooners* segment of the Gleason hour. Originally the *Honeymooners* had been a series of sketches on the DuMont show, with Pert Kelton as Ralph Kramden's wife Alice. Gleason had been so taken with radio's *The Bickersons* (Don Ameche and Frances Langford) that he optioned the rights to bring the constantly arguing couple to the

small screen. He then proceeded to do his own version, with blue-collar bus driver Ralph Kramden. Something happened along the way however. The characters, and the writers, evolved a softer version – one with warmth and sentiment as the soft underbelly of the laugh-provoking personality clashes. The antagonism of Ralph and Alice would always melt in an embrace, and the addition of the emotion was really a multiplication of facets to the interesting characters. Kramden is like Lucy: childlike – he can be blustery one moment and then innocently contrite the next.

Added to the fine comedic acting and quality writing on the *Honeymooner* skits was the family upstairs, Ed and Trixie Norton, played by Carney and Randolph. Art Carney brought perfect second-banana skills to his role; Ed Norton could be straight man, a perfect fool, or inevitable dupe for Ralph's schemes. Norton was a sewer worker ('where time and tide wait for no man,' as he would intone with literary flourish) and somehow lived better than longtime bus driver Kramden, but not for lack of financial dreaming on Ralph's part. KranMar's Appetizer, wallpaper that glowed in the dark, Chef-of-the-Future's Handy Housewife Helper – all were exploded get-rich-quick brainstorms of Ralph Kramden aimed at elevating him and Alice from their dreary flat in Bensonhurst, Brooklyn.

So popular did the *Honeymooners* become that Gleason retired his hour format in the 1955–56 season to offer half-hour episodes. In a rare bit of foresight, they were filmed on the ElectroniCam System of the wheezing DuMont Labs, and these episodes have become the 'Classic 39' that have

Above: The Honeymooners bunch – Jackie Gleason (Ralph Kramden), Art Carney (Ed Norton), Audrey Meadows (Alice Kramden) and Joyce Randolph (Trixie Norton).

Opposite: Ralph and Alice argue about whether he should go bowling or not. **Following spread:** The Honeymooners *gang on Ralph's bus.*

been on TV endlessly since then. But the *Honeymooners* lived elsewhere and lived longer (although never, to Alice's dismay, leaving their Bensonhurst apartment): other segments from early Gleason hours, although not in neat half-hours, finally saw the light of re-runs in 1986 on the ShowTime Cable system; he revived the sketches in his revamped Saturday night variety show (1962–70, which occasioned his attempt to make Miami a new TV production center); and periodic *Honeymooners* specials on network TV have appeared since the 1976 season. Sue Anne Langdon and Sheila MacRae played Alice in later versions, and Patricia Wilson and Jane Kean portrayed the curiously undeveloped Trixie Norton character; but Ed has always been – and always will be – Art Carney.

Gleason and Carney teamed for a TV movie in 1985 as *Izzy and Moe*, the true-life story of two Prohibition cops, and the magic was wonderful between them. But the remarkable magic and chemistry engendered by Ralph, Alice, and Norton – as vital 30 years later as when originally produced under the breakneck demands of weekly TV – has eternal appeal. The *Honeymooners* represents enormous creative and comedic qualities, but also stands as a testament to what TV could do, and how it could endure.

Above: *Debbie Weems, Bob Keeshan (the Captain) and Hugh Brannum on* Captain Kangaroo. *Before Keeshan began this children's program, he had played Clarabelle the Clown on* Howdy Doody.

Opposite top: *An* American Bandstand *telecast in the 1950s.*

Opposite bottom: *Four stalwarts of* The Mickey Mouse Club — *Emcee Jimmie Dodd, Annette, Tommy and Doreen.*

On the more reserved side was *Omnibus*, truly one of the remarkable shows in American television history. Hosted by Alistair Cooke — American correspondent for the *Manchester Guardian* and the BBC — the program was a cultural potpourri of interviews, live drama, music, education and even comedy. Originally funded by the Ford Foundation, the Sunday-afternoon program was clearly too intellectual, and too varied in content, to have maintained its own commercial audience, although several imitations were spawned (albeit in TV's back-closet, Sunday afternoons), including John Houseman's *Seven Lively Arts* and NBC's *Kaleidoscope*.

'Education' was not entirely a dirty word in network programming offices, but the lines were clearly being drawn between entertainment and culture. Public affairs programs, religion, and news-discussions were being relegated to Sunday afternoons, and eventually sports events were to reduce that time-frame to Sunday mornings. Even talk shows of TV's early days, which had been largely informational, were now primarily entertainment/comedy/variety. Sarnoff's visions of art galleries in the home was firmly placed upon the trash heap before television was even a decade old.

Nevertheless the educational programs that surfaced were valuable and memorable. Dr Frances Horwich pioneered childrens' programming in the guise of Miss Frances, hostess of *Ding Dong School*, a long-running program of pre-schooler activities and elementary learning. Marlin Perkins hosted *Zoo Parade*, and later *Wild Kingdom*, keeping America in weekly touch with natural history and conservation; from the 1950s through the 1980s the gentle Perkins has handled thousands of animals — cute,

arcane, bizarre and threatening — in virtually every part of the globe. In 1955 *Captain Kangaroo* debuted. An early-morning show aimed at children, host Bob Keeshan fashioned a program that gently combined pure entertainment with childrens' literature, basic education and storybook moralizing. A small ensemble of players (Mr Greenjeans was Kangaroo's neighbor) clearly prefigured the format and premise of *Mr Rogers' Neighborhood* and many, many other childrens' programs through the years. The charming Captain Kangaroo was eventually bludgeoned by his network's demographic rush to fill the morning slot with programming — and commercials — aimed at rising commuters, but he was also done in by a new wave of children's shows that were less relaxed and more formulized.

Debuting on the same day (3 October) as Captain Kangaroo was Walt Disney's *Mickey Mouse Club*. The afternoon show was clearly not 'educational' in intent, but marked a new approach toward young people's TV. Hosted by Jimmie Dodd (and Roy Williams, a bearish Disney animator), the show featured a regular crew of 'Mouseketeers,' routinely clad in mouse-ear caps and T-shirts (especially the budding adolescent Annette Funicello, heart-throb of millions of pre-pubescent American boys). But the show also featured songs, stories, animated cartoons, drawing lessons, viewer-participation activities, serial adventures and, again, storybook moralizing. It was truly a quality-production musical-variety show for children, and kids were conscious of the respect Disney paid them. The *Mickey Mouse Club* continued until its original audience, and its players, grew up; in the early 1980s a bizarre caricature of itself appeared. The Mouseketeers seemed to be chosen more by ethnic quotas than by talent screenings, and disco replaced the warm sing-alongs of Jimmie and his guitar. The mod version was quickly iced.

The thematic arrangement of the *Mickey Mouse Club* was as follows: Mondays, Fun with Music; Tuesdays, Guest-Star Day; Wednesdays, Anything Can Happen; Thursdays, Circus Day; and Fridays, Talent Round-up. Running features included serials like 'Spin and Marty,' and animated cartoons featuring Donald Duck, who was ironically more popular than the low-keyed nominal host, Mickey.

Howdy Doody was a rating loser to the Mouse, and he moved to Saturday mornings, where he dominated the scene for years. Also on Saturday mornings — in the days before animated cartoons wiped live performers from the screen — were *Winky Dink and You*, hosted by Jack Barry (featuring a 'magic screen' to be placed on the TV set and drawn upon with crayons); *Andy's Gang* (hosted by Andy Devine and featuring bizarre puppets like Froggy the Gremlin, he of the Magic Twanger) and *Ray Forrest's Children's Theater*. Forrest had been an NBC-TV news

pioneer in 1944 with *The War As It Happens.*

Other Saturday morning favorites were *The Paul Winchell and Jerry Mahony Show* (Winchell, one of the funniest of TV's ventriloquists, featured Knuckhead Smith and others, and three decades later was to be a voice of the Smurfs); and *Rockey Jones, Space Cadet,* whose vision of the future seemed to rely more on intriguing costumes than sophisticated gadgetry. Pinky Lee, burlesque comedian and TV pioneer in several comic functions, found his niche as host of a kiddie show, and Abbott and Costello actually began their television careers on Saturday mornings on CBS.

American Bandstand began a remarkable run on ABC, with the perennially labeled World's Oldest Teenager, Dick Clark, as its second host (the first host was bounced when arrested for drunk driving in the midst of his station's safe-driving campaign). It originated in Philadelphia and showcased two things: the latest dance steps, as self-consciously undulated by the city's teenagers; and probably every roll 'n' roll act since the music erupted. Remarkably, Clark was able to maintain his image and the show's popularity — and, arguably therefore, rock's very existence at several crucial junctures — through its eras of the bad-boy image, the payola scandals, the drug- and hard-rock period and punk. Clark, still doing *Bandstand,* has created a TV empire as producer of many prime-time entertainment specials and host of daytime game shows.

In the evening hours there was still experimentation, and a variety of talent both old and new. Bob Hope tried his hand at a weekly comedy and music show, but decided that his future was in monthly or periodic specials (it proved to be a winning formula). Ronald Reagan, his movie career winding down, assumed guest-host and occasional starring duties on *General Electric Theater* and the syndicated Western anthology *Death Valley Days*; his connection with GE led to his employment as a corporate spokesman for the company, including increasing numbers of political and free-enterprise speeches throughout America. In a very real sense TV was not the salvaging of Reagan's career, but the beginning of a new one.

Inquiries into Communist subversion and infiltration affected television in only peripheral ways during the 1950s. Legend has it that the entire communications industry was convulsed with fear of lynch mobs, but in actuality only several players with Communist affiliations (like Philip Loeb of *The Goldbergs*) were pressured off the air, while a left-wing backlash ensured the employment of others; Edward R Murrow and others, furthermore, made whole careers out of witch-hunting the witch-hunters like Senator Joseph McCarthy. One by-product of all this activity was the show *I Led Three Lives*, based on the real-life adventures of double agent Herbert Philbrick.

Sophisticated nonsense came to half-hour sitcoms in the fantasy comedy *Topper*, based on Thorne Smith's novels of the 1930s and the

Top: *Anne Jeffreys and Robert Sterling, as the ghosts, Marion and George Kirby on the* Topper *show, confuse the moving men.*

Above: *Betty White (left) and Bea Arthur discuss a problem on* The Golden Girls.

Opposite: *Jon Provost and his dog (right) with a friend and his dog in an episode of* Lassie.

Cary Grant motion-picture vehicle. Leo G Carroll, with a proper British combination of stuffiness, confusion and playfulness, starred as Cosmo Topper, whose house was haunted by the ghosts of George and Marion Kirby, and their martini-swilling St Bernard. Lee Patrick (who had a role in *The Maltese Falcon*) played the dippy Mrs Henrietta Topper, and supporting players included Thurston Hall as bank president Mr Schuyler, and Kathleen Freeman, the Toppers' maid Katie. The show was pixilated nonsense of high order, and featured much trick photography and special effects.

Betty White has been a familiar face through TV's history. She starred in the DuMont series *Life with Elizabeth* in the 1950s, where each show would end with the two married couples in a big argue-fest; the camera would pull back to reveal them on a stage, the announcer would request the actors to say 'good-night' – and then they would resume their arguing. She later starred in a network sitcom, *A Date with the Angels*, and was hostess of a weekday afternoon variety show. Married to the late gameshow host Allen Ludden, she was also a principal player on the *Mary Tyler Moore Show*; a shortlived follow-up sitcom bearing her name; an occasional guest on *St Elsewhere*; and a star of *The Golden Girls*.

George Gobel has also been a regular presence on TV screens through the years. The former child star and yodeling cowboy singer of Chicago's *WLS Barn Dance* was the host of an entertaining NBC variety hour on Saturday nights, reflective of his winsome and cerebral wit. He has also appeared on *Harper Valley PTA*, the *Tonight Show*, and many guest spots.

Television pre-empted later critics by throwing programming to the dogs in the canine persons of Rin-Tin-Tin and Lassie in the 1950s. Rusty and his dog *Rin-Tin-Tin* were sole survivors of an Indian raid and were 'adopted' by the men of Fort Apache, where they proved more resourceful than their adult, human protectors for 10 seasons. *Lassie* (through the years played by several collies, all males) had several masters, young Tommy Rettig and Jon Provost and then forest ranger Robert Bray, and several 'mothers,' including Cloris Leachman and June Lockhart. In the last of her 15-year run, Lassie would have no owner, drifting from place to place and solving problems in a manner that would baffle Mensa members. These shows fore-shadowed other animal epics of the tiny screen like *My Friend Flicka*, *Fury*, and *National Velvet* (horses); *Born Free* and *Daktari* (featuring lioness Elsa, and Clarence the Cross-Eyed Lion, respectively); and *Flipper*, about a dolphin whose speciality was saving the day.

Left: Flipper, *the dolphin, amazes his friends.*

Above: *The* Make Room for Daddy *clan — Rusty Hamer, Danny Thomas, Jean Hagan, Sherry Jackson.*
Opposite: *In* My Three Sons, *Fred MacMurray played Steve Douglas and two of his sons were played by Don Grady (center, as Robbie) and Stanley Livingston (Chip). Here they decide to keep*

Harry, the dog who will share the house with Tramp, their long-time canine companion.
Right: *The Anderson family from* Father Knows Best — *Lauren Chapin (Kathy/ Kitten), Robert Young (Jim), Elinor Donahue (Betty/ Princess), Jane Wyatt (Margaret) and Billy Gray (James Jr/Bud).*

The image of the American father has been much written about, especially by those anthropologists whose views of societies are seen through glasses colored Matriarchal or Patriarchal. Indeed many of the standard TV sitcoms have prospered on the *Blondie* formula of the American Husband and Father as Jerk — the mother may be dippy or scatterbrained, the father is a jerk (indeed two separate *Blondie* TV adaptations were mounted in the 1950s). Ozzie Nelson certainly played this role, and others — like Danny Thomas in *Make Room for Daddy* and the *Danny Thomas Show* (he was a showbiz star but not immune to problems of his own making) — followed suit to greater or lesser degrees. *Life With Father*, starring Leon Ames and derived from the Clarence Day stories and William Powell movie, was a classic costume piece that also capitalized on Father's eccentricities.

Leave It To Beaver departed from this mold to an extent, and so did *My Three Sons*. In these shows the prototypical suburban father-figures

of the 1950s and early 1960s lorded over households of innocently wayward sons; Dad was always there to correct, soothe, chastise and sermonize by show's end. If Ozzie Nelson was a Greek God to David and Ricky — an authority figure as flawed as a human — then Ward Cleaver (to Wally and Beaver) and Steve Douglas (to his three sons, who through the years included Mike, Robbie, Chip, and Ernie) were Greek Chorus figures coaching, chiding, commenting. Ultimately these characters and these shows were bland comedies of manners, reflections of a homogenized middle-America that became reality through TV's repeated images and the subliminal secret weapon of television, the Implied and Assumed Truth. When shows like *Leave It to Beaver* and *My Three Sons* are perceived as Everyman's typical home — as opposed to, say, the rather more modest milieux of *Life of Riley* and the *Honeymooners* — an Expectation Gap occurs. Added to the 'typical' households shown in hundreds and hundreds of television commercials, households that are plainly, upon examination, upper-class, we can see the television as an instrument of economic seduction and social subversion. These settings do not spur viewers toward a lifestyle to attain, but rather tend to fill them with resentment that they do not share what seems so obviously to be the American household norm.

Hollywood and Madison Avenue thereby provided impetus to a generation's complaints about class structure and social mobility. The Cleavers (played by Hugh Beaumont, Barbara Billingsly, Tony Dow, and Jerry Mathers as Theodore 'Beaver' Cleaver) and the Douglases (Fred MacMurray played the lead, with William Frawley and William Demarest as stereotypically irascible older relatives) were clearly not revolutionaries. They were icons, symbols of a bland 1950s family life in America that probably never existed in widespread ways, but because of TV's inertial law of Implied and Assumed Truths, are perceived today as mirrors of their time.

Probably the show that stands tallest among such shows is the one that largely inspired the genre, but whose similarities to the endless stream of imitators are only superficial. *Father Knows Best* starred Robert Young, making the transition from the radio serial of the same name, and adding the following cast: wife Margaret (Jane Wyatt); daughter Betty (Elinor Donahue); son Bud (Billy Gray); and younger daughter Kathy (Lauren Chapin). Yes, there were predicaments — this was a weekly sitcom — and yes, Father did get in binds, but so did everyone in the family. Father *didn't* always know best (the clever title has all but supplanted the phrase that it tweaked, 'mother knows best'), and this sitcom was arguably the most democratic of all family comedies on television.

All of the players supported and respected

each other, and when they didn't, there was common regret and forgiveness. None of the characters was clichéd – the children could be brash, but were sensitive and vulnerable – and they grew each week – in affection as well as maturity. The viewers of *Father Knows Best* were intensely loyal, and public reaction brought the show back after cancellation the first season, prefiguring many such salvations. The program ultimately ran for nine seasons, and if other family sitcoms remain with us as how television saw us in the 1950s and 1960s, then *Father Knows Best* stands as how American families saw themselves in that period; it was more a comedy of relationships than situations.

Meanwhile another bit of Americana received its television blessing in 1954. The *Miss America Pageant*, long hosted by toothy TV knockabout Bert Parks (television was now entering the age of the 'TV personality,' i.e., someone with few credentials from other media who presumably could do little else than TV activities) was representative, and foremost, of that peculiarly American phenomenon, the beauty pageant. When TV confers status, a property can be instantly absorbed into, and become a major element of, the mainstream of American culture. Televised beauty pageants proliferate, even unto Steve Allen's annual parodies, The *Miss Las Vegas Showgirl Pageant*.

Significantly it was television that served as a catalyst in a similar way when an already viable entertainment tradition sought new vistas. Walt Disney, after a generation of providing animated cartoons and a wealth of comics and stories, was, in the early 1950s, looking for backing as he planned a lifelong dream, the Disneyland amusement park for children and adults. Coincidentally, the fledgling ABC network was about to go out of business. Always the weak sister among the networks, not enough cities had stations at the time to be potential affiliates. Two factors helped ABC: DuMont was slowly leaving the network television field, which marginally reduced competition, and Paramount invested $30-million in ABC. This gave the network a financial shot in the arm, as well as movie and programming connections. But it also gave them $500,000 to invest, in turn, in Disneyland. Disney then signed a production agreement with ABC, giving them a weekly variety series (which could promote Disney characters and the new theme park) and other shows as well (*The Mickey Mouse Club* soon appeared, as well as *Davy Crockett, Zorro, Texas John Slaughter, Spin and Marty*, and other mini-series and specials). In less than a year Disney opened the entertainment miracle that is Disneyland, and the already formidable Mouse factory was off in new directions, including more theme parks and a steady flow of quality television production – all the result of virtual spare change in a television transaction!

Opposite: *Bert Parks, the long-time host of* The Miss America Pageant.
Above: *Ron Ely took over* The Miss America Pageant *from Bert Parks. Here he is with Cheryl Prewitt, Miss America, 1980.*
Below: *Guy Williams as Zorro.*

New variety shows continued to debut (it is difficult to imagine, in these days when the genre is virtually absent from television, how numerous and seemingly essential these shows once were), hosted by Tennessee Ernie Ford; Red Foley; Jimmy Dean (the country and rural audiences were duly, and demographically, served); Lawrence Welk, serving older viewers a mixture of genteel music-and-dance and schmaltz; Johnny Carson, bouncing around between game shows and morning and evening variety shows (he had a CBS summer evening show in 1955); and Jonathan Winters, squarely in the round-hole traditions of Ernie Kovacs and Steve Allen. Jimmy Durante graced television for a short while with the flavor of his speakeasy humor, his outrageous personality and his very real charm. It was a wonderful period in American cultural history, when new forms and formats were proliferating, but at the same time the very essence of older, treasured forms and performers could be captured, and transmitted, on television. All of Durante's silliness was eclipsed by his patented closing — a fade-out walk along a spotlight-footpath, after a melancholy 'Goodnight, Mrs Calabash, wherever you are,' a reference to his late wife.

Popular situation comedies included *The Peoples Choice*, with veteran child actor (now grown as an adult lead, and later a director Jackie Cooper; *The Brothers*, a wacky show with Gale Gordon and Bob Sweeney (Gordon's past was with *Our Miss Brooks* and future with *Lucy* spinoffs while Sweeney was TV's Fibber McGee); *Mr Adams and Eve*, starring film veterans (and real-life marrieds) Ida Lupino and Howard Duff; *O, Susanna!*, which was Gale Storm's second TV

hit, this time with delightful character actress ZaSu Pitts; and *The Real McCoys*, a classic rural comedy starring Walter Brennan, Richard Crenna and Kathleen Nolan.

As the networks entrenched their positions, so did independent producers, who served a growing number of local stations as well as network affiliates with free time on their schedules. Among the successful syndicated programs of the middle and late 1950s were *Highway Patrol* (with Broderick Crawford), *The Cisco Kid*, The *Lone Ranger*, *Racket Squad* (a Hal Roach production, indicating that nearly everyone was now entering TV), *Waterfront*, *Abbott and Costello*, *Casey Jones* (with Alan Hale Jr) and *Death Valley Days*.

The era of the game show arrived in the mid-1950s as well. Always a staple on radio, and an early staple of TV, the first prime-time block-buster was *The $64,000 Question*, hosted by Hal March. The quiz spawned many imitators, including its own *$64,000 Challenge*, and *To Tell the Truth*, *The Price is Right*, *Keep Talking* and *Twenty-One*. Daytime and evening TV blossomed with these games, which triggered viewers' greed glands with arrays of lavish prizes (losers on *The $64,000 Question* received Cadillacs). Sponsors loved the shows, because their products were hyped shamelessly. And producers loved them too — compared to drama and variety shows, they were ridiculously inexpensive to mount. Everyone was happy, and the formula seemed eternally satisfying, as long as the viewing public's tolerance for lightweight subject matter and brassy announcers held out.

In 1958 it came to an abrupt halt, however. A former contestant on the game show *Dotto*

Above: Four members of the Champagne Music Makers (Salli Flynn, Sandi Jenson, Tanya Falan and Andra Willis) help their boss, Lawrence Welk, celebrate his 65th birthday in 1968 on The Lawrence Welk Show.
Above left: The irrepressible Jonathan Winters.

Opposite: The beloved Jimmy Durante — 'The Schnoz.'

confessed to receiving answers; then Herbert Stempel outlined his elaborate coaching on *Twenty-One*. In his case it might have seemed like sour grapes, in spite of his considerable earnings, because he had been beaten on the show during one of Quiz's proudest moments – when Charles Van Doren, intellectual scion of one of America's brainy elite families – grimaced and sweated his way to winning $129,000. Van Doren, who had been ensconced in the famous soundproof 'isolation booth', at first stoutly denied that he had been given answers.

America was shocked at the scandal, and soon Congressional hearings were being conducted; there was the traditional American circus element at play, but also the country wondered whether its new toy – immediate, gratifying, kaleidoscopic – could also be devious. Witnesses swore their innocence until the glare of publicity grew too great, and finally ten were convicted of perjury. Producers thereafter defended the fraud by claiming entertainment value as the extenuating circumstance. The Game Show was wounded – but certainly not dead. For the next decade quiz programs were mostly confined to the daytime and were either so cerebral or inane that they were above suspicion. Jack Barry, producer and host of *Twenty-One*, left TV for a while but returned as producer of *Tic Tac Dough* and host of *The Joker's Wild*, shows in which contestants would have needed special coaching to answer the brain-twisters *incorrectly*.

Mostly, it seemed to damage not the genre so much as the medium itself. Television had reached majority and matured in many ways; now it had had its first illicit affair. For the first time the viewers' precious illusion was shattered: TV was *not* life, not an impartial carrier of truth. It was an entertainment business (read: profit motivation) that willingly subordinated truth, fairness, and – most insultingly – appearances, to further its private ends. To Americans who contemplated the state of affairs it all had troubling implications. But to most it was a momentary shock, half-disappointing and half-amusing; most folks were addicted to the tube by now anyhow.

A somewhat higher road was being trod on television by an unexpected genre, the Western. Previously the stuff of cheap fiction and children's time-slots on television, the hour-long drama *Gunsmoke* broke new ground. Creating a school dubbed 'adult Western,' *Gunsmoke's* plots were hardly psychological dramas or Ibsen on horseback – but they did eschew the formalized bankrobber/stagecoach holdup/kidnap/head-'em-off-at-the-pass clip-clops of so many successful Saturday morning Westerns. The players were low-key, and characters were developing beyond two dimensions.

Gunsmoke was actually spun off its radio incarnation (where William Conrad, later TV's *Cannon* and *Nero Wolfe*, was the voice of Sheriff Matt Dillon) and was first offered to John Wayne as a starring vehicle. But James Arness, the

second choice, was finally cast as the lead, and he found employment between 1955 and 1975. It was an incredible run atop TV's plethora of competing shows, and the series truly became an institution.

Other cast members included Amanda Blake (Miss Kitty of the Long Branch Saloon), Milburn Stone (Doc Adams), Dennis Weaver (the limping deputy, Chester), Ken Curtis (Festus Hagen), and Burt Reynolds (blacksmith Quint Asper). Coincidentally, another Western temporarily set in the same town, Dodge City, Kansas, premiered the same week: *The Life and Times of Wyatt Earp*, starring Hugh O'Brien. It was also seen as an Adult Western, and the rush was on – virtually resembling the Oklahoma Land Rush. In 1956 Dick Powell switched his anthology-set gaze to

the Western and hosted (often starring in) the *Zane Grey Theater*, named for the prolific author of horse-operas. Soon there was *The Texan*, with Rory Calhoun; *Wanted – Dead or Alive*, the exploits of Josh Randall, bounty hunter, starring Steve McQueen; and *Bat Masterson*, starring Gene Barry as a foppish dandy. Bat was totally divorced from historical accuracy, but he was similarly estranged from the stereotyped shoot-'em-ups of recent TV Westerns.

Cheyenne spun off a Warner Brothers' TV anthology series and found a life of its own, as did many other Warners' Westerns and those of other studios. In fact in the 1959 season alone there were 28 Westerns in network prime-time. Among these were *Tales of Wells Fargo; Sugarfoot; Bronco; The Rifleman; Laramie; Wichita*

Above: *The* Gunsmoke *crew – James Arness (Matt Dillon), Milburn Stone (Doc Adams), Amanda Blake (Miss Kitty), Ken Curtis (Festus Hagen) and, seated in front, Burt Reynolds (Quint Asper).* **Opposite top:** *Steve McQueen was Josh Randall, the bounty hunter, in* Wanted: Dead or Alive. **Opposite bottom:** *Clint Walker as* Cheyenne.

Above: *Ward Bond seems to be getting the better of his opponent in a fight on* Wagon Train.
Opposite: *Cool, calm, collected and a bit cowardly – James Garner as* Maverick.

Fuller provided the dose of brash inexperience and romantic interests to insure the show's appeal to all age groups. Another long-running Western was *Rawhide*, starring Eric Fleming as the trail boss and country-music comedian Sheb Wooley as the trail scout. But the real interest in the series centered on Rowdy Yates, the Ramrod, played by Clint Eastwood, who parlayed the role and his identification with Westerns to the superb, influential 'Spaghetti Western' movies of Sergio Leone – and superstardom beyond.

Have Gun – Will Travel was one of the most self-consciously offbeat – and successful – of the late-1950s' wave of different-flavor Westerns. Richard Boone starred as the surly, mysterious, macho hired gun. He served only the cause of the righteous and helpless, and was identified by two trademarks: the paladin symbol on his holster (Paladin was his only name as well), and his business card. Business card? It read 'Have Gun – Will Travel. Wire Paladin, San Francisco.' Among the regulars were his servants, Hey Boy and Hey Girl. Boone later starred in one of the most intelligent of television's Westerns, *Hec Ramsey*, in the 1970s, when his face and demeanor were even more craggy.

But the only real competition to *Gunsmoke* in the strata of TV Westerns was *Bonanza*. It ran from 1959 to 1972 and was high in viewers' affections. It too had a somewhat unorthodox premise – the father, Ben Cartwright (Lorne Greene) had to raise his three sons alone on the Ponderosa Ranch near the Comstock Lode in Nevada. The young men (Pernell Roberts as Adam, Dan Blocker as Hoss, and Michael Landon as Little Joe) manifested every character trait in Central Casting between them, so the episodes were varied in their themes and predicaments. The Cartwrights constantly found themselves protecting their land, helping the helpless and fighting corruption. With a cast of locals, and a host of convenient passers-through, the formula worked for a multitude of devoted viewers who kept *Bonanza* atop rating charts for years. Dan Blocker died and was absent from the final season, but the other stars each had rich television careers subsequent to *Bonanza*: Lorne Greene starred in *Griff*, *Battlestar Galactica*, and *Code Red*; Pernell Roberts starred as *Trapper John, MD*, a nominal spinoff of *M*A*S*H*; and Michael Landon achieved fortune as producer and star of both *The Little House on the Prairie* and *Highway to Heaven*.

The Warner Brothers factory did not manufacture only Westerns but many other genres. It was the first of the great movie studios to get smart about television; they had maintained a hostile attitude toward the tube well into 1950s. Studios reportedly blacklisted actors who would appear on TV and they refused to allow TVs as props in their movies. After World War II a Supreme Court consent decree allowed the major studios to keep their production and distribution monoliths, but required them to abandon their

Town; *Johnny Ringo*; *Law of the Plainsman*; *Man from Blackhawk*; *The Deputy* (starring Henry Fonda); *Lawman* and *The Rebel*.

One of Warners' most appealing vehicles was more a parody of Westerns than an adult Western: *Maverick*. Starring low-keyed James Garner as the fast-talking Bret Maverick who tried living by guile instead of guns, there was as much comedy as action, and it was a winning formula. Jack Kelly starred as brother Bart, and later a British cousin Beau appeared in the person of Roger Moore (later TV's *Saint* and the movies' James Bond). Garner's character provided a career-long durability: an early-1980s resurrection *(Young Maverick)* failed, but the very successful *Rockford Files* mystery series featured Garner similarly cast as a sweet-talking but hapless hero.

Wagon Train was another Western series that assumed the proportions of a saga. Ward Bond was the original trailmaster, and when he died John McIntire became the star. Young, handsome sidekicks Robert Horton and later Robert

systems of theater ownership. In retrospect this should have heralded the studios' cooperation with the nascent television industry, but TV was still seen as a threat — and in truth was hurting the theaters (as we have noted, movie attendance was down on Tuesdays, when Uncle Miltie was broadcast). In 1955 the struggling RKO broke the logjam when its parent company, desperate to survive, sold its entire film library to television packagers and its studio to Desilu, the TV production firm owned by Lucille Ball and Desi Arnaz. The other studios — none of them in rosy financial condition — followed suit through the late 1950s; Warners, Fox, Paramount.

But Warners was doubly smart — it drove directly into the television waters and found success. It signed a deal to produce the Disney TV series. Warners' own series debut was the anthology *Warner Brothers Presents*, originally including a 10-minute segment about upcoming theatrical releases as a sop to theater owners. Called *Behind the Scenes* and hosted by Gig Young, it was soon discovered that TV audiences just wanted the television episode, not a documentary commercial for movie houses. The anthology rotated three series: *Casablanca, King's Row,* and *Cheyenne.* Ironically — but significantly — the two movie spinoffs withered and died, but the TV creation, *Cheyenne,* starring Clint Walker as a loner trained in ways of the Indian and white man, succeeded impressively. It soon became an independent entry in prime-time.

Walker was also one of the first of television's contract holdouts, although not without reason He was hired for what was assumed to be a time-filler, at a salary even below that of his guest stars; he was guaranteed no residuals, and was required to act in three theatrical films a year for Warners on the same conditions. He left the series and saw the ratings collapse, prompting his return at more favorable pay.

Warners now concentrated on television production. Other Westerns included *Maverick, Colt .45, Sugarfoot, Bronco* and *The Lawman.* And it can be said that their other television action/ drama series were actually Westerns in other costumes and milieux. Good guys, bad guys, chases and fights were all formulas in series like *The Alaskans* (gold rush days with Roger Moore and Dorothy Provine); *The Roaring Twenties* (Prohibition gangsters with Rex Reason and Dorothy Provine); *Bourbon Street Beat* (New Orleans intrigue with Andrew Duggan and Richard Long); *Hawaiian Eye* (island mysteries with Robert Conrad and Connie Stevens) and *Adventures in Paradise* (high-seas exotica with Gardner McKay).

The most memorable of the Warner series was *77 Sunset Strip,* which typified the 'new' detective shows (now everyone was a Private Eye, or Investigator), much as *Gunsmoke* had ushered in the Adult Western. Trendy, slightly humorous, and featuring flashy action, the series starred Efrem Zimbalist Jr (son of concert

violinist Efrem Zimbalist and opera star Alma Gluck and father of *Remington Steele* star Stephanie Zimbalist) as Stu Bailey. His sidekick was Roger Smith, and later Richard Long joined the cast. But the real tone was set by a supporting player, Edd Byrnes as Kookie, the parking-lot attendant next to the detective agency at 77 Sunset Strip in Hollywood. Kookie was a stereotyped 1950s teenager, but hipper than Ricky and David Nelson. He was forever combing his hair in duck-tail fashion, and spoke in proto-beatnik lingo. He inspired a rock hit ('Kookie, Kookie, Lend Me Your Comb') and indeed the series' theme itself was a big-selling record.

The emphasis on trendy set-ups and jazzy music was also parlayed to success by TV crime mysteries *Peter Gunn* (with Craig Stevens and Lola Albright) and *Mr Lucky* (with John Vivyan and Ross Martin), which both featured Henry Mancini's music. *Pete Kelly's Blues,* a 1959 Jack Webb series based on the motion picture, was a period piece set in Kansas City during Prohibition, and featured traditional jazz and lonely cornet solos.

One of the most successful of TV's crime mysteries of the late 1950s and early 1960s was another period piece, *The Untouchables.* The Robert Stack vehicle was loosely based on the life of G-Man Eliot Ness, and guest-starred some of the medium's heaviest of heavies: William Bendix, Lloyd Nolan, Neville Brand, and Nehemiah Persoff. The escapades of the crime-busting squad (so named because they were incorruptible during the Gangster Era) were narrated by the staccato voice-overs of columnist Walter Winchell, a familiar voice to radio listeners, and one with appropriately dated associations.

Left: *Paladin (Richard Boone) throws a punch in* Have Gun, Will Travel. **Right:** *Hoss Cartwright (Dan Blocker) towers over his father, Ben (Lorne Greene), a they guard the Ponderosa Ranch in* Bonanza.

Above: *Robert Stack
(pointing) played Eliot Ness,
the crime-fighting Chicago
FBI man of the racketeer era,
in* The Untouchables.

Television comedy was still thriving despite the onslaught of action shows (it is interesting that many of them could only be classified as 'action' as they were not strictly detective or mystery or adventure plots: it was another indication of television's inherent supremacy of form over substance). There was Groucho Marx, who held forth on *You Bet Your Life*, a seemingly spontaneous but well-rehearsed game shows; *The Ann Sothern Show*; *The Eve Arden Show*; and *The Donna Reed Show*, another entry in the homogenized-suburban sitcom sweepstakes. Reed, a former Oscar winner, starred with Carl Betz as her husband Dr Alex Stone and, as her children, Shelley Fabaris and Paul Peterson. After the fashion of Ricky Nelson, who *must* have lived in the same neighborhood, the teenagers each became recording stars apart from the show.

One of the classics of television comedy debuted in 1955 and soon became the first show to beat Berle in the ratings. *You'll Never Get Rich* (later known as *Sergeant Bilko* and *The Phil Silvers Show*) was a perfect marriage of writing, actors and premise. Created by Nat Hiken (who was the show's chief writer, managing such other writers as Neil Simon), the show centered on a larcenous motor-pool sergeant on somewhat

remote US Army bases, his protector/leech relationship with his hapless platoon, his skirt-chasing, and his schemes perpetrated under the nose of the base commanders. Phil Silvers, the veteran burlesque comedian, was superbly cast as the fast-talking Ernie Bilko, and Paul Ford — paunchy, exasperated, hangdog — played his foil as Colonel John T Hall. In such a well-fashioned ensemble it seemed that every bit of casting was impeccable: Maurice Gosfield as Private Duane Doberman, who must have been designed by George ('Grin and Bear It') Lichty; Billy Sands; Herbie Faye; Mickey Freeman; Jack Healy; Allen Melvin and Harvey Lembeck. Joe E Ross mugged outrageously as Mess Sergeant Rupert Ritzik, but found it impossible to overplay. The characters were believable, even if caricatured — Bilko showed occasional flashes of compassion — and the brilliant construction of predicaments and situations made *You'll Never Get Rich* one of the richest moments of TV comedy.

After Andy Griffith made a guest appearance in the late 1950s on the Danny Thomas Show as a rural sheriff, he was cast as Andy Taylor, Sheriff of Mayberry, North Carolina, in *The Andy Griffith Show*. The unpretentious rural comedy of manners grew to be a remarkable

Left: *Efrem Zimbalist Jr, Edd Byrnes and Roger Smith starred in* 77 Sunset Strip. **Below:** *Donna Reed and Carl Betz played Donna and Alex Stone on* The Donna Reed Show, *which ran from 1958 to 1966.*

chapter in television; the program ran for eight years, spawned spinoff series, and inspired a great number of memorable character actors — but low-key, philosophical Andy was always the eye in the center of the hurricane, playing a widower who lived with his Aunt Bee (Frances Bavier) and his young son Opie (Ronny Howard, later Ron Howard of Happy Days). The remainder of the cast through the years included Don Knotts as Andy's partner Barney Fife (as the deputy sheriff in a sleepy Southern town he was always imagining great plots and threats); Jim Nabors (Gomer Pyle); George Lindsey (Goober Pyle); Howard McNair; Jack Burns; Howard Morris; Denver Pyle; the bluegrass-music Dillard Brothers and Ken Berry, who eventually starred in the series' next-generation spinoff when Griffith retired — *Mayberry RFD*. The Griffith show, no matter how trivial the townsfolk's problems seemed, or how silly Barney's antics became, was warm and believable.

There is an interesting family tree of television of which the Andy Griffith Show was one branch. Sheldon Leonard, former movie heavy, was the producer of the Danny Thomas and Griffith shows, and, later, *The Dick Van Dyke Show*, which starred Van Dyke and Mary Tyler Moore. Later she headed her own production

company with a dozen of TV's classic series. Tony Thomas, Danny's son (and brother of *That Girl*'s Marlo Thomas) produced shows like *Soap*, *Benson* and *The Golden Girls*.

Paul Henning began his own TV-production empire in 1957 with *The Real McCoys*, starring character actor Walter Brennan (possessor of three Oscars), and concerning a poor West Virginia family transplanted to California. The warm humor was well played by other cast members, including Richard Crenna (late of *Our Miss Brooks*, and later to star in *Slattery's People* and *It Takes Two*) and Kathy Nolan. Brennan later starred in *The Tycoon*, quite differently made up as a millionaire, and became active in rightwing politics.

Steve Allen's replacement on *The Tonight Show* was eventually settled when Jack Paar became host. With a retiring, cerebral image, Paar cultivated a group of character actors as regular guests – Cliff Arquette ('Charlie Weaver'), Genevieve, Jack Douglas, Oscar Levant, Alexander King – to mix with the occasional guests.

Paar made a specialty of wearing his emotions on his sleeve, whether it was gushing over liberal politics or weeping over network interference. Once he walked off his own show because the NBC censors deleted a reference to a toilet in one of his jokes. Equally astonishing was a major personality's split-level sophomoric performances, and the degree to which standards have changed at NBC (even unto *The Tonight Show*, which became under Johnny Carson a bellwether of barely permissible scatology in American society.)

As Steve Allen and Ernie Kovacs continued in cleaner, and more brilliant, paths, their fraternity was joined by Jonathan Winters, who hosted a Tuesday night NBC show in 1956 and has since appeared on TV with many guest appearances featuring his asylum of alter-egos and hair-trigger improvisations.

In the late 1950s children's television was enriched by *Rocky and His Friends*, a brilliant ensemble of characters and skits that surely must have sailed over the heads of many

Above: *Ken Berry played farmer-city councilman Sam Jones in* Mayberry, RFD, *a spinoff from* The Andy Griffith Show. *Here he discusses the state of the world with a Cub Scout. The show lasted two years on CBS and then went into syndication.*
Opposite: *The young Raymond Burr as* Perry Mason.

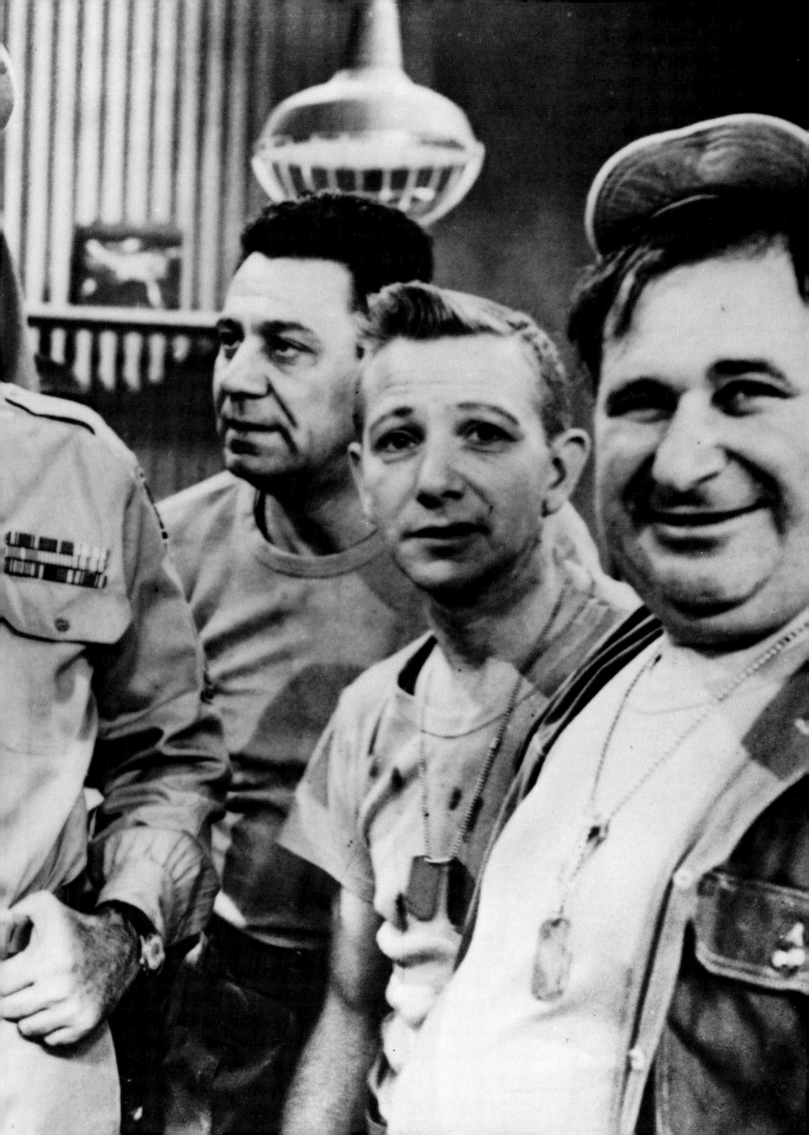

would be seen only by their arms in the doorway, and Reba's head was in a potbellied stove. Sale's routines brought baggypants burlesque to a new generation of Americans — his outrageous skits would invite kids to 'send in the green paper from Daddy's wallets' (it happened in great volume and resulted in a suspension) and admonishing kids to eat their Jello just like Soupy. When he did, his swallow was accompanied by the sound effect of a flushing toilet.

Other children's programs included Paul Terry's *Mighty Mouse*, the first Saturday morning animated-cartoon series (beginning a television tradition that has almost made 'Saturday morning' and 'cartoons' synonymous). Later *Heckle and Jeckle, Tom Terrific* and *Mighty Manfred the Wonder Dog* joined the Terrytoons. *Ruff and Reddy* were Hanna and Barbera's first TV animation after a long, honored career as 'Tom and Jerry' animators with MGM; their streamlined, low-budget animation processes for television revolutionized the industry and brought dozens of series under their direction through the years. *Gumby*, a stop-action animated series with clay figures, had a short but memorable life with TV youngsters in the late 1950s. The force of television-evoked nostalgia is such that Baby Boomers 30 years later would buy resurrected Gumby merchandising items for their own children.

Left: *Rocky the flying squirrel, Natasha and Boris Badenov standing on Bullwinkle J Moose in* Rocky and His Friends.
Opposite: *Soupy Sales — the kids' answer to Ernie Kovacs.*

Previous spread: *Phil Silvers (center) as Master Sergeant Ernie Bilko (serial number 15042699) with his platoon in* The Phil Silvers Show.
Below: Heckle and Jeckle — *ever the tormentors.*

younger viewers. Comedy, satire and parody were the hallmarks of this Jay Scott-Bill Ward animated series; featured were Rocky's sidekick Bullwinkle J Moose; the baddies Boris Badenov and Natasha; Sherman and Peabody (the genius-level dog who invented a time-machine); Dudley Do-Right and others. Among the voices were June Foray (the brilliant lady of a thousand voices), Paul Press, William Conrad and distinguished character actors Hans Conreid and Edward Everett Horton. The animation studio went on to create *George of the Jungle* and other children's favorites, but Rocky was in a tradition — already forged by *Crusader Rabbit* and *Beany and Cecil* — that appealed to adult viewers as much as their kids.

Squarely in the same tradition was Soupy Sales, a live-action host who similarly played (via references, puns and allusions, not to mention double-entendre) to the oldsters. Sales began in Detroit, moved to the ABC network, and then local stations in New York. His companions were puppets and unseen voices; White Fang (the sweetest dog in the world) and Black Tooth (the meanest dog in the world)

Left: *Ed McMahon, Richard Kiley, Selma Diamond and Johnny Carson in an early edition of* The Tonight Show.

Opposite: *Mary Linda Rapelye and Jacques Perreault tie the knot on* As the World Turns.

Below: *One of the sleaziest daytime quiz shows of all time was* Queen for a Day. *Here emcee Jack Bailey crowns a winner.*

In the daytime of late 1950s television came two new soap operas destined to have long runs: *The Edge of Night* (featuring the travails of Mike Carr) and *As The World Turns*. Among the quiz shows was *Tic Tac Dough, Truth or Consequences, The Price Is Right* and *Concentration,* which aimed, with its first host Hugh Downs, at a more intellectual image. Johnny Carson moved penultimately closer to superstardom when he hosted *Do You Trust Your Wife?* (later *Who Do You Trust?*), a free-format show that allowed him to parry comments with guests *à la* Groucho. Previously Carson had bounced around daytime and prime-time shows, California-local and network. When Jack Paar took his final peevish walk, his chair became Carson's for a quarter-century.

Surely one of the most bizarre of any quiz show concocted by the nameless army of quiz-show concocters was *Queen For a Day*. Smarmy host Jack Bailey daily decided just who among several sobbing ladies on the brink of personal disaster would receive the prop crown and assorted gifts; the other down-and-outers would contemplate their relative misery as they were ushered off the stage as losers.

Among variety shows Jaye P Morgan hosted several, one with her four brothers; Patti Page hosted a Saturday night show on NBC; Jimmy Dean brought down-home folksiness to mornings and prime-time on ABC; Pat Boone rode the wave of success as a young singer untouched by Presley's earthiness in his own variety show;

has little to do with that attraction — attested to by countless commercials with grotesque visages — and neither, evidently, do the traditional definitions of talent.

Two spinoffs from other media were notable hits. Cartoonist Hank Ketcham saw his half-pint terror somewhat tamed by the cute Jay North in *Dennis the Menace*, and Max Shulman's literary chronicles of lovelorn teenager Dobie Gillis were transferred to the tiny tube. Dwayne Hickman starred, with Tuesday Weld as Thalia Menninger, the most serious of his romantic preoccupations in *The Many Loves of Dobie Gillis*; Bob Denver as his beatnik pal Maynard G. Krebs; Frank Faylen and Florida Friebus as his eccentric parents; Sheila James as Zelda Gilroy, the tomboy with a crush on Dobie; Warren Beatty as Milton Armitage, Dobie's rival; and Steve Franken as the spoiled rich boy Chatsworth Osborne Jr. The predicaments seldom grew stale as the producers wisked Dobie and Maynard through high school, into the army, and then into college through the show's five-season run.

The decade closed with one of television's brightest — and, in its own way, darkest — series: *The Twilight Zone*. Rod Serling, already noted as one of young TV's most brilliant innovators and instinctive handlers (scripter of *Requiem for a Heavyweight* and other original teleplays), hosted the series and wrote a majority of its scripts. The anthology program sometimes served up science-fiction, sometimes fantasy, sometimes humor, but always 'What-If?' Top-flight writers contributed, and big-name stars acted, to make practically every episode a classic of tight writing, vivid characterization and invariably arresting premises, through 151 episodes. In recent years of re-runs it has developed a cult following.

If television's new maturity was an admixture of good and bad — such as live drama versus quiz-show scandals — so too was the medium's remarkable capacity as informer. Abstractly, any vehicle of mass communication would have a salutory effect on the populace in a democracy. Indeed such events as the coronation of Queen Elizabeth, coverage of the A-Bomb test and the documentary aspects of Khrushchev's US visit at least satiated people's curiosity and at best made them more informed as citizens — and, presumably, voters. But the impact of a mass-communication medium on a non-democratic society (as envisioned in horror by Orwell and others) was dangerous not only when the people were captive, but when the airwaves were un-democratic as well.

Consequently, because the TV hosts are cast in favorable attitudes, because narrators assure us of impartiality, because all the 'friendly' faces on the screen as perceived as neighbors, because commercials interrupt whatever is telecast and therefore make everything seem 'normal' — because of all these factors some very personalized points of view have been accepted as news or, more twisted yet, as fact.

Rosemary Clooney, Patrice Munsel and Polly Bergen each hosted their own shows. Frank Sinatra tried and failed with several attempts at a regularly-scheduled show and Walter Winchell challenged his cross-town rival Ed Sullivan on TV (Winchell was a columnist for the New York *Mirror*, Sullivan for the New York *Daily News*). Although Winchell arguably had more show-business experience, as a childhood member of Gus Edwards's troupe with George Jessel and others, there was no beating Sullivan at this new game, no matter how awkward and tentative he seemed. Sullivan's success and longevity was testament to the fact, slowly dawning on network executives and casting directors, that the little screen not only changed proportions but perceptions as well; as we have noted, in television like no other medium, a 'personality' with no other credentials than a presence or a certain aura can attract followers. Comeliness

In one of television's earliest and most effective displays of such persuasion, Richard Nixon, of all people – he who was ultimately undone partly by television – salvaged his political career with a television speech in 1952. Accused of accepting gifts, Vice-presidential candidate Nixon read an emotional speech defending his daughters' acceptance of a dog (instantly the soul-bearing episode was dubbed 'The Checkers Speech') and then attacked his opponents by referring to his wife's 'Republican cloth coat' – and at the appropriate moment the cameras panned to Pat Nixon sitting off to the side. It was masterful, it was persuasive and it was Television. Like a political Ed Sullivan, and in spite of the subsequent stereotypes about his image problems, Nixon proved that being telegenic is not the sole criterion for being a television communicator.

Senator Joe McCarthy was his own worst enemy. Almost. In one of the decade's most riveting television productions, the Army-McCarthy Hearings were transformed somehow at midpoint from Are there Communists in the Army? to Let's Watch Senator Joe self-destruct. Television cameras indeed turned the atmosphere of the investigations into a performance. The emotional apex of the hearings, when Army counsel Joseph Welch repeatedly asked McCarthy, 'Have you no sense of decency?', was perceived by viewers as the ultimate confrontation with witch-hunting tactics. Actually it was Welch's reaction to McCarthy's breaking a pledge not to raise an aspect of the past of Welch's aide Fred Fisher; Welch had similarly promised not to tread on an area in McCarthy ally David Schine's past. It was nothing more, but on television, it became *much* more, gaining the appearance of a momentous confrontation. Very appropriately, Welch parlayed his new-found fame from the Army-McCarthy hearings into a

modest career as an actor and master of ceremonies on television.

If there ever was a face on television that could have used coaching, it was McCarthy. Right or wrong, sloppy or evil, determined or possessed – it made no difference with McCarthy. He was ideally perceived as a bad guy, with his shadowy countenance, darting glances and whining monotone. If he had indeed been the super-ambitious conniver, he might have played more to the cameras, but television was new and McCarthy was, in the hot-media sense, naive. Edward R Murrow was not. When he reported on McCarthy, Murrow could control his own image – and by implication contrast it with the sinister Senator. When he displayed images or replayed footage, Murrow was the master of what to choose – and often selected the most unflattering shots of McCarthy. When Murrow 'reported' he actually engaged in editorializing, and whether it was presented as straight news or introduced as 'no time for men who oppose Senator McCarthy's methods to keep silent,' herein was the ultimate reality of television. For the viewer is forced to concentrate his vision and thoughts on the little screen, and this produces an intimacy. The television as a personal possession

Above: *Cliff Robertson starred as a possessed ventriloquist in a* Twilight Zone *episode.*
Above left: *The logo for the Rod Serling drama series.*

Opposite: *Jonathan Winters, in his television debut, and Jack Klugman, in the original* Twilight Zone *episode, 'A Game of Pool.'*

Above: Dorothy Collins, one of America's sweethearts when she starred on Your Hit Parade, *pushes the sponsor's product – Lucky Strike cigarettes. Today this commercial would be illegal.*

becomes a personal confidence between broadcaster and viewer; when adventure and crime shows are so close to reality, men in business suits looking straight at you must *be* reality.

So if the editorial *caveat* puts the viewer's defenses up, then the arched eyebrows, vocal inflections and myriads of other means of coloring perceptions are subliminal – and effective. The Army-McCarthy Hearings are worth considering not only because they were the best show of the decade, but also because of their implications about fairness, perceptions, and the larger role of television in a democracy.

One of the most brilliant pieces of editorial direction, coloring what could otherwise have been a purely impartial piece of news coverage, came at the request of the victim during the Kefauver Crime Hearings televised during the 1950s. Witness Frank Costello, a mobster, asked that his face not be shown on television. The cameras obliged, and millions of viewers focused on his nervous, sweaty hands during tough questioning.

The end of the 1950s brought a symbolic end to many of television's traditions – and illusions. Already Berle, Caesar, *Howdy Doody* and *I Love Lucy* were gone. Live television's image was fading from the screen. The new stars began their careers on TV, not having transferred popularity from radio or movies. Television had become a necessity, not a luxury; the set was like the telephone or the auto.

Television had not lost its virginity with the quiz show scandals. That had happened during the Checkers speech and Murrow's McCarthy crusade. TV was not only new, exciting, immediate and necessary, but the little box might just be something more than it seemed. If not a vehicle for political propaganda, then it was certainly a medium of commercial propaganda: advertisers geared up in ways that must have made the shades of totalitarian 'Information Ministries' jealous. TV was no longer innocent when the quiz scandals broke, but many viewers were. TV was going in two directions at once: its feet were slipping a little more in the mud, but its eyes were cast upward. It is difficult to proceed in such a manner, but the succeeding ages of television history in America may be seen through that imagery.

One factor cast TV's eyes a little higher than otherwise by the end of the decade. The Soviet Union had propelled a basketball-sized machine into orbit around the earth, and the government and educational establishments were shocked – and chagrined. Television was seen, again, as a potential tool for educational advancement. If Sarnoff's vision of lessons and art galleries in the homes had been detoured in the business office, then there were others to lead television's sometimes groping hands, if even through the mud of banality.

FREE TO PUBLIC
KEFAUVER TV
SENATE CRIME HEARINGS

FREE TO PUBLIC TODAY.

BROADCAST ON OUR THEATRE SCREEN

KEFAUVER SENATE CRIME INVESTIGATION HEARING

THE
SIXTIES

Television, a figure trudging through the mud of mediocrity, was characterized slightly differently by a public figure in the early 1960s. The Federal Communications Commission determined to play a stronger role in television programming and policies, or at least the new president, John F Kennedy — himself elected, by common consent, largely because of his telegenic performances of televised debates — sought to impose that vision. Newspapers and magazines were private enterprises strictly covered by Bill of Rights guarantees, but the airwaves were the public's and the stations merely the temporary trustees. Kennedy saw the government itself as the larger trustee, and foresaw government's role in directing its progress. He named a former law partner of Adlai Stevenson to be FCC chairman, and Newton Minow lost no time in chiding broadcasters (9 May, 1961): 'I invite you to sit down in front of your television set when your station goes on the air . . . and keep your eyes glued to that set until the station signs off. I can assure you that you will observe a vast wasteland . . . . True, you will see a few things you enjoy. But they will be very, very few. And if you think I exaggerate, try it.

'It is not enough to cater to the nation's whims — you must also serve the nation's needs. The squandering of our airwaves is no less important than the lavish waste of any precious natural resource.'

If the answer was in more quality programming — live drama, for instance — the networks were in a retreat from which they would not deviate. If the salvation was in more public-affairs programing and news specials, many segments of the public were awake to the potential bias, especially with an activist administration prodding the industry. (Already calls were issued for a multiplicity of channels and pay-TV — the 'free marketplace of ideas' — although it would be quarter-century before the vehicle, if not the content, was to be achieved.) And almost every voice that bothered to raise itself in response to Chairman Minow was in agreement with his critique — yet ownership of sets and total viewing numbers steadily rose.

The Russians had Sputnik up, and Camelot was setting up camp on the Potomac. As the 1960s dawned, the nation at large had reasons to feel both bad and good, and television provided the escapist panacea for whatever ailed one. Comedies proliferated, as they have throughout almost every one of television's years.

Pete and Gladys was a successful spinoff from *December Bride*. It starred Harry Morgan and Cara Williams, whose character had never been seen on the established show. Gale Gordon and Verna Felton completed the cast in this series about an insurance salesman and his scatterbrained wife. *Harrigan and Son* brought Pat O'Brien to TV as a conservative lawyer who insisted on loose interpretation of the law to accommodate clients. He quarreled with his son, just out of college, who insisted on strict interpretations and going by the book. The Sixties had obviously only begun.

The Flintstones debuted in 1960, and became the first animated cartoon series in prime-time. It was another in the growing production-line of cartoons from the Hanna-Barbera Studios, but a cut more sophisticated than the rest; ostensibly aimed at adults, it would never tax a pre-schooler's capacities but was a unique diversion (it inspired a few imitators, like H-B's own *The*

Above: *Television covered the 1961 Summit Meeting between President John F Kennedy and Russian Premier Nikita Khrushchev.*
Previous spread: *Neil Armstrong — the first man to walk on the moon, televised in June 1969.*

Jetsons, but none with the staying power of the Flintstones). The series was a stone-age version of *The Honeymooners*, featuring Fred and Wilma Flintstone and their neighbors Betty and Barney Rubble (the voices, respectively, of Alan Reed, Jean Vanderpyl, Bea Benaderet and Mel Blanc).

As Hanna-Barbera refined limited-animation techniques, animation purists squirmed but the industry could afford to bring cartoons to a new generation. Among the (mostly daytime) cartoons that proliferated during the 1960s were: *Alvin and the Chipmunks; Clyde Crashkup; Top Cat; Calvin and the Colonel* (based on radio's *Amos 'n' Andy*, featuring the originals' voices, Charles Correll and Freeman Gosden); *Johnny Quest; Tom and Jerry; Atom Ant; Secret Squirrel; The Beatles; Magilla Gorilla; Road Runner; Cool McCool; The Fantastic Four; Spiderman; George of the Jungle; The Archies; Scooby-Doo* and *The Pink Panther*.

Robert Young was unable to parlay his Father Knows Best popularity to *Window On Main Street*, which lasted just the 1961 season although it was a well-written, cozy show. Neither could the TV versions of the movie classics *Going My Way* (with Gene Kelly and Leo G Carroll) and *Mr Smith Goes to Washington* (starring Fess Parker) make the grade. *Mrs G Goes to College* (with Gertrude Berg); *The Joey Bishop Show; The New Bob Cummings Show* and — especially *The Hathaways*, about a bunch of chimps living with a suburban family, were unlamentable, short-lived series.

A winner in 1961 was the CBS Comedy Spot, a tryout-format that featured, in one segment, Harpo and Chico Marx as bungling thieves in 'The Incredible Jewel Robbery,' truly one of the great moments of television. It also offered a half-hour called *Head of the Family*. In it, Rob Petrie, a comedy writer, tries to assure his disillusioned son that Daddy does indeed have a job as important as his friends' daddies. It starred Carl Reiner, but when it was picked up as a series, Dick Van Dyke became the star (Reiner continued as chief writer and occasional guest player). It was cancelled after its first season — as the Dick Van Dyke Show — having placed 80th in the ratings. But it was resurrected and soon

Right: *Three popular children's cartoon shows of the 1960s:*
Top: The Flintstones.
Center: The Road Runner Show.
Bottom: The Jetsons.

found its audience, and a place in history. Witty as well as funny, the show was able to cover both domestic comedy in the Petrie household (Mary Tyler Moore played wife Laura) and in the office where Rob was chief writer on a TV comedy/variety show. Morey Amsterdam and Rose Marie played his staff, Richard Deacon was the oafish producer and Reiner the temperamental star. The writing was literate, and the program was the first among many shows built on quality material and basically strong relationships between the players.

Another comedy debuted in 1961, a cult favorite of exquisite quality reminiscent of the *Bilko* show because its creative crew and many cast members were alumnae of Fort Baxter. *Car 54, Where Are You?* was created by Nat Hiken, and it starred Joe E Ross and Fred Gwynne as police officers Gunther Toody and Francis Muldoon. Other officers and assorted neighborhood nuts were played by Al Lewis, Jack Healy and Carl Ballantine; Beatrice Pons and Charlotte Rae also had featured roles. Toody was earnest but thick-headed, and tall, laconic Muldoon was placid and cerebral.

Producer Paul Henning played a variation on his *Real McCoys* theme when he created a program about Ozark hillbillies discovering oil on their land and moving to posh Beverly Hills. *The Beverly Hillbillies* became a monstrous hit and was an unpretentious comedy about rural folks' difficulties with urban life and society — and sophisticated folks' reactions ranging from bewilderment to protectiveness to larceny. Veteran song-and-dance man Buddy Ebsen looked quite at home unshorn and in tattered clothes; his cranky mother-in-law was played by Irene Ryan; and his nephew and daughter were portrayed by Max Baer, Jr and Donna Douglas. Douglas, as Elly May, wore tight dungarees and may have started the trend of blue jeans worn by females.

Adjusting to modern life in the city was hard on all the show's characters, and stories revolved about Jed and Granny's desire to return to mountain life. Elly May was determined to find a beau and live among her 'critter friends,' and Jethro, a thick-headed lunk, got into predicaments and searched for sweeties. A supporting cast of character types kept the program fast-paced and varied. The local banker (Raymond Bailey) was desirous of keeping the Clampett's account; his wife (Harriet MacGibbon) wanted them out of the neighborhood. The banker's secretary (Nancy Kulp) was a stuffy society-type, while his son (played by Louis Nye) was a wastrel. Local doctors fought Granny's home brews and oil executives prostrated themselves before the Clampetts. Bluegrass legends Lester Flatt and Earl Scruggs portrayed themselves as friends from back in the hills, although their wives were played by Hollywood bombshells Joi Lansing and Midge Ware. The program allowed for great interplay of personalities as well as malaprops and situational misunderstandings.

Above: *Eddie Albert and Eva Gabor starred as Oliver and Lisa Douglas in* Green Acres, *a spinoff of* Petticoat Junction.
Opposite top: *Buddy Ebsen (Jed Clampett), Irene Ryan (Daisy 'Granny' Moses), Max Baer Jr (Jethro Bodine) and Donna Douglas (Elly May Clampett) in* The Beverly Hillbillies.
Opposite bottom: *Buddy Sorrell (Morey Amsterdam) entertains Laura Petrie (Mary Tyler Moore), Rob Petrie (Dick Van Dyke) and Sally Rogers (Rose Marie) on* The Dick Van Dyke Show.

The success of the program led to two notable spinoffs. Bea Benaderet occasionally appeared as Jethro's mother, Pearl, and she became the star of *Petticoat Junction*. Set in rural Hooterville, Benedaret played the widowed proprietress of the Shady Rest Hotel, where her three lovely daughters (Bobbie Jo, Billie Jo, and Betty Jo) and a well-meaning blowhard (Uncle Joe Carson, played by Edgar Buchanan) also lived. Stories revolved around the girls' romances, silly intrigues involving the dilapidated local railroad and a woman doctor's problems finding acceptance in the countryside (after Benedaret's untimely death toward the end of the show's run, June Lockhart assumed the 'matriarchal' role as Dr Janet Craig).

Truly inspired nonsense – even surrealism – followed in the next spinoff also set in Hooter-

ville: *Green Acres*. This was *The Beverly Hillbillies* in reverse, with prosperous urban lawyer Oliver Douglas (Eddie Albert) moving to farm country for peace of mind. His absurdly aristocratic and dumb wife Lisa (Eva Gabor) made inane but sincere efforts to adapt to the country-spartan lifestyle. The humor flowed from bizarre characters – the bumbling Agricultural Agent Mr Kimball; the constant conniver Mr Haney played by Pat Buttram; the inane hired man Eb Dawson (Tom Lester); Fred Ziffel the pig farmer (Hank Patterson) – but also touches of Dada: when a letter is read, the sender's voice replaces the reader's; Lisa comments on the show's credits, appearing on the screen, dirtying her hanging wash; everyone's (except, inevitably, Oliver's) assumption that Arnold Ziffel, the pig, is a real person.

O.K. Crackerby, with Burl Ives as a burly oilman determined to enter Palm Springs society, was another attractive comedy set in a similar mode. Critics were universally unkind to these shows, but the public supported them. *Green Acres*, especially, maintains its quality after years on the shelf and in syndication.

Lucille Ball returned to TV in 1961 with *The Lucy Show*; it seemed she would never be away from the screen too long before her virtual retirement in the 1980s. Foreshadowing Mary Tyler Moore always casting herself as a Mary, Lucille Ball followed her Lucy Ricardo character with, in 1961, Lucy Carmichael and, in 1968, Lucille Carter. In the 1968 show *(Here's Lucy)* she co-starred with her two children, Dezi Arnaz Jr and Lucie Arnaz. Through the two 1960s shows she brought along her co-stars, Gale Gordon and Vivian Vance.

McHale's Navy was virtually a spinoff; except for a few of the supporting characters being in both series, there was no formal relationship with Sergeant Bilko, but the parallels were obvious. The branch of the military changed, as did the time (*McHale's Navy* was set during World War II), but the premise – a group of gold-brick servicemen led by their fast-talking leader, scheming under the nose of the commander – was the same. It was an impossible challenge to duplicate Bilko's quality, but some comic moments were provided by the mugging of Ernest Borgnine as McHale, Tim Conway as bumbling Ensign Parker, and feisty Joe Flynn as Captain Bingham-

ton. *Broadside*, about WAVES, was a spinoff of *McHale's Navy*.

Above-average acting and writing graced the sitcom *I'm Dickens, He's Fenster*, starring John Astin and Marty Ingels as two carpenters. But within two seasons (in 1964) Astin was starring in a new show, *The Addams Family*, based on the macabre population of Charles Addams's *New Yorker* cartoons (Carolyn Jones and Jackie Coogan co-starred). It was a season for monsters, as two *Car 54* alums starred in *The Munsters*. Fred Gwynn played a Frankenstein look-alike, Herman Munster, and Al Lewis portrayed grandpa, a Dracula figure. Yvonne De Carlo played Mrs Munster, and Beverly Owen (and later Pat Priest) played the very normal niece Marilyn who had to cope with her bizarre family and their impact on the neighborhood.

It was a time for the supernatural in TV shows. *My Favorite Martian* (with Ray Walton in the title role, and Bill Bixby); *I Dream of Jeannie* (with Barbara Eden as the genie and Larry Hagman as her reluctant master) and *Bewitched* (starring Dick York, and later Dick Sargent, as the befuddled husband of pretty witch Elizabeth Montgomery and her shrewish mother-in-law Agnes Moorehead) all debuted in 1964.

More conventional entries of the day included *The Patty Duke Show*, wherein the child star played twin cousins via trick photography; *The Farmer's Daughter*, with Inger Stevens as the nanny to a Congressman's (William Windom) children; and *The Baileys of Balboa*. This was

one of TV's famous fizzles, but was actually an inspired show with an excellent comedy ensemble. Located in Balboa Beach, California, and focusing on the disputes between a tug captain (Paul Ford) and an aristocratic yacht owner (John Dehner), the cast also featured Sterling Holloway, Rosemary DeCamp, and Judy Carne.

The New Phil Silvers Show transferred the Bilko routine to a factory, where Silvers played Harry Grafton, foreman of a motley crew; but the show's failure proved that others could swipe his format better than he. Other short runs during the period were endured by: *The New Loretta Young Show*; *The Bill Dana Show*; *The Bing Crosby Show*; *Wendy and Me* (George Burns's post-Gracie effort, with Connie Stevens); *Many Happy Returns*; *No Time for Sergeants*; *The Cara Williams Show* and yet another fantasy entry, *My Living Doll*, featuring Julie Newmar as Bob Cumming's gorgeous robot.

Valentine's Day was a sophisticated comedy starring Tony Franciosa as suave publishing executive Valentine Farrow, and Jack Soo as his cynical valet. On the other side of the sophistication coin were two comedies that debuted in 1964 and had long runs. *Gomer Pyle, USMC* was a spinoff of *The Andy Griffith Show*, with the rube Gomer in the Marines, making life miserable for his Sergeant Vincent Carter. Pyle was neither larcenous nor a schemer, yet Frank Sutton as the sergeant would go into weekly paroxysms over Pyle's ineptitude in manners

that would have made Edgar Kennedy jealous.

Gilligan's Island proved there was life after Dobie Gillis for Bob Denver, who was Gilligan in this nonsensical comedy about a varied group of castaways never able to make contact with civilization. This in spite of the fact that visitors came and went, and the show's definition of 'stranded' included wardrobes, hardware and other amenities. As in *Green Acres*, however, the inconsistencies were deliberate, and the show never took itself as seriously as did the critics — who deplored the show with near-unanimity. Also in the cast were Alan Hale, Jr as the Skipper; Jim Backus as millionaire Thurston Howell; Russell Johnson as the Professor; Dawn Wells as Mary Ann; Tina Louise as Ginger the starlet; and Natalie Shafer as Mrs Howell. The show inspired TV movies years later, as well as two animated series: *The New Adventures of Gilligan* and *Gilligan's Planet*. The Henning shows, *Gomer Pyle* and *Gilligan's Island*, all successes, were on CBS, which was developing a reputation as not only a ratings leader, but as the network of rural, unsophisticated comedy.

NBC evidently wanted to show that it could not be out-schlocked. In 1965 it presented *My Mother the Car*, one of the most deserved disasters in sitcom history. Jerry Van Dyke (Dick's brother) was the hero whose late mother possesses his vintage jalopy; Ann Sothern mercifully lent only her voice to the mother character. Avery Schreiber played the voracious antique car collector who sought Van Dyke's mother after it was refurbished to try to meet the family's objections. Not only the family objected: the program was gone within a year.

Besides hicks and monsters, the television

industry in the mid-1960s was preoccupied with category programming — but only a few categories. Romantic comedies staked their claim, with Marlo Thomas and Ted Bessell starring in *That Girl*. *He and She*, starring real-life marrieds Paula Prentiss and Richard Benjamin, was a short-lived but literate romantic comedy several cuts above TV's average. The lead players brought an element of interaction that made the series about a cartoonist and his exasperating, scatterbrained wife more than another *Lucy* ripoff. Ted Cassidy (as the TV hero Jetman based on cartoonist Benjamin's comic strip) and Hamilton Camp (as the apartment building's handyman) rounded out the ensemble. *Love, American Style* was an interesting format concept: an anthology series with longer segments starring guests, interspersed with blackouts performed by ensemble players. It

Above: *Marlo Thomas played Ann Marie, an aspiring actress in New York in* That Girl, *which ran from 1966 to 1970.*

gave the nation several joke crazes via *Get Smart!* with his catch lines 'Would you believe . . .' and 'Sorry about that, Chief.'

On the adventure side of the dial, but with comedic touches, was *The Man from U.N.C.L.E.* (if its intent was parody of James Bond, it succeeded fairly; if it was imitation it was poor). The organization's acronym stood for United Network Command for Law Enforcement, and the show's two agents were Napoleon Solo (played by Robert Vaughn) and Ilya Kuryakin (David McCallum), who reported to Mr Waverly (Leo G Carroll). The enemy command was initialed T.H.R.U.S.H. Bond's creator, Ian Fleming, actually had a hand in fashioning the series by revamping a character from *Diamonds Are Forever* for the Solo character. The chases and gadgets kept viewers watching from 1964 to 1968, and prompted a spinoff, *The Girl from U.N.C.L.E.*, starring Stephanie Powers.

Crimefighting was elevated to even higher camp on *Batman*. The perennial third-place network ABC ventured with the comic-book spoof on Wednesday and Thursday nights, and discovered a smash hit. The series was a satire on every cliché of TV and comic books, and even of itself. The dialogue was in stilted pulp jargon, and during fights, visual sound effects appeared on the screen. Adam West and Burt Ward played Batman and Robin (and have been trying to shake that identification ever since), and while the nation was Batman-crazy for a couple of years, so was Hollywood: there was a mad scramble to be cast as a villain in Batman episodes. Among such absurd villains as the Joker and the Bookworm were actors Burgess Meredith, Art Carney, Pierre Salinger, David Wayne, Victor Buono, Vincent Price, Cesar Romero and Roddy McDowall.

In rapid order (sooner, as Robin would say, than you could say 'Holy Ripoff!') there were three other comic-book-inspired shows on the air. *The Green Hornet*, a direct adaptation, starred Van Williams and an unknown Bruce Lee as his Oriental assistant Kato; and Stephen Strimpell was *Mr Terrific*. Buck Henry tried to exploit his own *Get Smart!* and the superhero craze with *Captain Nice*. The program concerned a timid scientist who discovered a formula that would change him into a crimefighter, albeit in baggy costume. The short-lived series is notable at least for showcasing its star in character modes he has not displayed since – the bumbling scientist/crimefighter was played by William Daniels, later Dr Mark Craig on *St Elsewhere*.

Youth was served, too, in the latter part of the 1960s, the time of the Youth Generation. *The Brady Bunch* was largely about the pitfalls and pratfalls of adolescence. Two widowed parents (played by Florence Henderson and Robert Reed) met and married and created an instant family of six kids from the previous unions. Ann B Davis, once Bob Cumming's TV secretary, was the housemaid to the menagerie.

allowed for different writing and acting styles and kept the program fresh. It also – with its 'liberated' suggestiveness and trendy fashions and mores – reflected the changes then occurring in American society during its run (1969–74).

Another trend that television comedy reflected in the 1960s was the spy genre. Not only was international intrigue on the front pages, but James Bond was big stuff; President Kennedy had even praised it as favorite fiction. Naturally TV was there with multitudes of permutations. *Get Smart!* was clearly the best of the lot. It was a clever spy spoof with Don Adams as Maxwell Smart (Agent 86) of C.O.N.T.R.O.L. The romantic interest (eventually 86's wife) was Barbara Feldon, known only as Agent 99, and patient, exasperated Chief was played by Edward Platt. The bad guys were agents of K.A.O.S., and Bond spoofs abounded – eccentric spies, ridiculous threats and unbelievable gadgetry. The program was created by Mel Brooks and Buck Henry, two of the generation's finest comedy writers; and Don Adams, a former stand-up comedian,

Left: The Monkees – *David Jones, Mickey Dolenz, Peter Tork and Michael Nesmith.*

Left: The Monkees – *David Jones, Mickey Dolenz, Peter Tork and Michael Nesmith.*

Below: *Adam West listens to the mayor as Burt Ward looks on in* Batman. *Another adventure for the Dynamic Duo.*

Above: *The Green Hornet was another superhero show, spun off from the old radio thriller. Bruce Lee (right) played the faithful servant Kato.*

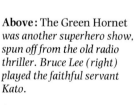

A large family plus a widowed mother plus music were the ingredients of *The Partridge Family*: Shirley Jones (and her real-life son David Cassidy) and the other kids played rock music of the soft variety, and parlayed their performances into occasional hit records and an animated-cartoon spinoff, *The Partridge Family 2200 AD*. As long as youth and rock music were being served and exploitation was TV's name of the game, *The Monkees* appeared as a stone-cold copy of the Beatles and their madcap musical movie *A Hard Day's Night*.

Actually, for all the formula and pastiche, The Monkees was a respectable show. The premise and special-effect gimmicks were patterned after the Beatles, but inspired writing and zany acting combined for memorable performances. And the music – not usually played by the troupe – turned into a string of hit records. The four Monkees were Mickey Dolenz (who, as Mickey Braddock, had appeared as TV's earlier *Circus Boy*), Michael Nesmith (a legitimate musician who later recorded country-music hits and developed the first music videos), Peter Tork, and Briton David Jones. Contemporary rock stars made guest appearances on the free-form half-hour sitcom, and in testimony to the series' more substantial aspects (today the

Above: *David McCallum
(Ilya Kuryakin), Leo G
Carroll (Mr Waverly) and
Robert Vaughn (Napoleon
Solo) in* The Man from
U.N.C.L.E.

Previous spread: *Hollywood
personalities would kill to be
guest villains on* Batman.
*Here Shelley Winters (center)
has captured Batman (Adam
West) and Robin (Burt Ward)
and strapped them into
futuristic electric chairs.*

tapes and songs are cult favorites) are the
credits of Paul Mazursky, respected film director,
as writer of the pilot, and director Bob Rafelson
and actor Nicholson as co-writers of the
Monkees' 1969 theatrical release, *Head*. Maybe
television was not the *only* place where Central
Casting could assemble a group for a program
about a famous rock ensemble that would in
reality become a famous rock ensemble — but
it was the surest place.

Consideration of 1960s comedies cannot pass
without mentioning the gamut of some forgettable and some never-to-be-forgotten programs: *Please Don't Eat the Daisies*; *Mr Roberts*;
Pistols and Petticoats (with Ann Sheridan); *The
Jean Arthur Show* (also with Ron Harper, about
a mother-and-son legal team); *Family Affair*,

with Brian Keith and Sebastian Cabot; *The
Pruitts of Southampton* (the first of several bombs
for Phyllis Diller, but one that resurrected Grady
Sutton, once a foil of W C Fields); *Love on a
Rooftop*; *The Flying Nun* (with Sally Field); *Julia*
(with Diahann Carroll helping to break color
barriers in sitcoms); *The Debbie Reynolds Show*;
The Courtship of Eddie's Father; *Room 222*; *The
Doris Day Show* (in five seasons it had four
premises and settings); *The Ghost and Mrs Muir*
and *The Don Rickles Show* (or at least the first of
several Rickles flops).

Dramatic series in the 1960s served as TV's
transition format from live drama and as such
many of the crime, police, doctor and Western
series were formularized, but many were innovative and experimental. *The Defenders*, for

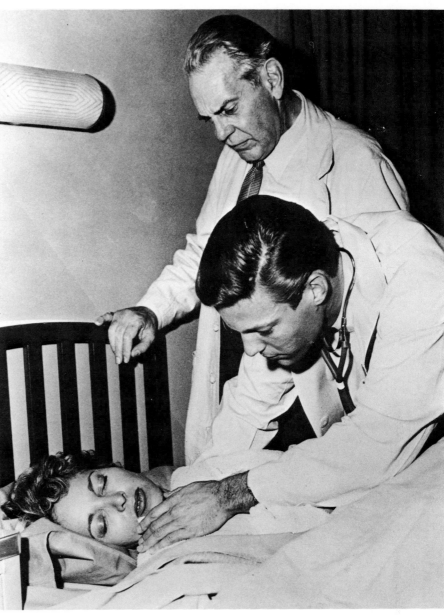

instance, spun off a 1957 *Studio One* play by Reginald Rose. Father-and-son lawyers E G Marshall and Robert Reed involved themselves in thought-provoking cases and liberal causes, and the well-fashioned program represented the new type of packaged TV drama that did not rely on chases, fights and 'action.' *The Westerner*, starring Brian Keith (and directed by Sam Peckinpah) was a realistic, sensitive series that went against the newly established grain of even many Adult Westerns. *The Law and Mr Jones* was a bit lighter than *The Defenders*; James Whitmore starred in the comedy/drama that also tackled contemporary issues. *The 87th Precinct* was a memorable cop show, displaying more personality but less procedure than Jack Webb's *Dragnet*, and it starred Robert Lansing, Norman Fell and Ron Harper. A decidedly different sort of crime-show premise was effected in *Checkmate*, wherein Sebastian Cabot and Doug McClure played criminologist-consultants. The show was famed as much for its opening motif (swirling colors, like unto an oil slick, behind the credits and titles) as its performances. Barry Sullivan played Pat Garrett and Clu Gulager played Billy the Kid in *The Tall Man*.

In the beginning of the decade two medical shows became instant hits. *Ben Casey* starred Vince Edwards as the strangely brooding and wooden doctor, with Sam Jaffe as Dr Zorba, his older mentor. *Dr Kildare* was transplanted from movies and radio with young Richard Chamberlain in the Lew Ayres title role and Raymond

Massey in Lionel Barrymore's role as *his* older mentor. At the end of the decade Robert Young returned to television as *Marcus Welby, MD*, for a long and successful practice; and Chad Everett and James Daly ministered on *Medical Center*. Other medical series were *Nurses*, with Zina Bethune, which ultimately moved to daytime as a soap-opera; *The Breaking Point*, about two psychiatrists and *The 11th Hour*, also about psychiatry.

War drama also proliferated after the success of *Combat!*, a grisly program that often used stock footage of battle and starred Vic Morrow and Rick Jason. Following were *Convoy*; *The Wackiest Ship in the Army* (a drama with moments of light comedy, based on the motion picture); *Rat Patrol*; *Jericho*; *Twelve O'Clock High*; *The Gallant Men*; *The Lieutenant* and *Court Martial*. Significantly, very few TV programs sought to glamorize the Viet Nam experience, even before opposition was widespread across America.

Before 'relevant' became a television-synonymous word for 'maudlin,' George C Scott appeared in the superb *East Side, West Side*. He

Above: *Raymond Massey (Dr Gillespie) looks on as Richard Chamberlain (Dr Kildare) examines patient Beverly Garland in Dr Kildare.*
Above left: *Don Adams (Maxwell Smart, Agent 86) mistakenly draws on Edward Platt (the Chief) as Barbara Feldon (Agent 99) looks on in Get Smart!*

In 1962 *The Virginian* formally bridged the chronological gap between live drama, theatrical movies and television series by becoming TV's first 90-minute Western. Loosely based on the Owen Wister book, dedicated to Theodore Roosevelt, and the Gary Cooper movie, it starred James Drury as the Virginian, and through its nine-year run, featured Lee J Cobb, Roberta Shore, Doug McClure, Randy Boone, Clu Gulager, Charles Bickford, John McIntire, and Farley Granger.

In one of TV's cleverest premises, Dr Richard Kimble is wrongly accused of murdering his wife, and spends four seasons chasing the one-armed murderer while eluding the police. *The Fugitive* starred David Janssen – an actor whose talents seemed at their best on the small screen – and its denouement, when he convinces the police of his innocence is the most-watched episodic program of the decade, foreshadowing the 'Who Shot J R?' ballyhoo 15 years later.

The Saint, a British import with Roger Moore, and *Burke's Law*, starring Gene Barry as a suave millionaire crime-fighter who encounters eccentric suspects like puppies attract fleas, are fanciful, light dramas where crime never pays. Closer to reality were shows like *Slattery's People* starring Richard Crenna. The program cast him as a state legislator battling corruption and dealing with constituents; it was uniformly excellent, but played only one season. *Mr Novak* similarly dealt with problems of all varieties in a high-school setting. James Franciscus played the title character, with Dean Jagger as yet another older mentor.

The Trials of O'Brien was another program cut from a different cloth. Peter Falk played a rumpled attorney, brilliant but dissheveled, juggling his cases and his worries about personal debt and divorce. The premise should sound familiar to viewers who watched Falk's later *Columbo*, in which his personality was virtually identical. One of television's brightest moments came with *The Rogues*, broadcast on Sunday nights on NBC. It starred, as members of an international family of wealthy con artists, David Niven, Charles Boyer, Gig Young, Robert Coote and Gladys Cooper. The cousins conspired elegantly to rob from the rich, from those who deserved being unburdened of ill-gotten baubles and from other crooks. Even sophisticated larceny was an unwritten television taboo, so the Rogues occasionally assisted police in troublesome cases. Despite the stellar cast, impeccable acting and clever writing, the program lasted one season. Later in the decade Robert Wagner, in *It Takes a Thief*, reprised the premise.

While young Kurt Russell, in the TV version of Robert Lewis Taylor's Pulitzer Prize-winning *Travels of Jamie McPheeters*, walked the dusty roads, an army of actors walked the low road in another successful ABC gamble, *Peyton Place*. The nighttime soap-opera, originally broadcast twice a week, chronicled the doings in a New

Above: *It's another fight for Roger Moore, as* The Saint, *in an episode called 'The Golden Frog.' This time his opponent is Alvaro Fontana.*
Right: *David Niven and Dina Merrill in an episode of* The Rogues.
Opposite: *Pursuer and pursued find themselves handcuffed together on* The Fugitive *– David Janssen (right, as Dr Richard Kimble) and Barry Morse (as Lieutenant Gerard).*

was a social worker in this urban drama, and the show broke ground by including a black woman, Cicely Tyson, as a co-star. David Susskind, before he was reduced to tawdry and superficial preoccupations as host of a talk-show, produced the series, which consistently featured mature scripts and fine acting. Scott, of course, went on to greater success in the movies but in the mid-1980s returned to television and mini-series biographies of *Mussolini* and *Patton*, because, he said, motion pictures had been kidnapped by 'the pimple set.'

Above: *Barbara Parkins (right) starred as the powerful and seductive owner of the Peyton Mill, and John Beck played Dorian Blake in* Peyton Place: The Next Generation.
Opposite: *Joyce Jillson and Michael Christian starred in* Peyton Place.

England town obsessed with sex and nastiness. Mia Farrow, Ryan O'Neal and Dorothy Malone starred in the adaptation of the Grace Metalios novel.

Other dramatic entries of the early 1960s include: *The Third Man; Bus Stop; Route 66* (the Corvette Saga starring Martin Milner and George Maharis); *Stoney Burke; Destry; Voyage to the Bottom of the Sea* (produced by Irwin Allen, who later produced *The Time Tunnel, Land of the Giants* and *Lost in Space* before going to Hollywood with *The Poseidon Adventure* and *The Towering Inferno*); *Branded; Honey West* (starring Anne Francis); *Daniel Boone* played by Fess Parker; *Daktari; Felony Squad;* a new *Dragnet* with Jack Webb and Harry Morgan; *Hawk,* a crime series starring Burt Reynolds that was repeated in many time slots when this superstar began to rise; *T.H.E. Cat; High Chapparal; N.Y.P.D.,* a precursor of *Miami Vice,* with hard scripts, unorthodox camera angles, and clever film editing; *Gentle Ben; Adam-12* and, thanks to demographic pandering to guidelines concerning 'relevance,' *The Mod Squad.* It featured a young white man, a young black man and a young white woman as minor lawbreakers recruited into a big-city police squad to infiltrate and 'relate' where the cops could not. Pete Cochran, Clarence Williams III and Peggy Lipton were described in ABC publicity as having had no acting experience before being cast for the show, which sounded like typical network hype to increase the series' aura of reality. But airing proved that network publicity departments occasionally do tell the truth.

Two Western series appeared to have been inspired by other programs, but were respectable in their own right. *The Big Valley* was a matri-archal *Bonanza,* with Barbara Stanwyck as head of the clan; also appearing were Richard Long, Lee Majors, and Linda Evans. *The Wild, Wild West* was a stylish spoof that could be termed a Western *Man from U.N.C.L.E.* Robert Conrad played Jim West and Ross Martin his sidekick Artemas Gordon; the pair traveled the West in a luxuriously appointed and equipped (with modernistic gadgets) railroad car. James Gregory played President U S Grant, and the outlandish plots inevitably concerned bizarre villains and fantastic threats.

The semi-documentary *Profiles in Courage* debuted exactly two weeks before President John F Kennedy, on whose book the series was based, was assassinated. *The FBI* was touted as semi-documentary too, but it was more of a straight action program. The Efrem Zimbalist Jr vehicle was publicly declared a favorite by FBI Director J Edgar Hoover, which was probably prompted by the show's fictional pizazz.

Although *Judd for the Defense* (with Carl Betz, once Donna Reed's TV husband, as a lawyer) and *Mannix* (with Mike (formerly Touch) Connors as head of a computerized detective firm) played along the new lines, other shows by decade's end indicated that TV drama series had descended from innovation to gimmicks. *Ironside* featured Raymond Burr as a wheelchair-bound police chief. *Hawaii Five-O* featured chases, explosions and wooden acting by Jack Lord against an island setting. *The Bold Ones* was an innovative format even if its themes and causes were otherwise predictable. It rotated several continuing series, each in a different category now familiar to TV programmers. *The New Doctors* starred E G Marshall and David Hartman; *The Lawyers* starred Burl Ives and Joseph Campanella; *The Protectors* starred Leslie Neilsen; and *The Senator* starred Hal Holbrook as a properly concerned, assembly-line liberal lawmaker named Hays Stowe.

Sheldon Leonard brought a literate, bright espionage caper to weekly TV in the form of *I Spy;* it was immediately seen as a groundbreaker because its co-star (Bill Cosby) was black. But Cosby and Robert Culp contributed mightily with their own presence and sarcastic interplay.

One of the most remarkable of television's phenomena commenced on 8 September, 1966 on NBC. Producer Gene Roddenberry created *Star Trek,* a science-fiction epic chronicling the starship *Enterprise* as it cruised the galaxy. The program featured sensitive plots and many parallels to contemporary life and issues. Roddenberry, moreover, managed to work a magical chemistry of actors, scriptwriters, premise and atmosphere that somehow did not maintain its initial run longer than three seasons but did bring it to virtual immortality afterwards. An army of devotees studies every episode and records every detail as avidly as 'Baker Street Irregulars' do with Sherlock Holmes, and attends Star Trek conventions in droves. In retrospect it

Left: *The model of the* USS Enterprise *used on* Star Trek.
Opposite: *Some of the crew of* Star Trek's *USS Enterprise —* DeForest Kelly (Dr McCoy), *William Shatner (Captain Kirk), Leonard Nimoy (Mr Spock) prepare to beam down.*

Below: *Patrick McGoohan starred as John Drake in* Secret Agent.

was a very 'Sixties' series, cured in the brine of humanism and utopianism. The cast included William Shatner as Captain Kirk; Leonard Nimoy as Dr Spock; DeForest Kelly as Dr McCoy; George Takei as Lieutenant Sulu; James Doohan as Chief Engineer Scott; Michelle Nichols as Lieutenant Uhura; Grace Lee Whiteny as Yeoman Rand; Majel Barrett as Nurse Chapel and Walter Koenig as Ensign Chekov.

The Name of the Game was a well-crafted anthology series under a tighter umbrella than *The Bold Ones.* The central premise was that individual staffers of *Crime Magazine*, based in Los Angeles, would conduct their own crusades, pursue their own stories, and star in their own episodes. Glenn Howard (played by Gene Barry) was the publisher, Dan Farrell (Robert Stack) his senior editor and Jeff Dillon (Tony Franciosa) his celebrity reporter; Susan St James played girl-friday Peggy Maxwell.

Great Britain provided several exceptional series in the 1960s. *Secret Agent* starred Patrick McGoohan as British intelligence officer John Drake. The show, a spinoff from *Danger Man*, featured rocker Johnny Rivers' 'Secret Agent Man' theme song and McGoohan's brooding, quirky acting style. The series, filmed in Portmeirion in Wales, was a splendid evocation of lonely outposts, sinister intrigue and very real danger attendant to the career of not-very-flashy-indeed intelligence operatives. *The Prisoner* ran for a season in 1968, and also starred McGoohan. The series was probably the most bizarre to ever appear on network television; the mysterious shows concern McGoohan, dubbed 'Number Six,' as a captive in a strange land dotted with strange symbols, paradoxical clues, and seemingly possessed people. It was all surreal and beyond solving, for Number Six or the viewer, but was wonderfully evocative and has become a cult favorite.

Above: *Gareth Hunt (Gambit), Joanna Lumley (Purdy) and Patrick MacNee (John Steed) in* The New Avengers.

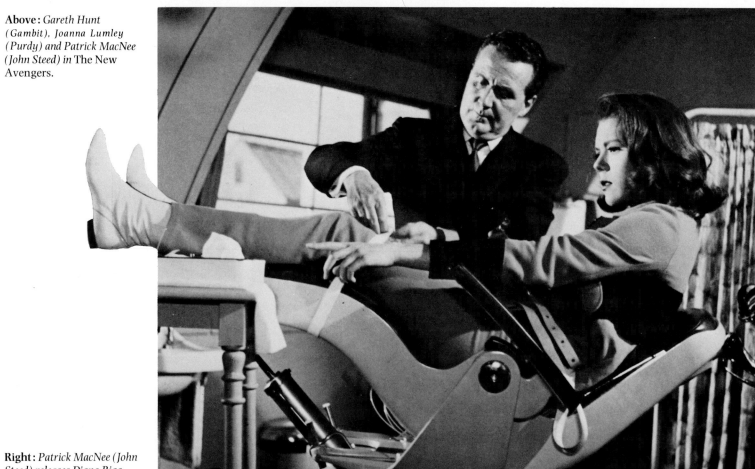

Right: *Patrick MacNee (John Steed) releases Diana Rigg (Mrs Emma Peel) from bondage on* The Avengers.

Then came *The Avengers*. Beginning in 1961 in England, the program went through several related premises. Dr David Keel (Ian Hendry), whose wife has been killed by drug traffickers, enlisted the aid of the mysterious dandy John Steed (Patrick MacNee). Later Steed teamed with Catherine Gale (played by Honor Blackman), and she was succeeded by Emma Peel (Diana Rigg), a sexy, emancipated widow who joined Steed for the fun of adventure. Steed and Peel never seemed to consummate a romance but were enjoined by duty, devotion, respect, affection, and – apparently – instinct. Solving bizarre crimes and threats to the British government, Steed used his steel-rimmed bowler, Peel used her martial arts training (she was frequently dressed in leather outfits), and both used their wit. The baddies and their schemes were delightfully elaborate and just as absurd, but the consistent flavor of the show was playful, with viewers gratefully willing to suspend disbelief. Once again a rare combination of superb writing, clever premises and the interplay of engaging personalities was the recipe for a television classic. *The Avengers* achieved what Dickens's magazine serials, the better nickelodeon cliff-hangers, and certain radio series did at their best: induce an affectionate craving on the audience's part.

The Avengers started as a mid-season replacement (for *Ben Casey*) on ABC. A fourth British version – with Linda Thorson as Tara King – ran after Emma Peel's husband was discovered alive in the jungles of Brazil. Yet another version ran (on CBS Late Night Movies in the US) as *The New Avengers*, with Purdy (played by Joanna Lumley) and Mike Gambit (Gareth Hunt) as Steed's partners.

Hot on the trail of the successful *Twilight Zone*, television came up with several similar series, and most of them were actually creditable. Alfred Hitchcock's anthology program was, of course, already treading some macabre ground, and Boris Karloff's *Thriller!* seemed to be a pastiche of the two approaches. Closer to pure science-fiction and fantasy were *One Step Beyond*, supposed case histories of supernatural events; and *Way Out*, hosted by Roald Dahl. It was an early video presentation, giving the appearance of live television but with bizarre special effects; where *The Twilight Zone* was frequently pixilated, *Way Out* was downright eerie. In the 1985 season, both *The Twilight Zone* and *Alfred Hitchcock Presents* – their hosts having long since passed away – were revived in new formats. Way out.

A spate of other programs in a related field also premiered in the 1960s and were also enjoyable. Nostalgia proved attractive – almost as if the public wanted one last touch of the passing days – and series devoted to older films and stars ran on networks and in syndication. *Silents Please* was an anthology-documentary that ran as a summer replacement on ABC in 1960, and was repeated endlessly in syndication. *Fractured*

Flickers was created by the 'Rocky and Bullwinkle' team, and featured bastardized voice-overs of old films (by people such as host Hans Conreid) but also interviews with movie celebrities. *Hollywood and the Stars* ran on NBC. Ken Murray regularly popped up with his Hollywood home-movies – candid footage of celebrities – and George Fenniman (Groucho Marx's announcer) turned the concept into a series, *Your Funny, Funny Films*, in 1963.

It took no crystal ball, only a slight dose of cynicism and pessimism, to see the glut of advertisements and the propensity toward schlock in television's future. Consequently, in TV's early days, in 1952, experiments in 'Public television' and 'educational television' were begun; at the time the terms were fairly interchangeable. Through the 1950s and into the early 1960s non-commercial television was mostly limited to language lessons, elementary arithmetic that was shown to huddled groups of schoolkids before portable sets, and low-budget drama. In 1962, amid much fanfare, WNDT was founded in the New York market as a

Above: Raymond Burr confined to his wheelchair in Ironside.

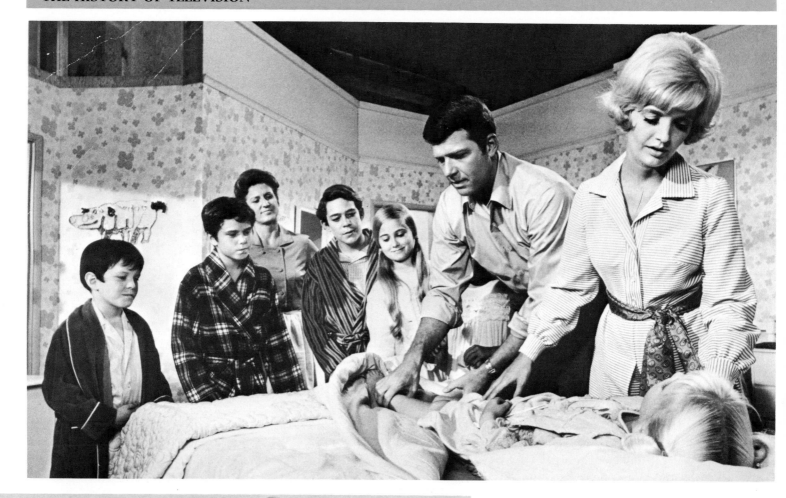

beacon of what Educational Television could be (its call letters stood for New Dimensions in Television).

Actually there were three factors at work in bringing public television to America. The first was a simple desire to see a new network, and it was composed of roughly equal parts of cultural elitism, anti-commercial dogmatism and disgust with quiz shows, payola and scandals. The second was the necessity, perceived by educators and government planners, to boost educational and scientific, if not cultural, levels among the school-age set. The third factor was probably the most compelling: The commercial networks were shedding all pretense of TV's missionary role to provide 'art galleries in the home'; they were economizing by cutbacks in live one-shot dramas; they found greater ratings and advertiser support in the lowest-common-denominator shows. Reviews, ratings, competition and image (or, to distill the ingredients, profits) all were increasingly making cultural programming an embarrassment to the networks.

So when Congress, in the midst of the Great Society spending spree, created the Corporation for Public Broadcasting in 1967, the commercial networks themselves were no doubt as jubilant as college professors and poetry readers. Indeed the networks lent support, including advertising time, especially during CPB's early years. The National Educational network fielded a shaky but full complement of programs on its schedule, and was fortunate to have a couple of stars emerge to help its visibility. Max Morath, playing

Above: *Jack Lord (right) gets his man, the villainous Wo Fat, in a* Hawaii Five-O *episode.*
Above right: *Boris Karloff was the host of, and sometimes acted in,* Thriller!, *a spine-chilling anthology series.*
Opposite top: *Robert Reed and Florence Henderson tend a sick child as the rest of* The Brady Bunch, *and Ann B Davis look on.*
Opposite bottom: *Shirley Jones (top right) played Shirley Partridge on* The Partridge Family. *A widow, she turned her family into a rock group. David Cassidy (top center) played her son (which he is in real life), Keith, the lead singer. Kneeling is Dave Madden, who played the group's agent, Reuben Kinkaid.*

(and teaching) ragtime music, donned period dress and definitely provided entertainment, but in 1963 Julia Child became the first certifiable 'personality' that NET could call its own. Her *French Chef* program provided recipes and cooking tips, as well as a view of Mrs Child preparing dishes. That the well-intentioned matron (and legitimate expert) bumbled, spilled and occasionally misspoke, only added to the charm, as well as to the appeal, of the series, which eventually broke the quarter-century longevity mark on NET. (On syndicated TV Graham Kerr provided one of many imitations of Mrs Child with *The Galloping Gourmet* in 1969; his specialty was appearing slightly tipsy and flirting with the females in his audience.)

In its early days NET provided programming for special-interest groups — its daytime schedule was exclusively aimed at classroom instruction — and it is thereby pioneered such series as *Black Journal* (1969). In the same year, on what was now to be called the Public Broadcasting System, *The Forsyte Saga* began. The superb BBC import starring Kenneth More, Eric Porter and Joseph O'Connor, based on John Galsworthy's novels, was enthusiastically received by critics and a surprising number of viewers. Public-TV bureaucrats were heartened, the networks were simultaneously surprised and relieved, and an embattled group of viewers finally saw at the end of the 1960s what had been promised at the start of the decade — and, indeed, at the advent of the medium itself; that is, programming based on quality, taste, and intrinsic merit.

Back on the networks, variety programming was proving to be the last holdout of live television. In retrospect, it would seem that the rapid turnover of series and stars should have told the network schedule chiefs earlier than they finally did realize that the public's stake in live performances was in fact evaporating. Perhaps the entertainment value of filmed sitcom and action shows was high enough that the public had cooled to spontaneity; perhaps, with film and video, live television had actually (and rapidly) grown to be an anachronism in the public's subconscious. But the effect was that a dying genre, the hour-long variety show, was dogmatically retained by the networks for a decade after they had largely abandoned live drama.

The decade opened with Mitch Miller's cloying good-times and forced-smiles of *Sing Along with Mitch*, proving that the bouncing-ball sing-alongs of old moving-picture theaters still had some bounce. Words to traditional and contemporary songs were flashed on the TV screen while the goateed Miller, his chorus and soloists like Leslie Uggams and Diana Trask warbled with the amateur singers at home.

Jackie Gleason hosted a game show, *You're in the Picture*, that was so terrible that he cancelled it himself after the first week; the following week he apologized to the audience and turned the balance of the season into a celebrity chat-show. Later he introduced his successful variety series *The American Scene Magazine*. It was a format that allowed for guests, skits, regular spots and

Above: *One of the most thrilling moments in television history was when Judy Garland had her young daughter, Liza Minnelli, as a guest on* The Judy Garland Show.

blackout humor. *The Honeymooners* continued as on his show of old, and he added new routines, some of them featuring Frank Fontaine as 'Crazy' Guggenheim. 'Crazy' was a character evidently meant to satirize the mentally retarded, so it was all the more striking when Fontaine would take off his hat and sing sentimental songs in a lush baritone. In a few years Jim Nabors too brought tears to the eyes of many in his audience with a similar bastard-operatic transformation.

Jack Paar, after making his last weeping exit from *The Tonight Show*, hosted his own Friday night variety hour in 1962, and it failed. Later he switched from NBC to ABC to try a variety program, and again met with no success. Through the early 1960s many other established entertainers hosted short-lived variety programs, including Art Linkletter, Roy Rogers and Dale Evans, Keefe Braselle, Danny Kaye, Edie Adams, Jimmy Dean, Jerry Lewis (like Paar, out of luck in several attempts and formats) and Steve Lawrence.

Above: *Television personality David Frost attends a theater opening with Bet Lynch, a star of* Coronation Street, *the long-running British TV series.*

music-and-dance programs included *Shindig, Hullabaloo, Shivaree* and *Shebang*; and through it all, of course, *American Bandstand* continued.

Even more contemporary was a comedy-variety show of topical humor. *That Was the Week That Was* – dubbed *TW3* like the British program that inspired it – began in 1964, just when the American public was starting to grow cynical about the war and big government and when the radical movement sprouted wings. *TW3* tapped into this restiveness, and much of its humor was political. In the ensemble were David Frost (a member of the British cast previously); Henry Morgan, TV's original barbed wit; Phyllis Newman; Nancy Ames ('The *TW3* Girl'); Buck Henry and Burr Tillstrom's puppets. The program lasted one season, but made an impact and paved the way for other shows like *The Smothers Brothers* and *Laugh-In*.

Coming and going seemingly as fast as the hooks could be readied offstage, were other variety formats: *On Broadway Tonight* (a 1964 show hosted by Rudy Vallee); *The New Christy Minstrels; The King Family; Fanfare; The Sammy Davis Jr Show; John Davidson; Hippodrome; The John Gary Show; The London Palladium; Wayne and Schuster; Continental Showcase; The Roger Miller Show; Milton Berle* (!); *Danny Thomas; Jonathan Winters; Dom DeLuise; Don Rickles; Phyllis Diller; What's It All About, World?; Jimmy Rodgers; Liberace* and *Turn On*, hosted by Tim Conway and featuring Chuck McCann, Hamilton Camp, and Teresa Graves. *Turn On* is distinguished in television history as being the shortest-lived of short-lived programs. It debuted and was cancelled the same night, 5 February, 1969, reportedly because of off-color and offensive material. It took longer — about two years — for the Smothers Brothers to be given the axe. They encountered trouble from CBS censors for off-color and politically slanted material, and perennial schedule and production problems. The folk-singing comedians were picked up by ABC, but lasted two months.

Faring slightly better than other variety shows, and certainly better than *Turn On*, were *The Dean Martin Show, Carol Burnett, Jim Nabors, Leslie Uggams, Laugh-In, Hee Haw* and *Johnny Cash*, several of which are worth noting. Dean Martin continued his life after Jerry Lewis with apparent ease and much success. He parlayed his recording and movie appeal to the small screen and proved perfect for the intimate atmosphere of television. Always in a mellow fog, he was self-deprecating and low key as host, and was adept at comedy routines on his variety show. He fashioned his own summer replacement hour starring the Gold Diggers, his female chorus, and later transformed his variety show into a series of staged celebrity 'roasts,' wherein a panel of guests paid sarcastic tribute to one of their fellows.

Carol Burnett fashioned one of the classic ensembles of all television variety programs, and

In 1964 *The Entertainers* debuted. It was a lively 1950s-style revue (it didn't take long for 1950s nostalgia to begin) starring Carol Burnett and Bob Newhart; among the repertory players were John Davidson, Art Buchwald, Jack Burns, Tessie O'Shea, Dom DeLuise and Caterina Valente. But it was withdrawn after half a season.

The Judy Garland Show had the same disappointing, truncated lifespan as *The Entertainers*. Hers was also a quality show, and offered the eerie bonus of seeing the great trouper's life unravel during this difficult period; Garland ultimately committed suicide. *The Hollywood Palace*, a weekly variety show, harkened back to vaudeville of the 1920s and the English music hall for its inspiration, and it worked; the series ran from 1964 to 1970 on ABC. Also successful, but feeding off the contemporary rather than the nostalgic, was *Hootenanny*, a country music program that featured live dancers and sometimes live performances (often the singers 'lipsynched' – short for synchronized – which has become a television practice as ubiquitous as recorded laughter and applause). As the discotheque craze established itself, with miniskirts and high boots, and as the Beatles led the resuscitation of rock music, copycat programs appeared like puffball mushrooms on a dewy lawn. Such

infused it with superb writing and her own amiable personality. As a hostess, she could sing, dance or perform comedy with any guest (her Carnegie Hall TV shows with Julie Andrews are landmark TV events), and the running routines – 'Mrs Wiggins the secretary,' 'Momma's Family,' etc. – became instant favorites with fans. In her talented ensemble were Harvey Korman, Vicki Lawrence, Lyle Wagonner, and Tim Conway. Her program ran 12 years, and continues in syndication.

Laugh-In was television's perfect compromise with the iconoclastic spirit of the times (it debuted as a special in 1967). It was irreverent, naughty, psychedelic (at least in decor) and mildly political but the hosts, Dan Rowan and Dick Martin, were reportedly Republicans, and many of the politicians who were spoofed (including Richard Nixon) actually made guest appearances on the show. Thereby any real political zing was co-opted, but in the end the show was meant more as comedy than commentary. The pace was frantic, with dozens of skits and black-out gags, standing routines and one-liners. Among the ensemble were Goldie Hawn, Lily Tomlin, Judy Carne, Arte Johnson, Richard Dawson, Jo Anne Worley, Alan Sues, Henry Gibson, Jud Strunk, Ruth Buzzi and Gary Owens – and they were responsible for many catch-phrases that swept the country, like 'You bet your bippy,' 'Sock it to me,' 'Look *that* up in your Funk and Wagnall's,' and 'Here come de judge!' *Laugh-In* had a five-year run and was rated Number One for its first two seasons.

Hee Haw could be termed a country-music *Laugh-In*, but the comparisons between it and anything else in TV history ceased there. The comedy-variety program was about 200-proof country, unlike the efforts New York and Hollywood invariably botch to add regional or ethic flavor to programming. Produced in Nashville and featuring black-outs, skits, standing routines and corn, *Hee Haw* also programmed live music by country superstars and guest appearances by songwriters, sidemen and celebrities. Hosted by rustic superstars Buck Owens and Roy Clark, the cast included certifiable (in more ways than one) country singers and comedians, some of them long-time veterans: Roy Acuff, Minnie Pearl, Grandpa Jones, Stringbean, Junior Samples, Archie Campbell, Don Harron (a Canadian who fit like a glove), Lulu Roman, Misty Rowe, and, in later years, George 'Goober' Lindsey, Jack Burns, the Reverend Grady Nutt, Barbi Benton, Ronni Stoneman and Gailard Sartains. Nashville studio musicians provided an excellent backup for the singers who appeared as guests. *Hee Haw* proved remarkably popular, and when CBS dropped it unceremoniously from its schedule in its 'hick purge' of the early 1970s, it went on to even greater success, in terms of number of stations, in syndication. Roy Clark celebrated this triumph of justice in a hit record, 'The Lawrence Welk-Hee Haw – Counter-Revolutionary Polka.'

The Johnny Cash Show was representative of several other moderate successes in the variety field centered on country-music stars. The show had strong country flavors but, unlike *Hee Haw*, frequently featured pop and rock guests. Cash's show was dominated by his hulking but gentle

Above: It was Ed Sullivan who introduced The Beatles to the United States cn his Ed Sullivan Show.
Opposite: Dan Rowan (left) and Dick Martin introduced America to a different kind of comedy show on Laugh-In.

presence, and offered as regulars his comedienne/singer wife June Carter, the legendary Carter Family, Carl Perkins, and a remarkably talented group of singers, songwriters and comedians, The Statler Brothers. Glen Campbell, on his *Goodtime Hour* variety show, featured as regulars Mel Tillis, Jerry Reed, and John Hartford, at that time all virtually unknown.

Mickey Finn's was a pleasant diversion, an hourly musical show set in Gay 90s surroundings with rinky-tink pianos. ABC fielded Joey Bishop against the already-formidable Johnny Carson in 1967; the stone-faced comedian, his fawning announcer Regis Philbin, and awkward band-leader Johnny Mann would likely have flopped against Shari Lewis's puppets without Shari. ABC was grooming another challenger in the wings: Dick Cavett, a former joke-writer for Carson. His calculated underplaying and super-cilious manner endeared him to many intellectuals — but never enough of them to maintain a regular slot for Cavett. He has jumped from daytime to prime-time to late-night, and between commercial networks to PBS and finally to cable's USA Network thus far in his career. In 1969 CBS picked Merv Griffin from a successful syndicated slot (to which he was eventually to return) and challenged Carson. Again the effort failed. David Frost, the *TW3* alumnus, hosted a syndicated talk-show that many markets ran opposite Carson, from 1969 to 1972.

The success that CBS didn't have in late-night hours was compensated for by its domination of daytime television in the early part of the 1960s. In 1960 the network had nine of the top 10 shows, and newcomer Fred Silverman, the 26-year-old programming chief, advanced the lead in 1963 to 14 of the top 14 daytime shows. Among their soap operas are *As the World Turns*, *Brighter Day*, *The Edge of Night*, *The Guiding Light*, *Search for Tomorrow* and *Secret Storm*; many of the titles sound almost spiritual, but in fact the serials dealt increasingly with adultery, conniving and betrayal.

Above: *The country/western star singer, Johnny Cash, hosted* The Johnny Cash Show.
Left: *Buck Owens and Lisa Todd, two of the country stars of* Hee Haw.

Opposite top: *Dick Cavett, the intellectual's Johnny Carson.*
Opposite bottom left: *Monty Hall (left) and two of his nutty contestants on* Let's Make a Deal.
Opposite bottom right: *Haila Stoddard and Peter Hobbs in* Secret Storm.

Above: The brash, yet lovable, Bugs Bunny cooks his favorite food.

Right: Jonathan Frid played Barnabas Collins, the vampire, on the macabre daytime soap, Dark Shadows.

Opposite: Big Bird of Sesame Street *poses with Fred Rogers of* Mr Rogers' Neighborhood.

equivalents of snake-oil pitches, the FTC called claims for products of Lever Brothers, Standard Brands, Colgate-Palmolive and Alcoa 'phony,' and characterized a campaign for Rapid-Shave 'deliberate fraud.' The dust soon settled, however, and commercials continued as before. It seems the public was incapable of having its intelligence insulted, and either stared blankly at offending ads or were amused by their humorous trappings.

Several notable daytime programs debuted in the 1960s. *Let's Make a Deal*, with Monty Hall, was a game show that encouraged studio-audience participants to dress and act outlandishly in order to gamble away their gifts for the chance of bigger gifts behind closed doors. *Supermarket Sweep* was able to make everyday folk act even sillier by equipping contestants with empty shopping carts and letting them loose in supermarkets. *Hollywood Squares* was a game show on a grand scale: nine celebrities participated, parrying their answers against the contestants'; for years Paul Lynde in the center square (the premise was based on tic-tac-toe) was the featured celebrity. Jack La Lanne and a host of imitators did for exercise at home what Julia Child was doing for cooking (La Lanne seemed perennially better preserved than Mrs Child's cured hams). And a soap opera with a new wrinkle was served up by ABC in 1966 in the form of *Dark Shadows* — a gothic horror serial replete with machine-made fog, creaking doors and vampires.

The 1960s were really ABC's decade in sports coverage. This was in spite of CBS's purchase of the New York Yankees in 1964 (or maybe the purchase was symbolic of CBS's instincts in the field; the network presided over the worst period of Yankee performance in decades). No less a disaster was a 1968 football game between the Oakland Raiders and the New York Jets. Oakland scored two touchdowns in the last nine seconds, but NBC had just switched away from the game to begin a broadcast of the movie *Heidi*.

Meanwhile ABC's brilliant sports chief (later also head of the news division) Roone Arledge instituted regularly scheduled major-league baseball games. With Jim McKay he began the weekend *Wide World of Sports*, which not only proved a quality standard of sports programming, but also helped seal the doom of public-affairs and religious programming on weekends. *The American Sportsman* debuted to acclaim in 1965. Arledge gambled on giving the abrasive Howard Cosell a prominent role in ABC Sport's image, and invested in video technology, such as the slow-motion and instant replay cameras. In 1967 the first Super Bowl was jointly telecast by CBS and NBC, an unusual procedure; ABC was excluded, but such was not to be the case for long in television sports. As the decade ended, the big sports stories were the triumphs of New York underdogs Mets and Jets. Similarly as the 1970s dawned, ABC was finally setting its own corporate sights on climbing from the cellar.

Many of the daytime game shows — in the wake of the industry scandals — were low-key and slightly cerebral, including *Password* (with former College Bowl host Allen Ludden), *Jeopardy* and *Concentration* (with Hugh Downs as host).

The Today Show was NBC's place in the daytime sun. Conceived by programming wizard Pat Weaver in the 1950s, it is an early-morning wake-up program of information, news and humor. Urbane Dave Garroway was the original host (mixing sophistication with appearances by chimpanzee J Fred Muggs), and the show later featured, among its hosts and 'editors,' Jack Lescoulie, Charles Van Doren, Betsy Palmer, Frank Blair, John Chancellor, Hugh Downs, Joe Garagiola, Barbara Walters, Frank McGee, Gene Shalit, Jane Pauley, Bryant Gumbel, and Willard Scott. For most of its years of existence it dominated its time slot, losing it to ABC's *Good Morning America* in the late 1970s and early 1980s, but regaining it in 1985.

In 1960 the Federal Trade Commission surprised many by cracking down on the absurd advertising claims that had become a trademark of television. Confronting the electronic-age

Above: *Fred Rogers accepts a rocking horse from delivery man Mr McFeely on* Mr Rogers' Neighborhood. **Above right:** *The irrepressible Daffy Duck.*

Children's programming in the 1960s reflected some innovation. Animated cartoons continued as before, since the technical revolution of Hanna-Barbera. No longer did children watch old silent cartoons by Paul Terry of Farmer Al Falfa and thousands of little mice hiding behind skinny trees. In the 1960s Terry was producing *Mighty Mouse* and *Heckle and Jeckle*. Companions on the screen were *Quick-Draw McGraw; Casper the Friendly Ghost*; the entire Warner Brothers crew including Bugs Bunny, Daffy Duck, Tweety and Sylvester and the Road Runner; *Tennessee Tuxedo* and *Huckleberry Hound*. An innovative humorous adventure series for children was presented in *H R Pufnstuf*, starring Jack Wild, heart-throb to a generation of adolescent girls. In the series he sails to a danger-filled island populated by the puppets of Sid and Marty Krofft (who provided many programs and puppet creations for children's TV through the years).

In 1967 Fred Rogers introduced *Mr Rogers' Neighborhood* to the nation via NET; he and his ensemble, through plays, secular sermonettes, and experiments in science and values, aimed beyond cognitive levels to behavior patterns. It was part of a movement in educational circles to bring humanism to children's television, and in 1969 censors cracked down on violence in kiddie cartoons.

The Children's Television Workshop (CTW) was founded in 1968, backed by money from the Ford Foundation, the Carnegie Corporation and the Federal Office of Education. Its first success was *Sesame Street*, which debuted on NET in 1969. It based its techniques on the very obvious (but clever, because it had never been employed) system of presenting children's entertainment and education via the techniques of TV commercials. Thereby sight and sound, graphics and persuasion, were all summoned to teach kids the pronunciation of diphthongs and counting by fives. With likeable actors and the incredibly engaging puppets of Jim Henson (Kermit the Frog, Big Bird, Oscar the Grouch, Bert and Ernie, the Cookie Monster, *et al.*), the formula proved irresistible to children. The producers have also sought to impart social values as well as educational ones, too; an ironic joke on the parents who moved to suburbia to escape urban slums and changing neighborhoods was the fact that *Sesame Street* is largely set on a ghetto street and featured a well-integrated cast. Spanish is even taught on the program to children who have not yet a command of English. But even if parents wanted to pry their young addicts away from the *Sesame Street* screen — in some markets shown four times a day — they would find it easier to separate a cookie from Cookie Monster. *The Electric Company*, which followed *Sesame Street* by two years, aimed a bit more to older viewers and concentrated on phonics and numbers more exclusively.

In the areas of public-affairs programming and specials, television was about as exciting as the decade, a period of ferment and changing lifestyles. In 1960 alone, *Macbeth* was presented on *The Hallmark Hall of Fame*; Graham Greene's *The Power and the Glory* starred Lawrence Olivier; *An*

Hour with Danny Kaye featured Louis Armstrong; and Gary Cooper hosted a remarkably accurate documentary, *The Real West*. In the 1960s, television offered notable tours, with memorable tourguides: *Jacqueline Kennedy's Tour of the White House; Princess Grace Tours Monaco; Liz Taylor's London; Sophia Loren's Rome; Charles Boyer Tours the Louvre;* Dwight D Eisenhower and Walter Cronkite visited Normandy in *D-Day Plus 20.* Jacques Cousteau began his voyages underwater, and *David Brinkley's Journal* presented notable overseas reports.

Musically, television presented *The Gershwin Years* and Ethel Merman in *Annie Get Your Gun.* Newcomer Barbra Streisand hosted *My Name Is Barbra,* and crooning legend Frank Sinatra offered *A Man and His Music.* A few live productions survived, including *Inherit the Wind* with Fredric March and Ed Begley; *Death of a Salesman* with Lee J Cobb; *Brigadoon; Mark Twain Tonight* with Hal Holbrook reprising his stage persona; and Robert Shaw in *Luther.* But live drama had just about disappeared by the decade's end, replaced in part if not in consolation by the genre of one-man specials. These included Vladimir Horowitz and Artur Rubenstein at one end of the spectrum, and Mama Cass, Woody Allen and Flip Wilson at the other. A pair of Christmas traditions began in the 1960s, with *A Charlie Brown Christmas* (not only has the animated cartoon been repeated endlessly, but it inaugurated dozens of 'Peanuts' cartoons) and Truman Capote's classic, autobiographical *A Christmas Memory,* starring Geraldine Paige.

Bright spots and routine spots during the decade include Stan Freberg's clever commercials; the science reporting of ABC's Jules Bergman; the predictable New Year's Eve celebration with Guy Lombardo from the Waldorf-Astoria; the Jerry Lewis telethons; and the regular coverage of Winter and Summer Olympics. In 1968, in the midst of a very turbulent period in American society, viewers saw black American athletes raise defiant fists against their country's racial climate when accepting medals at Mexico City.

It is in this very arena of societal ferment and volatile politics where television asserted its superiority over other media, and the public instinctively regarded their TV sets as primary sources of news, information and even solace. In generations before, during times of distress, Americans would pour onto the streets, or gather at newspaper offices or telegraph stations; in the 1930s they would listen to radios or boo, cheer or cry at movie-house newsreels. But in the 1960s – through wars, crises and assassinations – the TV set became the primary source of contact.

Appropriately, John F Kennedy, who used TV to such advantage (it was his massive spending in the medium that caused Hubert Humphrey to withdraw from the presidential primaries after West Virginia went for JFK) had his presidency virtually etched in television's terms. He won the Nixon debates, by common consent, because of his TV image. He was the first president to hold live, televised press conferences. He appointed

Above: *Oscar the Grouch lives in a garbage can on Sesame Street.*

129

Above: Sandy Koufax, the acclaimed Dodger pitcher, joined NBC as a sports broadcaster after his retirement from baseball in 1966.

Top: President and Mrs John F Kennedy watch the 5 May 1961 Allen Shepard space flight.
Right: Regis Philbin, who went from Joey Bishop's show to a cable network.

Edward R Murrow (a man more identified with television than anyone else except Milton Berle) to be head of the U S Information Agency; later newsman John Chancellor would also hold the post. When the Cuban missile crisis broke, it was to TV that Kennedy immediately turned to talk to the American people (and in so doing backed his diplomatic bluffs against the Soviet Union). And when Kennedy was assassinated in Dallas, television was there to report it and every moment of the aftermath (the tragedy made the career of a local reporter, Dan Rather). Ultimately symbolic of television's new role — participating in history as well as chronicling it — Jack Ruby murdered Lee Harvey Oswald, live, before millions of viewers.

Throughout the decade, America's incredible space program was followed on television. It was not only entertainment and thrills of the highest order; the government recognized television's role in creating and sustaining public support for the effort, and assisted networks in the coverage of each blast-off. In what now seems like the most primitive sorts of exercises — on TV and on the launching-pad — millions of schoolchildren huddled around portable sets in auditoriums and gymnasiums to watch Allen Shepard arc through the sky and John Glenn manage a single earth orbit. By 1986 none of the networks was even present to broadcast the symbolically important shuttle lift-off with the nation's first civilian astronaut; a cable-TV crew captured the disastrous explosion that years of routine had

Above: *David Brinkley, one of the most respected of all the anchor men/analysts/ commentators in the business.*

Top: *The world was shocked and grief-stricken at the television coverage of the assassination of John F Kennedy — 22 November 1963.*

Following spread: *Neil Armstrong, the first man on the moon, was seen by millions on TV — 20 July 1969.*

suggested was impossible. Like its very own technology, TV's saturation coverage of events had made the extraordinary seem mundane. The last big thrill seemed to be when Americans walked on the moon — perhaps the most impressive TV hookup to date.

As color became standard by mid-decade, TV news became standardized. The John Cameron Swayzes — eccentric news readers — were gone, replaced by news readers of more sober countenances. Chet Huntley and David Brinkley were the ratings stars, trading stories between each other in New York and Washington studios. Network nightly news expanded to 30 minutes in length, and Walter Cronkite replaced Douglas Edwards as anchor, only to be dumped by CBS for Roger Mudd and Robert Trout in the coverage of the 1964 political conventions. (CBS, in turn, was dumped on by the Republicans. Barry Goldwater and former president Eisenhower each led the convention crowd in lusty boos directed at the liberal press.)

The enduring trademark of Lyndon Johnson's campaign against Goldwater in 1964 was a television commercial — not a speech or slogan or newspaper ad. An animated cartoon showed a little girl picking a daisy one moment and vaporized by an atom bomb the next, with the tag line urging a 'safe' vote for LBJ. In that year a Roper Poll reported that a majority of Americans cited TV as their primary source of news, and the following year a television studio was built in the bowels of the White House.

The civil-rights march on Washington was covered extensively on television, and Pope Paul's visit was viewed in approximately 90 per cent of American homes. (Dr Carl McIntire, a fundamentalist radio preacher, asked for equal time to counter religious propaganda.) In 1968 Robert Kennedy was shot, and TV cameras were literally by his side to record the event.

But television's most significant role in events of the decade was its participation, not its documentation activities. In covering the Viet Nam war, its very coverage — footage of battles and carnage — is today regarded as the sufficient motivator in changing Americans' attitudes toward the war. But in truth it was the *way* the news was reported, the selection of material, and the very evident bias of reporters and anchors (as the hosts of the evening news programs were now called) that recast American opinion. The Tet Offensive was clearly a defeat for North Viet Nam, but it was uniformly reported — and shown, night by night — as a victory for the Communists. Correspondents grew open, on the air and in public statements, about their opposition to the war. As early as 1965 Walter Cronkite, after

Opposite: *The long-time anchorman for CBS News — Walter Cronkite.*

Right: *Four panels from the infamous commercial from the Johnson campaign.*

visiting South Viet Nam, reported disillusionment with American aims.

There was a second way that TV news participated in events in addition to covering them: in domestic politics, when radicalism was abroad in the land, it was clearly evident that a majority of network news personnel was leaning leftward. Cronkite exploded emotionally during the besieged Democratic Convention of 1968 in Chicago; many of the rioters who were not ringleaders (and, in fact, some who were) later reported that network camera crews would ask them to stage riots and demonstrations; and it was all theater, if not subversion, of the highest order. Television news was subverting its proper function, which was at the least to be impartial. One delicious moment that broke the tension occurred when NBC newsman John Chancellor was arrested on the floor of the Democratic convention for a trespassing violation. Seizing upon the silliness of the scene he signed off: 'This is John Chancellor, somewhere in custody. . . .'

The convention, for all its ugliness, was also great entertainment. To be caught up in the exigencies of such an event would allow anyone, or any medium, to be forgiven. But television news had come to view *all* events through political glasses. It had come to view all presidential statements not as news, but merely the first half of a debate; networks regularly pounced on speeches and press conferences with 'analyses' to interpret for viewers what they had just seen – and, by implication, had been unable to digest and understand by themselves.

The boos offered at the 1964 Goldwater convention had spread nation-wide as more people resented force-fed views instead of news, and bias in reporting and selection. Just as the media moguls were unelected and nameless, so did the public lack a spokesman to air this particular grievance.

In 1969 a spokesman presented himself. Vice-President Spiro Agnew was then perceived as a Rockefeller Republican and a moderate chosen by Richard Nixon as an ideological balance to his ticket. In the autumn of 1969 he showed new stripes, however, and called critics of the administration's policies 'an effete corps of impudent snobs.' Then – after a major policy speech on Vietnam by President Nixon was 'analyzed' unfavorably on each of the three networks immediately upon its conclusion, Agnew spoke the words that many had been thinking.

'When Winston Churchill rallied public opinion to stay the course against Hitler's Germany, he didn't have to contend with a gaggle of commentators raising doubts about whether he was reading public opinion right, or whether Britain had the stamina to see the war through. When President Kennedy rallied the nation in the Cuban missile crisis, his address to the people was not chewed over by a roundtable of critics who disparage the course of action he'd asked America to follow.

'. . . How is this network news [presentation and analysis] determined? A small group of men, numbering perhaps no more than a dozen anchormen, commentators and executive producers, settle upon the 20 minutes or so of film and commentary that's to reach the public. . . . They decide what 40 to 50 million Americans will learn of the day's events in the nation and in the world. . . .

'Nor is their power confined to the substantive. A raised eyebrow, an inflection of the voice, a caustic remark dropped in the middle of a broadcast can raise doubts in a million minds about the veracity of a public official or the wisdom of a government policy.'

The fact that within four years both Agnew and Nixon had reasons to be concerned about the public's perceptions of their veracity does not lessen the correctness of his analysis. Agnew was not, he said, calling for governmental censorship, but a recognition that censorship and management of the news was already occurring.

He continued, drawing a very precise portrait of television's inherent processes – and dangers: 'The labor crisis settled at the negotiating table is nothing compared to the confrontation that results in a strike, or, better yet, violence along the picket lines. Normality has become the nemesis of network news.'

Agnew had virtually dared the networks to air his speech (delivered on 13 November 1969,

Above: *Chet Huntley, who for many years teamed with co-anchorman David Brinkley, on NBC's* The Huntley-Brinkley Report. **Opposite top:** *Roger Mudd, long a leading political correspondent for NBC.*

in Des Moines, Iowa) and all three accepted his challenge; within moments of the speech's conclusion they issued statements of condemnation. Officials like Steve McCormick, vice president of the Mutual Broadcasting Company – a radio network – 'heartily endorsed' Agnew's 'call for fairness, balance, responsibility and accuracy in news presentation,' but among media moguls McCormick was in the minority. Thomas P F Hoving, then chairman of the National Citizens Committee for Broadcasting, said: 'Agnew's disgraceful attack tonight against network television news officially leads us as a nation into an ugly era of the most fearsome suppression and intimidation. . . . Should the people believe Agnew's ignorant, base attack on the only regularly worthwhile arm of American broadcasting, it is the beginning of the end for us as a nation.'

When public response was reported, it seemed in favor of the vice president's side or 'about even,' according to *The New York Times*. NBC reported that after the speech 614 calls were in agreement and 554 opposed. In cities around the country (Dallas was one cited) the reaction was to endorse the criticism. *The New York Times* quoted one caller, however, who shared Hoving's apocalyptic vision: 'I was horrified by the Agnew speech,' said Sidney Unger of New Rochelle, New York. 'It reminded me of speeches of Hitler before he got into power and he was brainwashing the German people against opinions that were against him.'

Agnew's critique had the salutory effect of inaugurating a debate on the very real condition of news selection, bias and the public's right to know. For all the real arguments and false arguments, however, there have been no institutional changes in network news policies. The public may have grown more lethargic on the subject; the newsmen may have drifted more to the political center (the David Brinkley who reportedly invited radical Abbie Hoffman to his home during the 1970 Moratorium in Washington has certainly mellowed) and the news may well have become less political and more fluffy – but the fact remains that a small band of nameless, faceless, unaccountable executives in two or three concentrated geographical neighborhoods decide the content of daily news presentation to what is supposedly the most enlightened nation on earth.

The inherent economic contradictions in the American system were not removed by the New Deal; it was World War II that succeeded in ending the Depression, and America has in a sense been on a war footing ever since. Similarly, the weaknesses in television news presentation that Vice President Agnew recognized are yet with the medium. And yesterday's weaknesses can be tomorrow's danger.

Left: *Walter Cronkite, now considered the dean of television news broadcasting, began working in television in the 1950s.*

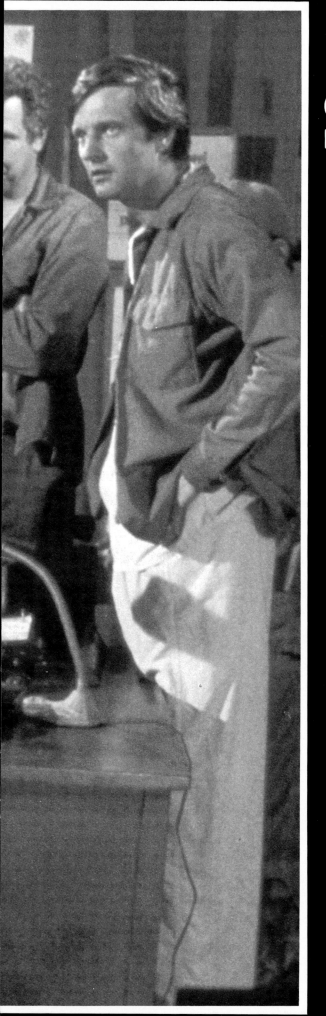

THE
SEVENTIES

Cultural trends never run in sharply defined patterns and neat schedules like railway time-tables (or perhaps one could say that they run like American railway schedules but not like European ones). Books like this try to sort out history by offering categories and defining trends in order to focus, and not be awash in, the multitude of data. We talk of the Gay Nineties, but (a) they weren't all that gay, with a major Depression smack in their middle years; and (b) the elements that suggest such classification started before, and extended after, that decade. In the same fashion, the supposedly placid Eisenhower years were really rather volatile – James Dean, Elvis Presley, rock 'n' roll, civil-rights protests, beatniks; all were residents of the 1950s.

So it is with television history and the pigeon-hole-by-decade approach. The 1960s are remembered as the decade of protest, but it was in the 1970s when television programming was radicalized. Social changes, integration, anti-war messages, even the sexual revolution – for the most part these phenomena did not enter the mainstream of TV in the 1960s via news departments, Spiro Agnew notwithstanding. Rather they entered American homes via entertainment programming, mostly through situation comedies. It began in the 1960s but was institutionalized in the 1970s.

The decade of the 1970s opened with the 'hick purge.' Many shows that appealed to rural and older audiences were cancelled, 12 top-rated programs in 1970 and 1971 alone. CBS led the pogrom (the network had become identified with these types of shows, even though they were top-rated) and axed The Beverly Hillbillies; Hee Haw; Mayberry R F D; Gomer Pyle; Hogan's Heroes; The Wild, Wild West; Petticoat Junction; Green Acres; and even The Ed Sullivan Show. The corporate pronouncements stated that CBS, the most prosperous and sophisticated of the networks, was concerned about its image. But the real reason was in the footnotes.

Pure numbers – in the TV ratings systems – were not enough any more; it was the numbers represented. When the A C Nielsen and Abitron companies delivered ratings numbers for shows and time slots, there was now a profile of viewership – and the rural and older viewers weren't the buyers. Already the seeds of an 1980s stereotype were being planted: it was the young, urban, professional viewer – and purchaser – about whom the advertisers concerned themselves with reaching and influencing.

Along the lifelines of television's growth, the entertainment people attached themselves to the industry (escapist-entertainment-at-all-costs, that is; resulting in quiz-show scandals and the

Previous spread: M*A*S*H starring MacLean Stevenson, Wayne Rogers and Alan Alda, was one of the most popular series in the 1970s.
Opposite top: *The Mary Tyler Moore Show gang – Betty White (Sue Ann Nivens), Gavin MacLeod (newswriter Murray Slaughter), Ed Asner (producer Lou Grant), Georgia Engel (Georgette Franklin), Ted Knight (newscaster Ted Baxter, later Georgette's husband), and Mary Tyler Moore (Mary Richards).*

Below: *Oscar Madison, played by Jack Klugman, and Felix Unger (Tony Randall) enjoying their stay in a hospital in* The Odd Couple.

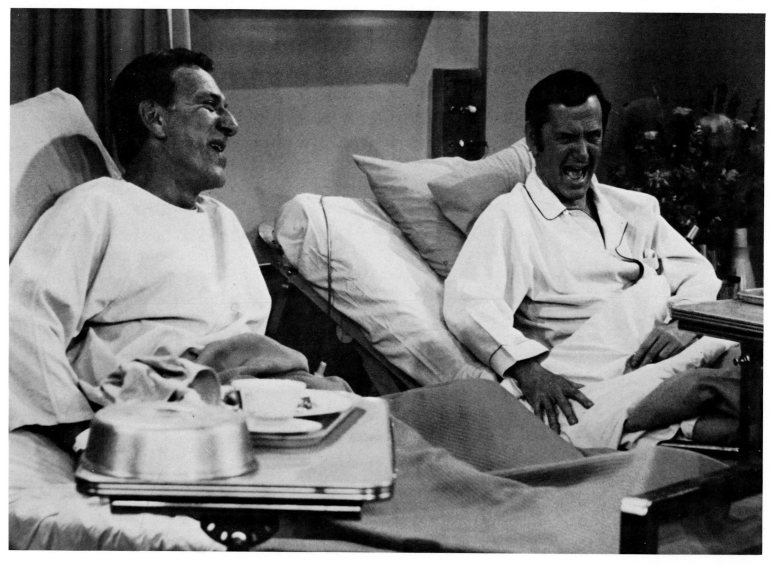

gradual demise of live drama) in the 1950s. In the 1960s the advertising people asserted themselves. In the 1970s it was to be the marketing people who would dictate programming policy. When rural-oriented shows returned to the networks, it was in the form of series like *The Waltons*, surely a rubber-stamped Madison-Avenue executive's proper image of what a country program should be like.

While relevance and demographics were becoming the name of the game, the decade opened with a varied offering overall, especially in the comedy category. Gary Marshall optioned the rights to Neil Simon's Broadway smash *The Odd Couple* and fashioned a television smash. Clever writing that maintained Simon's verve if not quality combined with a winning premise about two divorced men — one a slob, the other a prig — and superb characterizations in the roles. Tony Randall played photographer Felix Unger the Fastidious, and Jack Klugman played sportswriter Oscar Madison the Casual. The series ran from 1970 to 1975 on ABC, and presaged more success for both the network and producer Marshall.

Another show that laid the cornerstone of a dynasty was *The Mary Tyler Moore Show*, also debuting in 1970. Moore, veteran of the *Richard Diamond, Private Eye* series (where she played the secretary but was never shown above the hips) and *The Dick Van Dyke Show*, formed a production company with her husband Grant Tinker, and launched this comedy about a television newsroom. Mary Richards was the central character,

an associate producer at WJM, a small Minneapolis station. Other characters included Ed Asner as Lou Grant, head of the newsroom; Ted Knight as Ted Baxter, anchorman; Gavin MacLeod as Murray Slaughter, news writer; and Betty White as Sue Ann Nivens, hostess of the station's *Happy Homemaker* show. The brightness of the series grew from consistently superb writing and direction as well as the obvious contributions of story editors and creative consultants — the characters were kept consistent with strong personality traits that would interact (Baxter was oafish; Sue

Above: Rhoda, *starring Valerie Harper (left) as Rhoda and Nancy Walker as her mother, Ida Morgenstern, was a spinoff from* The Mary Tyler Moore Show.

141

Above: *Marla Gibbs (as Florence, the maid), Sherman Hemsley (as George Jefferson) and Isabel Sanford (as Louise Jefferson) in* The Jeffersons.
Opposite top: *The usual type of argument from* All in the Family: *the bigoted Archie Bunker (Carroll O'Connor, left) is defending himself against his liberal daughter Gloria (Sally Struthers) and son-in-law Michael Stivik (Rob Reiner).*
Opposite bottom: *Like* The Jeffersons, Maude *was a spinoff from* All in the Family. *Here Beatrice Arthur (as Maude) pleads with Bill Macy, her husband.*

Ann was man-hungry, etc). The series was strong enough to last until 1977 — and would have lasted longer but for the decision by MTM Productions to quit while on top.

Two of Mary's friends eventually got their own series. Valerie Harper played Rhoda Morgenstern, a Bronx transplant, who in her own show *Rhoda* returned home to contend with her love life, her mother (Nancy Walker) and sister (Julie Kavner). Cloris Leachman, who played Mary's landlady, Phyllis, had less success on *Phyllis*, probably because her personality — carping, two-faced, egocentric — held more humor for an incidental character than appeal as a main character. Ed Asner's turn was toward more serious, as his character of *Lou Grant* spun off into a dramatic series.

Another dynasty was being erected by another production company, that of Norman Lear. In 1971 *All in the Family* quietly began in mid-season (12 January), but that's not all that was different. It was recorded on video tape, so it once again brought the feel of live TV to the screen. Further it was based on a British series *Till Death Do Us Part*, inaugurating a method of creative inspiration that was to become virtually epidemic in Hollywood for 15 years. But *All in the Family*'s major contributions to American television were more revolutionary.

In what seemed like a mere gimmick for the series alone, several trends were begun in situation comedies. 'Relevance' was the *a priori* ele-

ment, and Archie Bunker, the lead character, had black neighbors and a daughter who espoused feminist issues. But Lear multiplied relevance to the *n*th degree and either shattered TV's restrictive taboos or pioneered offensive new vistas of bad taste, according to one's view. Menopause was discussed, as was homosexuality, abortion and all manner of personal parts and preoccupations. Fair game was material that children had heretofore never known, and adults were uncomfortable discussing even with each other. In these matters Lear was a revolutionary; what *Playboy* and liberal sociologists sought hard to do to American society in their segregated realms, Lear blithely did week after week in living rooms, with the cloak of acceptance provided by CBS, and laughing approval stamped by hundreds in the studio audience.

The other breakthrough was the manner of comedy. Archie Bunker yelled at his son-in-law, who yelled back. Neighbors shouted epithets at Bunker, and he called them names. Ethnic jokes abounded. And the audience howled. After *All in the Family*, every TV season would have at least one program on the schedule where players shouted insults or punchlines, and the audience reaction was as if the idiot-lights indicated 'howl' or 'hoot' instead of 'laugh' or 'applaud' as used to be the case. Civility was *passé* and subtlety was as forbidden as references to gonorrhea once had been.

Subtlety was reserved for the creative formula.

Archie Bunker, played by Carroll O'Connor, was a racist and a bigot; he was also a self-destructing jerk, so there was hardly a viewer who wouldn't like to watch him for one reason or other. His character was so overplayed that he lacked basic sympathy-points with his audience, yet he remained a favorite butt. O'Connor played Bunker to great comic effect, and was aided by memorable co-stars: Jean Stapleton as his set-upon wife Edith; Sally Struthers as daughter Gloria; Rob Reiner (Carl's son) as Mike Stivik, Gloria's husband. Mike was originally a pro-fessional college student supported by Gloria, and then a college instructor; in both roles he incurred the derision of Archie, especially when the couple lived under his roof.

As in the case of *Mary Tyler Moore*, Lear's *All in the Family* spawned a group of spinoffs. The first was *The Jeffersons*, with Isabel Sanford and Sherman Hemsley, concerning the Bunkers' black neighbors who 'moved uptown' after striking it rich in the dry-cleaning business. The family's maid Florence (played by Marla Gibbs) later starred in her own series, and when it flopped she returned to *The Jeffersons*. *Gloria* starred Sally Struthers as a single mother — the setting is after she and Mike have moved and divorced, and *Archie Bunker's Place* kept O'Connor alone in the neighborhood after Edith's death and the children had moved. In the spinoff he retired as a factory worker to operate his own pub, surrounded by friends and neighborhood crazies

played by Allen Melvin, Martin Balsam, Anne Meara and others. *Maude* starred Bea Arthur as Edith Bunker's much-divorced, liberal cousin of Westchester County; her show featured her efforts to get along with husband Number Four, played by Bill Macy, and her own divorced daughter, played by Adrienne Barbeau. In yet another spinoff, Maude Finlay's maid Florida (Esther Rolle) became the central character in *Good Times*, a series concerning the pitfalls and pratfalls of a black family living in a Chicago housing project. John Amos played husband James Evans, and Jimmie Walker played son J J, in a memorable performance of comic reactions and exaggerated expressions. Each of these shows featured brassy insults, and on-cue audience howls when traditions were flaunted.

Sanford and Son brought the noted nightclub comic Redd Foxx to television, which had previously been off-limits to him due to his invariably blue material. The program was an American version of the British *Steptoe and Son*, and concerned the lives of a junkman and his son, played by Desmond Wilson. The clever turns were assisted by other members of the mostly black cast, including Lawanda Page, Slappy White and Scatman Crothers.

Bob Newhart, star of the ill-starred *Entertainers* with Carol Burnett, and veteran of many talk-show appearances, starred in MTM's first

major spinoff in 1972 (and in fact shared a CBS comedy hour with *The Mary Tyler Moore Show* on Saturday nights, drawing extremely loyal viewership), *The Bob Newhart Show*. Playing Bob Hartley, psychologist, Newhart was joined by Suzanne Pleshette as wife Emily, and one of the most inspired casts ever assembled for a situation comedy. Included were Bill Daily as neighbor Howard Borden; Peter Bonerz as office-neighbor Dr Jerry Robinson; Marcia Wallace as secretary Carol Kester and Bob's looney patients played by Jack Riley, Oliver Clark, Florida Friebus and John Fiedler. The humorous situations revolved around the personalities of Bob and Emily, who were basically the only normal people among their friends and acquaintances, who were crazy in varying degrees. And once again the mark of creative control was evident in the quality scripts and essentially believable situations.

The run of *M*A*S*H* constituted a special period in television history. Spun off the popular movie, the series was originally presented as an anti-war polemic and treatment of brittle relationships amid the absurdities of war. It grew to be a well-crafted series built on warm relation-

Below left: *Bob Newhart, as psychologist Bob Hartley, tries to help his wife, Emily (Suzanne Pleshette) to overcome her fear of flying on* The Bob Newhart Show.

Below: *Redd Foxx (center) displays his irascibility to Don Bexley (left) and Desmond Wilson on* Sanford and Son.

Above: *Jimmie Walker (as J J Evans, left), Bernadette Stanis (as Thelma Evans, second from right) and Ja'net DuBois (as Willona Woods, right) co-starred in* Good Times.

Below: *Henry Winkler (The Fonz, Arthur Fonzarelli) and Ron Howard (Richie Cunningham) in* Happy Days.

145

Above: *Captain B J Hunnicutt (Mike Farrell), Major Margaret 'Hot Lips' Houlihan (Loretta Swit) and Captain Benjamin Franklin 'Hawkeye' Pierce (Alan Alda) look for choppers bearing incoming wounded in M*A*S*H.*

ships amid the horrors of war. Set in Korea in the early 1950s, the acronym of the title stands for the 4077th Mobile Army Hospital Unit. Captain Benjamin Franklin 'Hawkeye' Pierce (Alan Alda) is the main character around whom the action occurs (and who remained with the series during its entire 1972–1983 run); his major sidekicks are 'Trapper' John McIntire (Wayne Rogers) and, later, B J Hunnicutt (Mike Farrell). Other memorable characters through the years included Lieutenant Colonel Henry Blake (MacLean Stevenson, who left the series to star in a record number of TV flops); Margaret 'Hot Lips' Houlihan (Loretta Swit); Radar O'Reilly (Gary Burghoff); Frank Burns (Hot Lips' romantic interest and the butt of Hawkeye's practical jokes, played by Larry Linville); Corporal Max Klinger, who dressed like a woman to effect a discharge (Jamie Farr); Colonel Sherman Potter (Henry Morgan), who replaced Blake; and the Boston Brahmin Major Charles Winchester (David Ogden Stiers). The major actors participated in story conferences, leading to a very organic growth of ethos and characterizations. Only two characters did not fully evolve during the show's run. Major Burns was never elevated above a caricature;

and Hawkeye himself, who, played by Alda, was so adept at doing Groucho Marx turns that his eventual mental breakdown in the series' finale episode managed to lack believability and evince little compassion. Nevertheless *M*A*S*H* stands as a superb example of what time and talent can produce in episodic television. In its first season it was hovering only around Number 50 in the season ratings, but after CBS renewed it, it shot to Number 4 and remained popular all of its days.

Happy Days was the result of good critical reaction to a one-shot story on the anthology *Love, American Style* entitled 'Love in the Happy Days.' It was a nostalgic piece about the 1950s, and was itself inspired by the success of the movie *American Graffiti*. Ron Howard had been in both the movie and the skit, and he starred with Anson Williams (they played friends Richie Cunningham and Potsie Weber). Also in the cast were Tom Bosley and Marion Ross as Richie's parents and Erin Moran as his sister Joanie; Pat Morita and Al Molinaro as owners of the local malt shop and Henry Winkler (Arthur 'The Fonz' Fonzarelli) and Scott Baio (The Fonz' cousin Chachi) as leather-jacketed, tender-but-tough guys, who became teen heart-throbs around

Above: *Jailbird Laverne De Fazio (Penny Marshall) is visited by her best friend, Shirley Feeney (Cindy Williams) in an episode of* Laverne and Shirley.
Left: *Mork and Mindy — Robin Williams and Pam Dawber.*

Below: *In* Three's Company, *Janet Wood (Joyce DeWitt), Chrissy Snow (Suzanne Somers) and Jack Tripper (John Ritter) shared the same apartment, and (later in the series) Don Knotts became their suspicious landlord, who was constantly trying to catch them in the act.*

America. Nostalgic references eventually took a back seat as the series built upon the characters' interplay and the lessons of growing up.

Three series spun off *Happy Days*. In November of 1976 two characters named Laverne and Shirley appeared in an episode and reaction supposedly was so favorable that they had their own series two months later (it helped that one of the stars, Penny Marshall, was the daughter of producer Gary Marshall; her co-star was Cindy Williams, who had been in *American Graffiti*). *Laverne and Shirley* became a major sitcom hit for ABC, and had some moments recollecting the madcap physical comedy of Lucy, Joan Davis, *et al.*, of the early 1950s. *Mork and Mindy*, a clever farce starring Robin Williams as a being from outer-space planted on Earth to study humans, and Pam Dawber as his confidant, developed from a dream episode of Richie Cunningham's — and ran for four popular and critically acclaimed years. Finally, *Joanie and Chachi* starred in their own series that was the lone failure in the Marshall stable of programs.

There were other notable comedy shows of the early 1970s that received favorable audience response: *The New Andy Griffith Show*; *The Jimmy*

Above: *Captain Merril Stubing (Gavin MacLeod), the skipper of* The Love Boat, *referees a grudge match between two of his guest star passengers – Milton Berle (left) and Alan Hale.*

Opposite top: *The* Welcome Back, Kotter *gang. Teacher Gabe Kotter (Gabriel Kaplan) is in the center and Assistant Principal Michael Woodman (John Sylvester White) is in raingear. The Sweathogs were Freddie 'Boom Boom' Washington (Lawrence Hilton-Jacobs, left), Vinnie Barbarino (John Travolta, third from left), Juan Luis Pedro Phillipo de Huevos Epstein (Robert Hegyes, fifth from left) and Arnold Horshack (Ron Palillo, sixth from left).*

Opposite bottom: *Two of the waitresses in Mel's Diner in* Alice – *Linda Lavin (left), who played Alice Hyatt, and Beth Howland, who played Vera.*

Stewart Show; *Bridget Loves Bernie* (starring Meredith Baxter and David Birney as an Irish girl and Jewish boy defending their romance; the show was popular – Number Five for the season – but pressured off the air by ethnic groups); *Chico and the Man*; *The Ghost Busters* (with Larry Storch and Forrest Tucker); *Doc*; *Fay* (with Lee Grant, who publicly blasted the floundering NBC for its precipitous cancellation); and *Welcome Back, Kotter*, a show with Gabe Kaplan and John Travolta about high-school miscreants, possibly the most aggressively anti-intellectual series mounted by the American television industry.

Fully half of the shows mounted in the early 1970s were self-consciously 'relevant,' dealing in their premises with newly visible ethnic groups as lead players (Freddy Prinze in *Chico and the Man*), social issues as bases for scripts (Maude had an abortion), and previously taboo character types (prostitutes and homosexuals in *Hot L Baltimore*). Other comedy series from the period included: *Barefoot in the Park*; *The Tim Conway Show*; *Arnie* (with Hershel Bernardi); *Nanny and the Professor*; *The Smith Family* (with Henry Fonda); *Shirley's World* (with Shirley MacLaine); *Funny Face* (with Sandy Duncan); *The New Dick Van Dyke Show*; *Don Rickles*; *Temperatures Rising*; *The Paul Lynde Show*; *Thicker Than Water*; *Lotsa Luck* (with Dom DeLuise); *The Bob Crane Show* and *When Things Were Rotten*, a much-touted creation of Mel Brooks that spoofed the Robin Hood legends. It starred Dick Gautier, Misty Rowe, Dick Van Patten and Bernie Koppel, and

lasted, alas, but one season.

Two of the great shouting shows debuted in 1976. *What's Happening?* revolved around the experiences of a group of young blacks, and *Alice* – based on the movie *Alice Doesn't Live Here Anymore* – was set in Mel's Diner. Mel the grouch (Vic Tayback) was invariably complaining; Vera the dumbbell (Beth Howland) was invariably stupid; Flo the sassy waitress (Polly Holliday) was invariably caustic; and Alice (Linda Lavin) was invariably long-suffering. And somehow the audience invariably howled at clever, shouted lines like 'Kiss Mah Grits!'

One Day at a Time, over several successful seasons, traced the pains and joys of Bonnie Franklin (as Ann Romano) raising two daughters (played by Mackenzie Phillips and Valerie Bertinelli) alone. *Eight is Enough* was a gently humorous series about a large family headed by Dick Van Patten. *Three's Company* was, on the other hand, a raucous physical comedy that played for broad laughs; the premise centered on three young singles who couldn't afford to live each on their own. They decided to share an apartment, but problems arose from one's gender: Jack Tripper (played by Jack Ritter, the son of cowboy star Tex Ritter) was male, unlike his two comely roommates Suzanne Somers and Joyce DeWitt. The show concerned the myth that Jack was a homosexual, the landlords' reaction and their own faded love life (they were played by Norman Fell and Audra Lindley, and eventually starred in a spinoff, *The Ropers*) and the inevitably

ill-fated romances of the roommates. Ritter, especially, proved adept at farce, and *Three's Company* was possibly the closest television has come to old-fashioned vaudeville: excessive titillation; double entendres; slapstick humor; but all technically clean and played for laughs.

The Love Boat began in 1977 and quickly established one of episodic television's classic formats. An hour-long comedy-drama, the program was set on the cruise ship *Pacific Princess* and featured a regular crew (Gavin MacLeod as the captain, and crew members Bernie Kopell, Fred Grandy, Lauren Tewes and Ted Lange, among others who embarked later). Each week there were three or four plots that would intertwine, featuring all manner of guest stars — players from contemporary TV hits, faded movie stars, rock singers etc. It seemed that everyone who was anyone — as well as anyone who was nobody — at one time guested on *The Love Boat*, but actually guest stars were willing to appear on the short segments before a national audience — and receive an actual luxury cruise in the process. In mid-season 1977 ABC quickly duplicated its format success of the *Love Boat* and fashioned *Fantasy Island*, a drama about a place where one could travel to have dreams come true. Ricardo Montalban starred with the bizarre, diminutive Herve Villechaise, and the exodus was again on — both viewers and guest stars flocked to this new series. *Hotel* booked a similar format, starring James Brolin, Connie Sellica, Shari Bellafonte-Harper and Bette Davis.

Opposite: *The cast of* Soap. *The program made stars of (top row): Diana Canova (left), Richard Mulligan (center), Robert Mandan (third from right), Billy Crystal (second from right) and (bottom row): Jimmy Baio (left), Arthur Peterson (second from right) and Katherine Helmond (right).*

Left: WKRP in Cincinnati, *set in a radio station, starred Loni Anderson (center) and Howard Hesseman (center back).*

One of television's classic parodies and satires was premiered by ABC in 1977. Parody and satire are two distinct forms; they are hard to combine; and they have traditionally been hard to effect on television. But *Soap* was successful, and was a memorable series. Created by Susan Harris, the series satirized everything in sight — family life, suburbia, senility, homosexuality, death — in a format that lampooned TV's traditional soap-operas. A large ensemble cast was assembled with care, and included many actors who have since gone on to successful roles in other areas of television and in movies. Among such players were Richard Mulligan, Robert Mandan, Katherine Helmond, Billy Crystal, Ted Wass, Diana Canova, John Byner, Robert Urich and Robert Guillaume. A spinoff starring Guillaume, who, as butler Benson, was really the only character in *Soap* not made ridiculous, commenced in 1979. He played household manager, and finally cabinet-level assistant, to a state governor in *Benson*.

Several genre comedies asserted themselves with success in the late 1970s. *WKRP in Cincinnati* took the Mary Tyler Moore premise to a radio station filled with the usual assortment of stretched-to-the-limit personality types. *The Dukes of Hazzard* returned hick comedy to CBS; the rural action-comedy was invariably so thin on plot as to make it classifiable as a kiddie show, and indeed the likenesses of the major characters and their 'General Lee' hot-rod car festooned with children's lunchboxes and plastic toys were quite juvenile. *Diff'rent Strokes* was for a few years practically the only bright ratings spot in the line-up of NBC, which fell on incredibly hard times as a network in the late 1970s; even the importation of programming wizard Fred Silverman — after CBS secured its dominance under him and ABC in turn toppled CBS under him — was to no avail. But *Diff'rent Strokes* also distinguished itself by being the first of several shows to have black children adopted by white parents (*Webster*, with Alex Karras and Susan Clark, was another). Conrad Bain played a millionaire who adopted the two orphaned sons of his housekeeper; the young blacks were played to fine comic turns by Gary Coleman and

Todd Bridges. The series's housekeeper got her own show: *The Facts of Life* starred Charlotte Rae as housemother to girls (including Lisa Welchel, Nancy McKeon, and Kim Fields) in a boarding school; later her character Mrs Garrett took some of the graduates to help her operate a gourmet shop, and as the girls grow older their problems grow more complex. *The Associates* was a brightly written series centered in a law office, starring Wilfred Hyde-White and Martin Short. Failing on network TV, the comedy moved to cable TV, where it found a comfortable berth. The same

Above: *A tense moment between* The Associates' *Martin Short and Shelley Smith, who played first-year lawyers Tucker Kerwin and Sara James.*

Right: *Juliet Mills and Richard Long starred in the title roles of* Nanny and the Professor.
Opposite: *Conrad Bain, who plays millionaire Phillip Drummond, has some words of wisdom for his adopted sons, Willis (Todd Bridges, left) and Arnold (Gary Coleman), on* Diff'rent Strokes.
Below: *Tootie (Kim Fields) has a discussion with her housemother, Mrs Garrett (Charlotte Rae) on* The Facts of Life.

scenario was played by other sitcoms whose audiences were modest but loyal – *Too Close for Comfort* (with Ted Knight, Nancy Dussault, Deborah van Valkenburgh and Lydia Cornell) and *United States* (with Beau Bridges and Helen Shaver) – and even a dramatic series, *Paper Chase*, chronicling life on campus, with John Houseman.

House Calls chronicled life in a hospital, and starred Lynn Redgrave, Wayne Rogers, and David Wayne; and *Detective School* chronicled life as we hope it's not in the law-enforcement business. *Me and Maxx* was a warm comedy starring Joe Santos (late of the *Rockford Files*) and young Melissa Michaelson; and *One in a Million* was a promising but short-lived situation comedy whose situation was a street-wise young black cab driver (played by Shirley Hemphill, formerly of *What's Happening?*) inheriting a fortune from one of her fares. Carl Ballantine and Richard Paul co-starred.

Other comedies included *Ball Four* (the baseball rain-out starring, and based on the book by, Jim Bouton); *The MacLean Stevenson Show*; *The Tony Randall Show*; *The Nancy Walker Show* (after she played second banana simultaneously on *Rhoda* and *McMillan and Wife*); *The Practice* (with Danny Thomas); *Holmes and Yoyo* (an offbeat comedy about a mechanical man, starring two irrepressible character actors, John Shuck and Richard B Shull); *Mr T and Tina* (Pat Morita after *Happy Days* but before *The Karate Kid*); *All's Fair* (a bright comedy starring Richard Crenna and Bernadette Peters) and *CPO Sharkey*, a Don Rickles vehicle.

Carter Country, about a rural police station, attempted to capitalize on Jimmy Carter's name, if not popularity, and was doomed to failure; *The Betty White Show* co-starred John Hillerman and

Left: *Detective Stanley 'Wojo' Wojohowicz (Maxwell Gail), Officer Carl Levitt (Ron Carey) and Captain Barney Miller (Hal Linden) discuss a problem on* Barney Miller.

Below: *David Powlett-Jones (John Duttine, right) found a good friend in Algy Herries (Frank Middlemass), the headmaster of the British boys' school where he taught, in* To Serve Them All My Days.

Georgia Engel; *Tabitha* sought to update the theme, and the appeal, of the earlier hit *Bewitched*; *In the Beginning* was yet another MacLean Stevenson show (NBC, deep in the cellar, had little to lose in recycling the luckless *M*A*S*H* dropout); *The Bad News Bears* had a short season with Jack Warden as coach of the unlikely baseball team; *Quark* was a bright but short-lived science-fiction comedy with Richard Benjamin; *13 Queens Boulevard* was a brassy tale of two families, starring Eileen Brennan; *Angie* was an above-average sitcom about young marrieds, starring Donna Pescow, Robert Hays, and Doris Roberts and *Hello, Larry* was still another MacLean Stevenson attempt.

One way to trace motion-picture history is to date the years in which television rip-offs appeared. In 1979, after the success of *Animal House*, a spate of college fraternity-party pastiches were thrown at the viewing audience; all were flunked by the public – *Delta House*, *Brothers and Sisters* and *Co-Ed Fever*. Stockard Channing was unable to transfer her popularity from other media to TV in *Stockard Channing in Just Friends*. A theme concept called *NBC Carousel* failed to produce a hit among *Joe's World*, *Six O'Clock Follies* or *Good Time Harry* (none of them a MacLean Stevenson show). Georgia Engel had less than a good time on the short-lived *Good Time Girls*, Ron Moody and Cassie Yates discovered all too well that *Nobody's Perfect*, even on ABC during its ascendency.

Finally, two comedies stand out among later 1970s offerings. *Barney Miller* was an ensemble format about detectives in a run-down New York police precinct; each week kooky criminals and

assorted nuts would provide subplots, running themes and fresh diversions. Outstanding comedy writing made every episode memorable, and the interplay between the cops — whether warm or abrasive, it was authentic — provided perfect balance to the absurd mass of humanity that passed through the police station. Hal Linden starred as Detective Captain Miller. Co-starring were Jack Soo, Abe Vigoda, Gregory Sierra, Ron Glass, Steve Landesberg, Max Gail, James Gregory and Ron Carey. *Taxi* was an exceptionally brilliant product featuring comedy writing and acting of high caliber. Once again, a simple premise — the setting was a New York cab company, and the show followed the lives of the drivers and, occasionally, the fares — allowed for fresh plots, incidental characters and thematic experimentation. Judd Hirsch, a respected dramatic actor, was excellent at comedy in *Taxi* as Alex Rieger, the reserved island of normality among the eccentrics. Tony Danza played Tony Banta, a driver who was really an aspiring boxer; Jeff Conaway played Bobby Wheeler, a driver who was really an actor between jobs; Marilu Henner played Elaine Nardo, who planned to drive until her career in the arts took off. Hirsch was the only driver who was content to be a cab driver, and accepted his place. The multi-faceted Andy Kaufman, a stand-up comic, portrayed the immigrant mechanic Latka Gravas, and eventually Carol Kane entered the picture as Simka, and married him. Christopher Lloyd appeared on an episode as an incidental character and stayed as a regular — the quintessential doped-out 1960s survivor, Jim Ignatowski. Perhaps the most colorful of all was the meanest scoundrel ever to

appear in a television sitcom, Louie DePalma (played by Danny DeVito), the sawed-off, insincere, mercenary delight of a dispatcher at the cab company. The series provided both pathos and hilarity during its route on two networks as it served its fairly large but cultish audience.

As noted, the decade of the 1970s turned rosy for the first time for ABC, turned sour for NBC, and finally turned big-league for the Public Broadcasting System. In 1971, William F Buckley's *Firing Line* moved from commercial syndication to PBS, which lent the conservative movement something of an establishmentarian air, and also provided some ideological balance to the leftish network. Another identification was probably PBS's ultimate programming salvation, a move that has made it indispensible to a large bloc of American viewers; *i.e.,* the American transmission of British television shows, particularly those of the BBC.

In 1970, *Kenneth Clark's Civilisation* was in itself a civilized series surveying man's progress and achievements through the centuries. Similar in format was *Alistair Cooke's America* which, although produced by the BBC, was broadcast in America by NBC. In spite of this, and despite Cooke's outstanding contributions to young television with *Omnibus* of the 1950s, the urbane essayist's major identification was formed in the 1970s as host of PBS's *Masterpiece Theater*.

Featuring the best episodic television drama from around the world (but mostly from Britain), *Masterpiece Theater* was produced for the PBS network of stations by WGBH, Boston, which represents a familiar production arrangement for shows on Public TV. *Masterpiece Theater* is un-

Above: Upstairs Downstairs *ended its run on a happy note – the marriage of Georgina (Lesley Anne Down) to the Marquis of Stockbridge (Anthony Andrews). The Bellamys' servants, including Hudson (Gordon Jackson) congratulate them.*

doubtedly the finest continuous program of television drama in America's history of the medium. The series have been of varying length and have covered all sorts of matter from historical costume-pieces to light detective fare, and have even emanated from commercial and non-commercial sources, enabling host Cooke merely to introduce or provide unique essays wrapping the installments.

Through the years the productions – the masterpieces – have included: *The First Churchills*; *Elizabeth R*; *I, Claudius*; *Clouds of Witness*; *Cousin Bette*; *The Gambler*; *The Golden Bowl*; *Jude the Obscure*; *The Last of the Mohicans*; *The Man Who Was Hunting Himself*; *The Moonstone*; *Pere Goriot*; *Point Counter Point*; *The Possessed*; *The Resurrection*; *The Six Wives of Henry VIII*; *The Spoils of Poynton*; *Tom Brown's Schooldays*; *The*

Unpleasantness at the Bellona Club; *Vanity Fair*; *Anna Karenina*; *To Serve Them All My Days*; *The Citadel*; *The Jewel in the Crown*; *The Last Place on Earth*; *Lord Mountbatten: The Last Viceroy* and *Bleak House*.

Masterpiece Theater's finest moment – and television's – however, was *Upstairs, Downstairs*. Co-created on British commercial television by Jean Marsh (who was also featured player Rose, the upstairs maid), the series documented a generation of an upper-class family and their servants in the early decades of this century. The premise allowed for a large ensemble cast and, through the years, covered changing fashions, attitudes and styles. But the series brought something more than might otherwise have been a generational soap-opera. *Upstairs, Downstairs* presented a stunning evocation of a bygone era

reflected, were supremely organic. This was television at its best.

Included in the cast were, besides Marsh, Simon Williams as James Bellamy; Rachel Gurney as Lady Marjorie; Gordon Jackson as Hudson the butler; Pauline Collins as Sarah; Nicola Paget as Elizabeth and David Langton as Lord Bellamy.

This chronicle of life on Eaton Place, which ran for four full seasons on PBS (and five seasons in Britain; the first episodes were never shown in the US), was eventually presented in more than 50 countries to an estimated audience of a billion people. It was surely responsible for the advent in America of the mini-series.

(Just as predictable as a US imitation of *Upstairs, Downstairs* was its bastardization at Hollywood's hands. *Beacon Hill* appeared on CBS in 1975 and injected its period-piece of Boston Society with 1970s political messages; *i.e.,* a character returning from World War I brought his black trench-buddy into his exclusive club to surprised glances, at which he grows outraged. The series finished the season in the bottom 10 of the ratings.)

Public Television's tentative youthfulness as well as its audacity as an experimenter were illustrated in the early 1970s. PBS killed a Woody Allen Special because of political material, and in 1973 PBS presented the much-touted *An American Family*. This 12-hour series 'documented' the daily life of the Loud family (of Santa Barbara, California) who agreed to let TV

Above: *As the Nawab of Mirat, Saeed Jaffrey (right) and his chief minister, Count Bronowsky (Eric Porter), a Russian emigré who had lost an eye during his colorful career, played key roles in* The Jewel in the Crown, *adapted from Paul Scott's epic* Raj Quartet.

and even further-lost class system; a sympathetic view of life from all sides, the noble as well as depressing side of aristocratic and domestic life.

Through splendid writing and performances, viewers easily grew to care about all the characters, and the series took on the nature of a realistic family portrait — and that of a documentary. It was a costume piece with a vengeance: every prop and article of clothing was correct, as correct as were the characters and their attitudes. A period of enormous social and economic change was covered in *Upstairs, Downstairs*, and the producers deftly let circumstances dictate their storyline. There was little drumbeating and no hidden meanings for space-age audiences, and therein was probably the series' ultimate appeal — the whole story, its human elements and the social changes subtly

Right: The Last Place on Earth *was a riveting British import about the Scott Expedition's race to the South Pole.*

Below: *Robert Ito (as Sam Fujiyama, left) played the assistant to Jack Klugman, who starred as* Quincy.

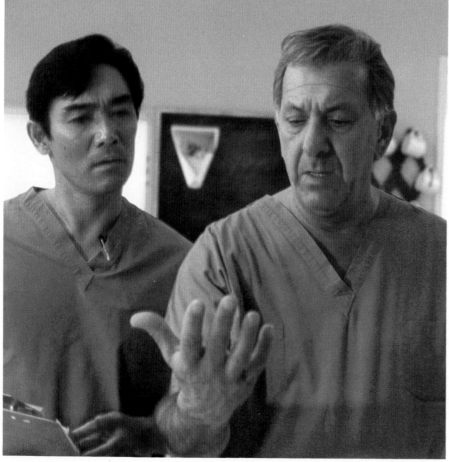

cameras record their every waking moment, good or bad, exhilarating or grief-filled. In the course of the series (culled from 300 hours of tape), the Louds' family life was a virtual soap-opera, including juvenile problems and the breakdown of the parents' marriage. Of course, only the most gullible among the Louds or any of the viewers could believe that TV cameras, equipment and personnel were invisible, especially in a household milieu. What the entire experiment represented at best was modern television's intimidating perversion of a 'normal' Middle-American family situation; at worst the nation witnessed a family allowed to be instant TV stars in a scenario of their own making, their response being to react in the way many new TV families were acting – bickering, scheming, engaging in confrontations. At one time, television met America; now America was fantasizing its role in a television syntax.

Back in the real world of TV dramas, not *all* of which were as morbid as the Loud Saga, NBC began the 1970s auspiciously with a unique format that rotated mystery stories for the better part of the decade. Beginning as *Four-in-One* and changing its name to the *NBC Mystery Movie* on Wednesdays and Sundays, a wide array of stars and premises were featured. Included in the shows were *McCloud* (Dennis Weaver as a

Above: *Danny Thomas, returned to television as Dr Jules Bedford, in* The Practice.

Western lawman assigned to a New York police station); *San Francisco International Airport*; Rod Serling's *Night Gallery*; *The Psychiatrist*; *Columbo* (Peter Falk as a rumpled, clever detective, with the first episode directed by Steven Spielberg); *McMillan and Wife* (Rock Hudson and Susan St James as a police commissioner and his wife); *Hec Ramsey* (Richard Boone as a turn-of-the-century cowboy lawman using modern techniques); *Amy Prentiss*; *McCoy*; *Quincy* (Jack Klugman as a big-city coroner with a detective's instincts) and *Lannigan's Rabbi*. Additional series in this anthology were *Banacek* (starring George Peppard); *Cool Million*; *Madigan*; *Tenafly* (about a black detective); *Farady and Co.*; and *The Snoop Sisters*, a delightful comedy-mystery starring Helen Hayes and Mildred Natwick.

Three Hollywood movie actors joined some fellows (generally motion picture actors have had poor luck with TV series) in ill-fated action shows: Glenn Ford starred in *Cade's County*; Anthony Quinn starred in *The Man and the City* and George Kennedy starred in *Sarge*, about a cop-turned-priest. Kennedy was more human and less caricatured than Robert Blake was to be more than a decade later in *Hell Town*.

James Garner, for all his success, one of the most underrated of TV or motion-picture actors, starred in *The Rockford Files* in 1974. As always,

he played himself, but the premise – he was a none-too-successful private eye, smooth-talking but with a penchant for getting punched out – was all the more attractive to TV audiences in an era of super-cool, street-wise fist-fighters. Co-starring with Garner were Noah Beery Jr and Joe Santos, and among those who frequently appeared in the humorous crime series were Rita Moreno, Stuart Margolin, Isaac Hayes – and even Mariette Hartley, with whom Garner appeared on a series of very popular TV commercials.

A similar feeling of playfulness amid deadly mystery was achieved in the series *Switch* starring Eddie Albert and Robert Wagner. Albert and Wagner played, respectively, an ex-cop and an ex-con, who joined their peculiar specialties to run an investigations office. Beyond that premise there was the obvious identification with the recent movie hit *The Sting*, but Wagner had already played the reformed con artist in television's *It Takes a Thief*. Sharon Gless, destined for promotion in *Cagney and Lacey*, played the PI's secretary in *Switch*.

Family, which began in 1976, was an extremely low-key drama series that sympathetically dealt with individual problems and relationships within a large suburban family. The series had a unique talent for seeing each member's

experiences on his or her level of maturity, and as such can be likened to a dramatic version of *Father Knows Best: i.e.,* warm, non-stereotyped, respectful. In the cast were James Broderick and Sada Thompson as the parents, and Meredith Baxter-Birney, Gary Frank and Kristy McNichol (later Quinn Cummings) as the children.

A product of the same production company that turned out *Family* was *Charlie's Angels,* a decidedly different sort of program. The premise had three pretty young women as detectives. Charlie, their boss, they would never see, but he would issue instructions by his voice (supplied by John Forsythe) and monitored by an office manager, played by David Doyle. The girls — originally Farah Fawcett-Majors, Jaclyn Smith and Kate Jackson — were each braless and sexy, each in her own way, better to cater to particular fantasies of male viewers. The popular series quickly provided all types of predictable situations: the girls being slapped around; bound; disguised as prostitutes, dancers or strippers. Through the years some faces changed (Cheryl Ladd, Shelley Hack, and Tanya Roberts became new Angels) but, for better or for worse, other things stayed the same.

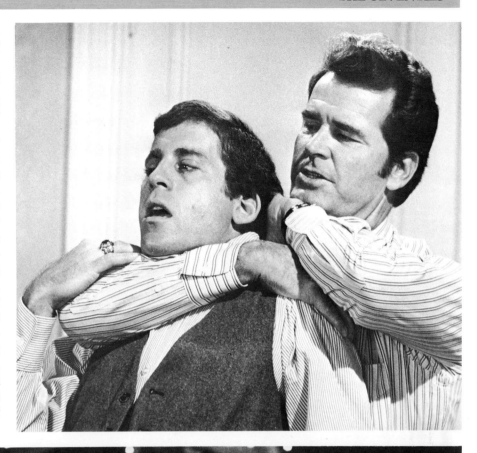

Right: *Dennis Weaver played the title role as a western marshal in the big city in* McCloud.
Above right: *James Garner, as Jim Rockford, the private investigator, subdues Paul Michael Glaser in* The Rockford Files.
Opposite: *Peter Falk, as police Lieutenant Columbo, asks questions of a murdered man's lover (Trish Van Devere), on* Columbo.

In 1978, as a replacement in Carol Burnett's time slot, *Dallas* premiered. In format it was clearly nothing new: it was an evening soap opera, and *Peyton Place* had done it before. The success of *Rich Man, Poor Man* as a mini-series two years earlier had confirmed the appeal of the big-cast angry-family formula. But *Dallas* brought something new to the genre. The clashing interests of money and oil seemed irresistible, and so was the trick of setting the characters amid unbelievable opulence and power. Some viewers could identify, some could dream, and the shnooks in the audience could find some relief in their own lives by seeing that rich people go through the same sludge as they do, albeit with designer labels.

The Ewings were the family, and it was a large family with enough members to love or hate, and enough problems to fuel several soap operas (and in fact there *was* a spinoff, *Knott's Landing*, about the Ewings in California). Jim Davis played the head of the clan, and Barbara Bel Geddes his wife (except for a brief period in the mid-1980s when Donna Reed replaced her). Other cast members included Steve Kanaly, Patrick Duffy, Victoria Principal, Charlene Tilton and Linda Gray. But the centerpiece of the show – besides the intrigues, backstabbing and adultery – was Larry Hagman as J R Ewing, the man every viewer loved to hate. With his smarmy smile and 79-cent hairpiece, he seemed to revel in betraying trusts and manipulating innocent people. It was hard to believe that he was the son of Peter Pan (Mary Martin played the fairy in early TV productions). One of the most-watched single episodes in television history was the historic 'Who Shot J R?' cliffhanger (Kristin Shepard, played by Bing Crosby's daughter Mary Frances, confessed).

Within a few years the evening soap opera was standard network fare, with stars competing

on the covers of supermarket tabloids, and scripts competing for the meaner intrigue, louder yelling matches and more shocking forms of cheating. *Knott's Landing* starred Donna Mills, Michelle Lee, Ted Shackelford, Joan Van Ark, William DeVane, Julie Harris, Lisa Hartman and John Pleshette; *Flamingo Road* starred Howard Duff, Morgan Fairchild, Mark Harmon, David Selby, Cristina Raines and Alice Hirson; *Falcon Crest* featured Jane Wyman, Lorenzo Lamas, Susan Sullivan and Robert Foxworth; *The Yellow Rose* starred Noah Beery Jr, Cybill Shepherd, Sam Elliott, Edward Albert and Chuck Connors; *Emerald Point N A S* starred Dennis Weaver, Susan Dey, Jill St John, Richard Dean Anderson and Andrew Stevens.

Dallas's main competition in style and notoriety came from *Dynasty*. Here the main characters, played by John Forsythe and Linda Evans, were basically nice guys, but Joan Collins managed enough venom for all. Also in the cast: Heather Locklear, Pamela Sue Martin (whose previous role had been Nancy Drew in the kids' mystery series), Al Corley, Lee Bergere, John James, Michael Nader, Diahann Carroll, Jack Coleman, Pamela Bellwood, George Hamilton and Catherine Oxenberg. Naturally there was a spinoff, and *The Colbys (Dynasty II)* featured Charlton Heston, Barbara Stanwyck, Katherine Ross, Ken Howard and Ricardo Montalban.

Some detectives with a difference appeared in the 1970s, inspired either by minority representation or the desperation of Hollywood program directors to find new formulas. In any event, included in this category were *Cannon* (an overweight detective, played by William Conrad); *Longstreet* (a blind investigator, played by James Franciscus); *The Rookies* (young cops); *Barnaby Jones* (a geriatric private eye, played by Buddy Ebsen, with Lee Meriwether as the wife of his murdered son) and *Baretta* (a unconventional undercover detective played by Robert Blake).

Some very sensitive and finely crafted dramatic crime shows appeared during the 1970s, although most with short service records: *Owen Marshall, Counselor at Law*; *O'Hara, US Treasury* (with David Janssen); *Hawkins* (with Jimmy Stewart); *Harry O* (another Janssen vehicle); *The Blue Knight* (with George Kennedy); *The Law* and immediately on its heels *DelVecchio*, both starring Judd Hirsch and *Tenspeed and Brownshoe* (a humorous detective series starring Ben Vereen and Jeff Goldblum that may have ushered in the 1980s' wave of humorous mysteries and crime shows).

Probably the finest in the genre of realistic police stories was *Police Story*, an anthology with no permanent cast. Ex-cop and award-winning author Joseph Wambaugh was creator, consultant and occasional scripter for the series which featured situations and cases based on files of police departments around America. Spinning off this series was the equally true-to-life *Medical Story* and the rather more glitzy

Police Woman with Angie Dickenson and Earl Holliman.

Alias Smith and Jones (1971) was an obvious takeoff on the movie *Butch Cassidy and the Sundance Kid*, but was a stylish one. *Kung Fu*, starring David Carradine, was a strangely brooding series about Kwai Chang Caine who, after killing a Chinese Mandarin back home, spent his life in the American West fleeing Oriental avengers and American bounty-hunters. *Little House on the Prairie*, produced by and starring Michael Landon, proved to be one of the most popular series in history, largely because of its emphasis on basic values and unpretentious characters. The series was based on Laura Ingalls Wilder's warm novels, and the TV show featured Karen Grassle, Melissa Gilbert, Melissa Sue Anderson, Merlin Olsen and Victor French during its long run.

Individual shows had strong followings during the 1970s. *Kojak*, a strong-willed plainclothesman (lavishly outfitted as the clothes were) was played by Telly Savalas; the show was probably more popular in Britain and throughout Europe than in the US. *The Six-Million Dollar Man*

Above: *Karen Black starred in the 'Confessions of a Lady Cop' episode on* Police Story. **Opposite top:** *Overweight though he was, William Conrad (left) was able to chase down criminals in* Cannon. **Opposite bottom:** *Inspector Steve Keller (Michael Douglas), Inspector Dan Robbins (Richard Hatch) and Detective Lieutenant Mike Stone (Karl Malden) in* The Streets of San Francisco.

starred Lee Majors as a man who underwent cybernetic surgery and received robot's powers. *The Bionic Woman*, with Lindsay Wagner, was a spinoff. *Kolchak: The Night Stalker* was a very compelling mystery series starring a superb TV actor, Darren McGavin, pursuing invariably weird, other-worldly cases. *The City of Angels* (Los Angeles) starred Wayne Rogers after *M*A*S*H* in a series, unfortunately short-lived, that was clearly inspired by the wave of 1930s-detective genre movies like *Chinatown*. Lynda Carter, who had been Miss USA of 1973, co-starred with Lyle Wagonner in a comic-book-inspired adventure called, interestingly, *The New Original Wonder Woman*. Science-fiction entries during the 1970s included *Logan's Run*, *Battlestar Galactica* (each of which *became* comic books), and the perpetually recycled comic strip dinosaur *Buck Rogers in the 25th Century*. *Hart to Hart*, starring Robert Wagner and Stefanie Powers, was a stylish, glamorized action program about husband-and-wife millionaires solving strange mysteries. But a murder a week turned out to be too much of a coincidence.

Above: *Lynda Carter, as Yeoman Diana Prince, aka 'Wonder Woman,' gives a baddie his comeuppance on Wonder Woman.*
Opposite: *Telly Savalas was New York Police Lieutenant Theo Kojak on* Kojak.

Nimoy, Lesley Ann Warren, Lynda Day George, and Sam Elliot as agents who received orders that presented enormous challenges. Each episode (which showed an agent receiving the assignment on a miniature tape-recorder that self-destructed) followed the team's masquerades and split-second schemes. In 1975, after contract disputes, two of the series' stars, the husband and wife team of Martin Landau and Barbara Bain, starred in their own program, *Space 1999*, an approximate cross between *Star Trek* and *Mission: Impossible*. Each of the networks rejected the series, but it became very popular in syndication.

As NBC sunk farther and farther in the ratings swamp, their hapless adventure shows became running jokes as much as running series. *Here's Boomer* was one such show; *B J and the Bear* was another. Almost as soon as *B J* premiered, Claude Akins (who had starred in NBC's ill-fated *Movin' On*, a truck-driver action adventure) spun off his character in a solo show *The Misadventures of Sheriff Lobo*. It was not instant popularity but instant desperation that prompted the network. Programming chief Fred Silverman had run out of the famous magic from his CBS and ABC days that had prompted his hiring by NBC. The network's most celebrated bomb during this period — at least in the dramatic field — was *Supertrain*, a highly publicized, high-budget, high-profile flop that sought to transfer *The Love Boat*'s successful formula to wheels. It was derailed by the dismal reality of a major TV network betting its chips on an imitation — no matter how good — of a basically superficial piece of fluff.

Other dramatic series from this decade of the best and worst of TV included 'relevant' shows like *The Young Lawyers, Storefront Lawyers, The*

Lou Grant was an interesting spinoff: Ed Asner played his character from *Mary Tyler Moore* but made a transition from comedy to drama as he became managing editor on a Los Angeles newspaper. The series was marked by mature scripts and fine acting (also in the cast were Nancy Marchand, Mason Adams, Robert Walden, Linda Kelsey and Jack Bannon) but as the scripts grew increasingly leftist-oriented — as did Asner himself in his public pronouncements — so did the audience support wane.

Mission: Impossible was a popular CBS series of the 1960s and 1970s that featured Peter Graves, Greg Morris, Peter Lupus, Leonard

Left: *Lee Majors (left) played Colonel Steve Austin, an astronaut who had been critically injured in a crash and had many of his parts replaced by atomic-powered electromechanical devices, in* The Six Million Dollar Man.

Interns, Silent Force, Matt Lincoln, The Immortal, Nichols, The Persuaders, Ghost Story, Banyon, Emergency!, The Streets of San Francisco, Love Story, The New Perry Mason, Toma, Griff, The Cowboys, Lucas Tanner (starring David Hartman before he became an alarm-clock host on Good Morning America), Petrocelli, Planet of the Apes, S.W.A.T., Starsky and Hutch, Ellery Queen, Matt Helm, Joe Forrester, Bronk, Black Sheep Squadron, The Life and Times of Grizzly Adams, What Really Happened to the Class of '65?, How the West Was Won (with James Arness), Eischied, Skag, Hunter, The Hardy Boys, Nancy Drew, Julie Farr, MD, Spiderman, The Hulk, CHiPS, The White Shadow, The Eddie Capra Mysteries, Vega$, Salvage-1, Mrs Columbo, 240-Robert (with Joanna Cassidy and Mark Harmon), A Man Called Sloane, Stone, BAD Cats and Paris.

In the area of 'specials' — a category-word that is an example of televisionese, turning an adjective into a noun — the 1970s saw the birth of the mini-series, a singular synthesis of the older dramatic presentation and the evening soap opera. Although the British had paved the way (with series like Upstairs, Downstairs and The Six Wives of Henry VIII), it was Rich Man, Poor Man (1976) that opened the floodgates in the US. The 12-hour dramatization of Irwin Shaw's novel (and the following season's 21-part sequel) concerned the affairs of Rudy and Tom Jordache (Peter Strauss and Nick Nolte). The large cast was studded with TV faces, including Lynda Day George, Dick Sargent, Craig Stevens, Dorothy Malone, George Maharis, Edward Asner, Murray Hamilton, Robert Reed, Norman Fell, Van Johnson and Dorothy McGuire. Mini-series proved a magical formula for television executives; they could be promoted in blitz campaigns; they could bring in big-name stars for relatively little money (since on-screen time was divided among the many) and they could serve as painless tryouts for season series.

Other mini-series through the decade included: Evening in Byzantium, The Bastard, Centennial, Ike, Blind Ambition, The Last Convertible, The Martian Chronicles, Holocaust, The Moneychangers, Moses the Lawgiver, Jesus of Nazareth and the most popular of all — a landmark in television history: Roots. On eight nights in a row America watched a total of 12 hours based on Alex Haley's best-selling docudrama of his family's origins in Africa, through slavery and then freedom in America. With almost every broadcast, ratings records were broken, and the last episode was the most-watched TV program to that time. Included in the notable cast were LaVar Burton (playing young slave Kunta Kinte), Ben Vereen, John Amos, Cicely Tyson (who was also to play Miss Jane Pitman in a celebrated mini-series about the 110-year-old former slave), Leslie Uggams, Robert Reed, Edward Asner and Lloyd Bridges. Roots — The Next Generations, bringing the tale up to date, featured Marlon Brando and James Earl Jones.

Other 1970s specials of the traditional variety included PBS's Hollywood Television Theater, which featured The Andersonville Trial, and Hamlet with Richard Chamberlain; Brian's Song, the TV-movie starring Billy Dee Williams as Gale Sayers and James Caan as fatally ill football player Brian Piccolo; Katharine Hepburn in The Glass Menagerie on the ABC Theater and two TV movies based on the lives of Franklin and Eleanor Roosevelt starring Edward Hermann and Jane Alexander.

Entertainment specials included Stand Up and Cheer, a patriotic musical program that became a syndicated offering; Elvis: Aloha from Hawaii, broadcast by satellite to an estimated audience of 1.5 billion people (if network publicists were to be believed); Liza With a 'Z'; Bob Hope's Road to China, a three-hour special (Hope continued his practice of hosting several specials a year, oftentimes before servicemen, all featuring the hottest talent of the day); The Johnny Carson Anniversary Specials, which have become an annual event, and Barbara Walters interview-specials for ABC.

Opposite: Dean Butler, Melissa Gilbert, Matthew Laborteaux, Michael Landon and Karen Grassle in 'The In-Laws' episode of Little House on the Prairie.

Below: Ben Vereen as 'Chicken' George in the popular mini-series Roots.

Above: *Robert Wagner (as Jonathan Hart), Stefanie Powers (Jennifer Hart) and Lionel Stander (as their faithful retainer, Max) in* Hart to Hart.
Right: *Peter Graves (as James Phelps), Greg Morris (Barney Collier) and Peter Lupus (Willie Armitage) on assignment on* Mission: Impossible.

Left: *Levar Burton (c) as young Kunta Kinte, aboard a slave ship in an early episode of* Roots.
Below: *The calm, cool, collected and ever pleasant Harry Reasoner — one of the anchormen of* 60 Minutes.

Walters had jumped from the *Today* show for $1 million a year and co-anchored, for a time, the evening news program.

Harry Reasoner had also moved to ABC, from CBS, and became anchorman of the evening news upon Howard K Smith's retirement in 1975. The networks maintained a shadow-dancing performance as they kept a semblance of their old news documentaries and Sunday-afternoon current-affairs programming. Weekends were taken by sports when the 1970s rolled around, so the networks offered a merry-go-round of mostly short-lived news-focus programs in prime time, including *NBC Reports, The Reasoner Report, NBC Weekend* (Saturdays at 11:30 PM, once a month) and *Conversations with Eric Sevareid.* And of course Public Broadcasting presented a higher percentage of news reports and documentaries; after all, at least in the view of the commercial networks, PBS was supposed to be the egghead ghetto.

CBS started a commercial trend by its successful introduction of the weekly news program *60 Minutes* in 1968. Through the years the on-screen reporters (sometimes they are the actual field reporters as well as narrators) included Mike Wallace, Morley Safer, Dan Rather, Ed Bradley, Harry Reasoner and Diane Sawyer, who have covered everything from trivial gossip to political scandal. *60 Minutes* has chased consumer fraud and told stories of governmental

inefficiency. As muckrakers of the classical sort – Theodore Roosevelt originally characterized the breed as, in *Pilgrim's Progress*, those who look down in the mud while never looking up at brighter things – *60 Minutes* has tended to wear its crusading heart on its sleeve. But it became the most popular program in America for many years. Helped by a Sunday-night lead-in from network football coverage, and little competition on early Sunday evenings – not to mention the glamorous headline-type stories producer Don Hewitt routinely produced – it garnered massive audience-shares in its time slot. ('Audience-share' is television parlance for the number of homes watching TV at a given time, factored with the percentage tuned to a particular program.)

60 Minutes also garnered massive imitation, which in American television is the sincerest form of laziness. Nevertheless, rival networks served up shows like *First Tuesday* (NBC). ABC's most successful imitation came with *20/20*, hosted by Hugh Downs, beginning in 1978. Correspondents through the years included Geraldo Rivera, Sylvia Chase (each of whom left in 1985 over ABC News' killing a story unfavorable to the Kennedy political dynasty), Dave Marash, John Stossel, Thomas P F Hoving and Barbara Walters. NBC introduced *Prime Time Sunday* in 1979, although host Tom Snyder smothered his material to such an extent that the program could not be called a strict news program. In fact, in the 1980s there have been tendencies at all three networks to produce 'information specials' of sorts – where personality pieces and 'lifestyle focus' reports tend to obliterate the line between news and entertainment.

In 1976 Richard Nixon was interviewed by David Frost over a network of independent stations after the Big Three rejected the package. Nixon shared in the profits – which arrangement was one of the odious elements to the networks – but the series of conversations attracted huge audiences. Also in 1976 there was a flurry of *Bicentennial Minutes* and bits of history and information. Stuffed between shows in the program schedules, they were often dwarfed by the accompanying commercials they were mostly designed to attract. But the cumulative images of America – all corners, all periods of history – should have reminded viewers that fewer than 25 years earlier, Edward R Murrow hailed the significance of showing the Atlantic and Pacific coastlines on one screen as the dawning of a new technological day through television.

In television's literal world of variety, the 1970s displayed a further devolution from the live-hour programs that dominated the medium's early days. In the 1970s virtually everything was on tape, and there were fewer series, with more short-run programs and late-night slots. But of course the big-name stars continued to shine. When the decade opened, variety shows were hosted by Englebert Humperdinck, Johnny

Cash (and his summer replacement show given to the Everly Brothers), Andy Williams (and *his* summer vacation covered by Ray Stevens), Don Knotts, and Pat Paulsen, who parlayed his popular somnambulent routines on *The Smothers Brothers Show* into ersatz media campaigns for the US presidency and his own variety show, *The Pat Paulsen Half-Comedy Hour*. Flip Wilson proved the variety program still had vitality when his hour on NBC became the Number Two show in its first two seasons. He also became the first certified black TV superstar, and part of his popularity stemmed from his 'characters' – Geraldine Jones ('What You See Is What You Get!'), the Rev LeRoy and others – providing some of television's most outrageous costume bits since Milton Berle. Another Wilson catchphrase that swept the nation was 'The Devil made me do it!'

On PBS, Marshall Efron hosted *The Great American Dream Machine*, a bright magazine-format variety program. On the commercial networks Pearl Bailey came home with her own variety show, and other hosts of their own series included Val Doonican, Marty Feldman, Jerry Reed, John Byner, David Steinberg, Ken Berry (*The Wow Show*), Bill Cosby, Julie Andrews, Helen Reddy and the comedy team of Burns and Schreiber.

Sonny and Cher, the slightly eccentric but very palatable rock stars (they broadcast anti-drug messages to the delight of network personnel), co-hosted a bright, loose comedy/music hourly series. *The ABC Comedy Hour* spun off to a very successful and extremely clever syndicated series, *The Copy Cats*, wherein the world's greatest

Above: *Ed Bradley joined co-editors Mike Wallace, Morley Safer and Harry Reasoner on the* 60 Minutes *team in 1981 – in the program's 14th season on CBS.*
Opposite top: *Eric Sevareid.*

impressionists formed an ensemble to do weekly lampoons and imitations. The crew included Frank Gorshin, Rich Little, George Kirby, Marilyn Michaels and Joe Baker. Dean Martin, whose own variety show was easy-paced and highly rated,

Left: The Mac Davis Show *began as a summer replacement variety showcase.*

spun off several other shows and replacements, including *The Bobby Darin Amusement Company* and *Music Country* (many of his own record hits were pop covers of country-music songs). ABC began to lose faith in Dick Cavett as a ratings magnet and cancelled his show but replaced it with *The Wide World of Entertainment*, at first rotating Cavett, Jack Paar and entertainment and mystery specials. An *In Concert* segment was aired late-night every other Friday, the counterpart of *Midnight Special* and other manifestations of rock 'n' roll's growing acceptance, in spite of drug- and sex-related lyrics, on television.

Throughout the decade ABC experimented with late-night variety formats to compete with Carson (while CBS stuck with movies and TV-series re-runs), all to no avail against the King of Late Night. In 1973 Carson's own network, NBC, introduced an insomniac follow-up to *The Tonight Show, Tomorrow*, hosted by Tom Snyder. The first program, devoted to octogenarian sex, appropriately set the tone for the show's tenure, as if Snyder felt compelled by a Truth in Packaging Law to reveal the level of taste to which he would stoop.

NBC tried the *Hollywood Palace* type of format with *NBC Follies*, which proved to be a folly, and was no match for ABC's *Saturday Night Live with Howard Cosell*, an embarrassment of major proportions; the egocentric Cosell, whatever he *was* suited for, was awkward and hokey as a master of ceremonies. To the millions of annoyed sports fans through the years who suspected that Cosell was out of his element as a color-man at football games and ringside announcer at boxing matches, his 1985 autobiography-of-sorts confirmed his basic displeasure with the assignments. He seemed most comfortable *shmoozing* and name-dropping at the celebrity *Battle of the Network Stars* competitions that were aired as specials throughout the 1970s and 1980s. He also hosted sports interview and anthology programs, but the self-anointed label of Sports Journalist fit him as well as his frequently ridiculed toupee.

Other entertainment stars hosted their own variety series through the decade, including Bobbie Gentry, Tony Orlando and Dawn, Dolly Parton, Mac Davis, The Smothers Brothers (again), Jim Stafford, Gladys Knight and the Pips, Ben Vereen (*Comin' at Ya!*), Rich Little, John Davidson, Bert Convey, Dinah Shore, Diahann Carroll, The Captain and Tenille, Shields and Yarnell, Marilyn McCoo and Billy Davis, Richard Pryor, Redd Foxx, Mary Tyler Moore (a short-lived attempt after her sitcom) and one of television's delicious moments — *Pink Lady*. During NBC's ratings swoon, panic reportedly reigned so confusingly under Fred Silverman that a Japanese singing duo, Pink Lady, was signed to host a variety show (with a spate of unknown comedians) before it was learned that the stars didn't speak English.

The Muppet Show was sampled as a pilot on

Opposite: *The special effects and costumes were splendid on* Battlestar Galactica — *a series that lasted less than two years.*

Above: *A* Star Wars *sendup, with guest star Mark Hamill, on* The Muppet Show, *made by puppeteer Jim Henson in England, which began in 1976.*

Below: *Howard Cosell — a sports broadcaster that one either loves or hates. Still, he is a tell-it-like-it-is commentator, and a muckraker of the first order.*

NBC, and the Henson Muppets, which had become popular fixtures via Sesame Street and clever merchandising, failed to earn a contract offer. None of the three networks was interested in this innovative program that featured puppets — Kermit the Frog, Miss Piggy, Fozzie Bear, the hecklers Waldorf and Statler — and was a parody of variety shows but was superb entertainment in itself. The show offered top-notch comedy, music and skits, and when Jim Henson went to England to put together a production arrangement, the resulting package was syndicated in the US with enormous success. As the networks regretted their rejection, they watched the biggest names in Hollywood stand in line for appearances on the newest 'in' booking.

Television — or rather the audience, whose interests can never totally be anticipated or fully manipulated — continued to produce surprises. Susan Anton, a hot property who seemed to have Las Vegas, movies and the world in front of her, starred in the variety show *Presenting Susan Anton!* in 1979 — and discovered that TV would not be one of the worlds she would conquer. On the other hand, a trivial replacement show starring Donnie and Marie Osmond — the two youngest and toothiest of the singing family that Andy Williams had helped bring to prominence — caught the public's attention. For several years, beginning in 1976, *Donnie and Marie* was a top-rated variety show.

In the late 1970s some new formats mani-

Above: *Chuck Barris in a fit of ecstasy on his television creation,* The Gong Show, *in which a variety of obscure performers displayed their unusual (and usually laughable) skills before a panel of celebrity guests.*
Right: *The clay figures, Mr Bill and Sluggo, were featured on* Saturday Night Live.

fested themselves. Unfortunately short-lived was *The Hanna-Barbera Happy Hour*, a free-wheeling comedy program that relied on improvisation and experimentation, and featured largely home-grown animation by some of the best talents in the business. There was also the spate of human-interest anthology shows that all shared several trademarks: a varied collection of news or personality items; a team of co-hosts and a patently false informal manner where awkward ad-libs were methodically read from teleprompters. Most prominent was *Real People*, hosted by Sara Purcell, Fred Willard, Skip Stephenson, Byron Allen and John Barbour; and *That's Incredible!*, hosted by Cathie Lee Crosby, Fran Tarkenton and John Davidson. Similar shows were *Those Amazing Animals* with Burgess Meredith, Priscilla Presley and Jim Stafford; *Speak Up America*, with Marjoe Gortner and Rhonda Bates and *The Big Show* with Charlie Hill, Shabba-Doo and Mimi Kennedy.

The Big Show also featured Graham Chapman, a veteran of Britain's *Monty Python's Flying Circus*, which had become an enormous cult favorite via PBS exposure. The comedy ensemble (including John Cleese, Chapman, Eric Idle and American animator Terry Gilliam) perpetrated crazy comedy that veered somewhere between gross iconoclasm and outright surrealism. Using *Monty Python* as obvious inspiration, NBC instituted *Saturday Night Live* as a late-night comedy/variety program. The sketches seemed to be self-conscious *Monty Python* imitations, and indeed the guest hosts — in a format that was regularly followed — would sometimes be personnel from the British show. The original American ensemble featured Chevy Chase, Dan Aykroyd, Jane Curtin, John Belushi, Gilda Radner, Laraine Newman and Garrett Morris. Later members included Bill Murray, Joe Piscopo and Eddie Murphy. The intended audience was obviously the youth market, for the musical guests were invariably rock stars, and the humor frequently scatological.

But *SNL*'s imitators were legion. ABC tried *Fridays* (featuring Melanie Chartoff, Maryedith Burrell and Larry David among its players); and in 1981 NBC brought on the *SCTV Comedy Network* after the *Friday Tonight Show*. *SCTV* (representing the call letters of a mythical TV organization, actually built on the troupe's origin, the brilliant Second City players) had been running for four years in Canada, although the comedy ensemble's origins were in Chicago. Brilliant comedy, satire and parody, much less political than *SNL*, was offered by *SCTV*, whose members through the years included Eugene Levy, Joe Flaherty, John Candy, Martin Short, Andrea Martin and Catherine O'Hara.

Daytime programming in the 1970s saw several successful new soap operas and some new types of game shows. *Another World — Somerset*, *Peyton Place* (on NBC, distilled from the prime-time ABC hit), *The Young and the Restless* and *Ryan's Hope* were among the soaps. It was during the 1970s that soaps expanded their lengths. *General Hospital* and *One Life to Live* became 45 minutes each in 1976, and *All My Children* ballooned to an hour the next year.

Game shows included the *Fun Factory* — with the set made up like a huge game-board for contestants to walk through, and starring Bobby Van — as well as *The Joker's Wild* and *Gambit*. In 1973 *The $10,000 Pyramid* made its debut and was one of the quiz shows wherein home viewers could legitimately participate in front of the screen with challenging and intelligent material. (The evening version became the *$100,000 Pyramid*). *Wheel of Fortune* began with Chuck Woolery as host, but an evening version later hosted by Pat Sajak turned it into a supershow among game programs. Another series fitting that description for many years was *Family Feud* with Richard Dawson (who had earlier been a regular panelist on *The Match Game*, which underwent a format transformation to great success in the 1970s). Chuck Barris, producer of *The Dating Game* and *The Newlywed Game*, was producer and host of *The Gong Show*, sort of a demented *Amateur Hour* where contestants would perform until 'gonged' off the stage by one of three celebrity misanthropes. The series overflowed with schticks, insults and double enten-

Below: *Dwight Schultz (Captain H M 'Howling Mad' Murdock on* The A-Team), *joins Pat Sajak (center) and Vanna White (left) on NBC's popular game show,* Wheel of Fortune.

dres. An answer to critics who scorned *The Gong Show*'s baser elements was the *$1.98 Beauty Contest*, with Rip Taylor, which made fun of contestants' physical attributes as well as their talent.

Following in the footsteps of daytime talk and variety show hosts Morey Amsterdam, Arthur Godfrey and Jimmy Dean, was David Letterman. His first guest was cartoonist Arnold Roth, who is such a funny personality that people often think he's a comedian; Letterman also featured an ensemble troupe of comedians who masqueraded as eccentric but legitimate guests. The resulting confusion may have had something to do with the show's brief lifespan, which may, however, have been a blessing in disguise, since Letterman was freed to host a late-night talk show (after *Tonight* on NBC) of notable quality and variety.

If rivals couldn't beat *The Tonight Show* in its time slot, they were certainly finding other cracks in NBC's ratings armor. ABC, which in mid-decade captured the prime-time lead from CBS for the first time, created *AM America* to challenge *Today*. It flopped. But when David

Hartman, occasional television actor, was added as host (at first with actress Nancy Dussault and then New York news-reader Joan Lunden), it was reborn as *Good Morning America* and enjoyed a steady ratings climb. Mixing light features with hard news, it became a comfortable companion to the wake-up crowd, and became a habit. In 1980 it passed *Today* in popularity, but NBC regained the lead in 1985.

The 1970s saw the virtual canonization of *Sesame Street*, *The Electric Company* and *Mr Rogers' Neighborhood* as must-watch programming for America's tots. Among the many kidvid shows of the 1970s were *Josie and the Pussycats*, *Sabrina*, *The Jackson Five*, *Pebbles and Bam Bam*, *The Brady Kids*, *Superfriends*, *Shazam!*, and the animated *Harlem Globetrotters*. *Hot Dog* was a series of informational spots by celebrities, an excellent educational tool for children. On Sunday morning Marshall Efron conducted *Marshall Efron's Sunday School*, a light but not sacrilegious non-denominational series of Bible stories retold for the television generation. On Sunday evenings, *The Hardy Boys* and *Nancy Drew Mysteries* ran in tandem as live-action for the younger set.

Opposite: All My Children *was the first daytime soap opera to run for an hour.*
Above left: *The childhood friends of comedian Bill Cosby, familiar from his monologues, became cartoon characters on* Fat Albert and The Cosby Kids.
Top: Walt Disney's Donald Duck *cartoons were rereleased for television.*
Above: *One of the newer cartoons for children was* Bad Cat.

Opposite top: *The* Today *show's co-anchors are Jane Pauley and Bryant Gumbel.* **Opposite bottom:** *Since the first televised game on 27 August 1939, baseball games have become a staple of the summer season, with millions of viewers.* **Below:** *The Watergate Hearings became popular TV fare. The questioners here are Senator Howard Baker of Tennessee (left) and Senator Sam Ervin of North Carolina.*

Fat Albert and the Cosby Kids was (as the credits read) hosted, created by, written by, and with the voice of Bill Cosby. Based on juvenile characters used in his stand-up comedy routines, Cosby was investing in a young audience that 15 years later would help make his *Cosby Show* a ratings leader.

The *ABC Afterschool Specials* premiered in 1972 on a schedule of one afternoon drama broadcast the first Wednesday of each month. The series has been of enormous importance, dealing with issues for children ranging from controversial to educational to simply entertaining. Broken homes, drugs at school, and child abuse have been tackled in dramatic contexts; the first program to air in the series was 'The Last of the Curlews,' a Hanna-Barbera production about the decimation of 35 million birds and the shooting of a lonely survivor that had met a mate. In general, ACT (a pressure group called Action for Children's Television) had been effective in campaigning against violence on children-oriented TV, although while they objected to the hard slapstick of 1930s and 1940s *Bugs Bunny* cartoons, their brush also indicted contemporary animation and film shows. The effect was the sissifying of Saturday-morning fare and frequent intimidation of innovative concepts.

In sports, ABC cemented its position as the network most adept at covering events and anthologizing them. In 1970 National Football League *Monday Night Football* premiered, with announcers Keith Jackson, Don Meredith and Howard Cosell (other voices calling the games included Fran Tarkenton, O J Simpson and Joe Namath). Football games – not to mention Olympic coverage – took on the aspects of grand Roman spectacles. In 1979 major-league baseball signed a pact with the television industry for broadcast rights; the astronomical package cost $54.5 million, although a few years later a new agreement was reached for $1 billion.

In the area of news that made its way to television – in certain ways the 1970s resembled the previous decades. In the aftermath of the George Wallace shooting, the words and scenes were reminiscent of the Kennedy and Martin Luther King Jr slayings of the 1960s. The settings and

drama of the 1950s' Army-McCarthy hearings were recalled during the Watergate Crisis, where accusations flew, and, finally, Congressional hearings were held. More than 300 hours of the hearings were covered by television — with the networks rotating their daily coverage and PBS presenting a nightly synopsis of developments — and it was ultimately such glare of publicity and the very implications of TV's brouhaha — as much as the damaging revelations themselves — that turned public opinion against Nixon and his cronies. Although newspaper reporters were far in the lead of television journalists, so called, in breaking all the Watergate details, it was, significantly, TV to which Nixon turned to make his resignation and farewell speeches. Television had finally come to a point where its requirement shaped public policy, or at least the exercise thereof: Nixon's trip to China, before his castle began to crumble, and his final summit trip to Europe, taken because of that disintegration, were timed so that the important visual scenes would arrive by satellite to the US in time for morning and evening news programs.

By the late 1970s, satellites were as common as experimental broadcast antennae once were. The pioneers had been Telstar at 22,300 feet above earth, followed by Relay, and Comsat's Early Bird, available to all who would bounce off its surface. By the 1970s the sky was full of them, assisting network 'feeds,' facilitating all types of communications and ushering in the nascent cable and home-receiver industries.

The apex — or nadir — of corporate-network's manufacture of news (as opposed to reporting of news) came with several CBS 'documentaries' of the time. *Hunger in America* had indicted the American economic system for allowing starvation and malnutrition in a jeremiad climaxed by the correspondent holding 'a dying baby.' The baby in fact, and unfortunately, did die shortly thereafter, but the doctors attending the case declared that other causes were responsible. There was also evidence that a network news department had staged, and even paid for, an invasion of a Caribbean island, in order that their cameras could be there to build a 'documentary.' Not only did the invasion fail, but newsmen at first claimed the CIA was the actual conspirator.

The worst incident of all was when CBS aired

Above: *'Weekend Update' on* NBC's Saturday Night Live. *Left to right: John Belushi, Jane Curtin, Bill Murray, Father Guido Sarducci (Don Novello).*

Top: *Some of the Jim Henson puppets from* Fraggle Rock, *a weekly kids' show on Home Box Office that features Fraggles, Doozers and Gorgs in their own fantasy land.*

Above: Good Morning, America. *Mary Tyler Moore (center) is interviewed by co-hosts Joan Lunden and David Hartman.*

The Selling of the Pentagon in 1971. It was a 'documentary' based on the Defense Department's power and operations, and the warning of President Eisenhower against a 'military-industrial complex,' which phrase became itself a virtual complex with TV news departments (it seems to be the only pronouncement of Ike's long career in the military, education and public service that television could remember). CBS was caught manipulating facts. One of the generals they interviewed had secretly hidden a tape-recorder during the filming session, and his prior suspicions proved correct: the producers spliced some of his answers to different questions, and edited portions of others, all to make *their* point, not his. There was a Congressional hearing, before Representative Harley Staggers' Commerce Subcommittee — somehow this one was not carried on television — and CBS executives firmly refused to cooperate with any proceedings, citing the 'chilling effect' such inquiries would have on freedom of the press.

Their stonewalling created some difficult precedents for television. First, it claimed that TV's self-appointed goals were more important than truth and their operations more important than public disclosure, allowing that the self-appointed goals might be uncovering corruption — *or* hyping ratings. It assumed that its electronic presentation of news was the legal equivalent of the print media's journalistic activities. Such was not clear, or even necessarily proper, since, as noted, the airwaves are the public's and not private enterprise's, like newspapers and magazines. In effect: when you propagandize in print you exercise your own free speech; when you propagandize on the air you impinge on the public's rights.

CBS never yielded an inch on the *Selling of the Pentagon* affair, and television, as an industry, still holds to the privileges claimed at that time. Television news has carried on since then clad in Emperor's clothing; the industry had revealed that its primary goals oftentimes were not journalistic but entertainment; that ratings (or sometimes politics) was the standard, not ethics; that instead of a news tradition, TV willingly planted itself in a show-biz tradition. As the years went on these truths were to confirm themselves, not only in network operations but in the peculiar subspecies known as local news. Sensationalism is a better selling point than the simple truth.

THE EIGHTIES

Previous spread: *Philip Michael Thomas (left) and Don Johnson (center) play detectives on* Miami Vice. **Above:** *J J Jackson (right), here with The Fabulous "T" Birds, is a VJ on MTV, the cable network that shows music videos.*

The year of 1980 provides a fairly clear demarcation line between eras and trends in television history. The variety hour was virtually dead, at least in a series format. The live drama production was now finally a relic of the quaint past, but had been firmly replaced by the mini-series, recently validated as a viable format by notable successes.

The advent of the cable and pay-TV was at hand in 1980, too. Long predicted and dreamed about, tentatively tried in fits and starts, the New Wave that would diversify America's programming, and end the networks' strangle-hold, finally arrived. As a Wave, its diversification was accepted with various levels of enthusiasm, and

the networks' viewing monopoly was bent — diminished – but definitely not broken.

In 1980 broadcasting maverick Ted Turner launched his Cable News Network, an all-talk service that blanketed the continent via free availability on the mushrooming number of local cable facilities. Networks seemed unconcerned until two years later when the CNN Headline Service was spun off. Local stations — including network affiliates — were buying the service to complement network news feeds, replace them, or sometimes pre-empt network prime-time programs.

The 24-hour CNN featured 25 news readers, a variety of field correspondents, footage bought cluding in the news division) and came at a time when their ratings lead was ended by a resurgent NBC.

Satellite use allowed Home Box Office to take off in 1972. This home service, among the types that require a special fee for unscrambling its transmissions, specializes in broadcasting current movies (as do The Movie Channel and Cinemax), but also serves up some original quality programming; among HBO's shows have been *Bizarre*, a Canadian-based cross between *Saturday Night Live* and *Benny Hill* starring John Byner; *Fraggle Rock* with Jim Henson's Muppets, and the brilliantly funny *Not Necessarily the News*. The Showtime pay-TV service has produced new episodes of the literate *Paper Chase* with John Houseman, a ratings failure when on CBS, and *Faerie Tale Theater*, a remarkable series of dramatized fairy tales, hosted by Shelley Duvall, starring major Hollywood actors and written by innovative screenwriters like Jules Feiffer. Showtime also negotiated the rights to broadcast 75 'lost' episodes of *The Honeymooners*, one of television's legendary series (these were 1950s episodes that were longer or shorter than the commercially mandated half-hour and were not sold by Jackie Gleason as part of the 'classic 39' shows for syndication).

As more and more viewers acquired video cassette recorders (VCRs) and rented contemporary first-run movies, the cable channels lost some of their allure as movie-theater replacements; consequently cable and pay-TV services turned to innovation and specially originated programming to survive. The wrinkle has furthered the cause of programming diversification.

CBS itself sought to enter the cable field with an arts channel that unfortunately expired after 14 months, but ABC, in partnership with the Hearst Corporation, launched ARTS (Alpha Repertory Television Service), later the Arts and Entertainment Network, with fair success. It has run British and American drama and documentaries; operas and ballet; the comedy hit *Alas Smith and Jones*; the first-run comedy series based at the legendary Los Angeles nightclub, *Evening at the Improv*; and movies. ABC/Hearst, in partnership with Viacom, also operate Lifetime, which is oriented rather more toward chat and self-help programming — diet, recipe, health exercise, religion, advice, and even sex therapy among its categories.

Nickelodeon is a children's specialty channel that offers hours of animated fare (most of it from outside America, providing a glimpse of the creative ferment that has emigrated from America); *Pinwheel*; *Livewire*, the comedy ensemble for kids; *You Can't Do That on Television*; and — recalling an old TV stand-by on TV's newest vehicle — the reassuring *Mr Wizard*. Don Herbert continues to teach basic science to youngsters in a simple, interesting and non-condescending manner.

Among other cable services, USA offers sports

Above: *Bruce Weitz plays undercover detective Mick Belker on* Hill Street Blues.

from news services around the world and a few big names like Daniel Schorr, who had left CBS in a dispute over ethics and sources. Inevitably, news stories and features were repeated throughout the day — as all-news radio stations or the BBC Worldservice inevitably must do — but the cable channel became a fixture in a lot of viewers' homes. Turner also inaugurated a 'superstation,' actually his Atlanta-based WTBS, spreading its availability around the nation. One of its aims was to broadcast to the entire nation Atlanta Braves baseball games (Turner also owned the team), and offer greater audience potential to his advertisers.

In 1985 Turner sought to buy one more toy, although how serious he was can be questioned — the CBS network. He announced plans to purchase outstanding shares of CBS stock, and hinted that he would make sweeping changes, like bouncing the liberal news anchor Dan Rather. CBS, at least, took Turner seriously, and scrambled to outbid him for every free share. They succeeded in buying up a great number — and in the process put themselves in a financial bind that ultimately caused severe cutbacks (in-

and re-runs; ESPN (Entertainment and Sports Programming Networks) offers major teams and minor sports to a nation hungry for such fare; The Weather Channel offers around-the-clock local, national and world weather information; The Financial News Network does the same for financial matters, also offering features and discussion; PRISM offers sports and movies; The Playboy Channel offers soft-core pornography to paying subscribers; C-SPAN (Satellite Public Affairs Network) broadcasts deliberations of House of Representatives, Congressional committees and speeches of all sorts.

The Christian Broadcasting Network has become one of America's major programming carriers. Its centerpiece is the *700 Club*, a 90-minute talk-entertainment-information-spiritual program similar in format to the late-night talk shows. Hosted by Pat Robertson, a typical show features a discussion of news events; several guests discussing their specialties, experiences or recent books; a filmed report on miracles or conversion experiences and prayers for healing. The show is co-hosted by Ben Kinchlow, and among its other activities, *The 700 Club* operates Operation Bread Basket, which has distributed many millions of dollars to the needy and disaster-stricken. CBN has grown to be a world-wide operation, including the production of animated Bible stories in Japan, and the opening of CBN University in Virginia Beach, Virginia, which offers degrees in TV production, law, and religion. Much of the CBN Cable network offering is vintage television re-runs, allowing TV addicts to recapture the memories of mostly black-and-white family-oriented sitcoms and Westerns. Other religious networks have been introduced, including Trinity Broadcasting.

MTV (Music Television) has proved popular, innovative, and influential. Consisting primarily of music videos — high-tech dramatized presentation, of current songs — the channel has done more than promote records. It has created a new entertainment form, with rapid editing, integration of animation, multiple images and the like. The techniques have influenced contemporary movies and some television production (its vaunted disciple being *Miami Vice*), but has also sparked protests that its sexual content is sometimes hotter than the Playboy Channel's.

The Disney Channel was started in 1983 when Disney's hour-long program finally left network TV (it returned in 1986). Offering classic Disney animated features and live-action films, it also provides a basic complement of children's television programming that has made the TV set a rather more palatable babysitter than traditional commercial television.

These new vehicles and others — carried by cable, microwave, pay-systems and the increasingly popular home-satellite dishes — are clearly where the future of television is in America. There will likely always be commercial, broadcast TV, but the genie is out of the bottle — and

he's not a monster; he's a creative, innovative, wildly varied, democratic servant. What was briefly termed (patronizingly at first) alternative programming in America rapidly became a living-room necessity as basic as the toaster, the radio, the auto, and – commercial television.

If there was another hallmark of the 1980s besides the technology and programming represented by the cable revolution, it could arguably be summed up in three letters: MTM.

Studios and production companies had previously originated, or represented, trends in television history. The flood of Warner Brothers genre shows in the late 1950s signalled new clichés in action programs, accelerated the demise of live drama and represented a major adjustment in the Hollywood-studio system. In the 1970s Norman Lear both produced and inspired the wave of relevant, political and high-decibel comedies. Although MTM (whose corporate symbol is a pussycat parody of the MGM symbol) began its successful series of programs with Mary Tyler Moore's own starring vehicle in 1970, it was the company's Phase II in 1980 that proved truly revolutionary.

A spate of their new shows, mostly dramas, raised the standards of commercial television when critical and market-based factors were predicting gloom. And MTM's president (Mary Tyler Moore's former husband) Grant Tinker personally moved over to the NBC presidency, bringing his taste and standards and resulting in the resurgence of that beleaguered network by the proven popularity of MTM-type shows.

In January of 1981 *Hill Street Blues* commenced on NBC. Critically applauded, the show was indifferently received by America's viewers;

Above: *Mary Frann and Bob Newhart play Joanna and Dick Loudon, who run an old inn in Norwich, Vermont, on Newhart.*

Opposite: *A somewhat befuddled Dr Victor Erlich (Ed Begley Jr, left) and Dr Wayne Fiscus (Howie Mandel) in the chaos that follows a nurses' strike at St Eligius Hospital, on St Elsewhere.*

two factors ultimately saved it: lame-duck Fred Silverman's determination to keep it against all odds and in whatever time slot (a determination born of both taste and desperation, no doubt); and a surprising amount of Emmy Awards, the television industry's Oscars. Soon people *had* to tune in to see what the excitement was about.

The excitement was about an ensemble show set in an urban police department. Thematically the show wove several major plotlines and many subplots. In form there were soap-opera elements, as characters were followed through activities and problems. There was explicit violence and a good deal of comedy and – in shots of the squad room – a documentary feel. Carrying the superb writing was a splendid cast, led by Daniel J Travanti as Captain Furillo; Veronica Hamel as Joyce Davenport; Charles Haid as Officer Renko; Michael Warren as Officer Bobby Hill; Keil Martin as Officer LaRue; Taurean Blacque as Officer Washington; Joe Spano as Lieutenant Goldblum; Bruce Weitz as Detective Belker; James B Sikking as Lieutenant Hunter; Ed Marinaro as Officer Coffey; Betty Thomas as Officer Bates; Michael Conrad as Sergeant Phil Esterhaus and Robert Prosky as Sergeant Stan Jablonski after Conrad's death; Barbara Bosson as Fay Furillo and Dennis Franz as 'Guido' Buntz (after he had first played a corrupt cop in a series of earlier episodes).

The show was created by Steven Bochco, who had fashioned *Delvecchio* and other gritty (and quality) dramatic and action series. *Hill Street* provided a weekly excursion into plot surprises and forceful characterizations to which there was

little subtlety – the viewer sees the action, knows how the character will react, sees the character react and oftentimes sees the character *discussing* his reaction. But that form of heart-on-sleeve openness is central to *Hill Street*'s purpose, and emblematic of its style; emotions, as well as actions and motives, are viewed under intense lights as if in the police interrogation room.

St Elsewhere was another MTM production that scaled new heights in quality writing and fine ensemble acting. Set in a decaying Boston hospital (actually St Eligius), the show was based on the same formula as *Hill Street* – a documentary atmosphere in general, and intense emotional close-ups in the specific. Operating-room realism was mixed with a rather high dose of comedy and eccentric personalities. In a trademark of the show, characters who departed didn't just fade away; they were raped, driven to suicide, shot and developed AIDS. Starring were William Daniels as Dr Mark Craig; Ed Flanders as Dr Westphal; Norman Lloyd as Dr Auschlander; Ed Begley Jr as Dr Erlich; Howie Mandel as Dr Fiscus and David Morse as Dr Morrison. Also appearing were Stephen Furst, Christina Pickles, Cynthia Sikes, Kim Mayori, Mark Harmon and Denzel Washington.

Bob Newhart returned to episodic comedy with *Newhart*, where he now played a free-lance writer (of how-to books) who ran a New England inn with his wife (played by Mary Frann). In the first season, the characters were obviously not defined or comfortable. Two of them – a pushy neighbor and a housemaid – were replaced, and the comedy took on tinges of surrealism. Sleeper

Right: *Stephanie Zimbalist and Pierce Brosnan play Laura Holt and Remington Steele — two private detectives — on* Remington Steele.

characters included Larry (with his brother Daryl and his other brother Daryl); Stephanie the pouting housemaid; and Michael, a yuppie played by Peter Scolari. The handyman George, played by Tom Poston, at first seemed either drunk or simple but soon settled into a one-man, homespun, ironic Greek chorus to the goings-on. The combination of talent like Newhart's own, and of patient creative work by MTM, brought the show to front-rank status.

Another MTM production emphasized a mature level of writing and characterization, as well as a unique premise. *Remington Steele* starred Stephanie Zimbalist as a private eye whose client-list was non-existent because, she concluded, she was a woman. She invented a male name to put on her agency's door — Remington Steele — and through humorous intrigues a man with no past (amnesia or shame? Neither Zimbalist as Laura Holt nor the viewers ever know) appeared and became the nominal boss. Pierce Brosnan as Steele was half-suave and half-klutz, and in addition to the mystery about his past (never fully exploited as a sub-plot in the series) there was the running hint of romance between the two leads. The experienced TV and commercials-actress Doris Roberts played the team's secretary, and the programs contained a high dose of comedy and irony.

Mary Tyler Moore herself returned in an MTM show in 1986. Entitled *Mary*, the series was inevitably compared to the classic *Mary Tyler Moore Show* of the 1970s — and the concept of *Mary* didn't dispel such speculation: instead of a TV newsroom there was a newspaper city room; instead of oafish Ted Knight there was oafish Ed

LaSalle (John Astin), etc. James Farentino, as Mary's boss, is however, more handsome, younger, and more aggressively romantic than Lou Grant was, and therein was the main difference between the two shows. *Mary's* humor is more explicit, and Mary's character is brash to a degree that the 1970s Mary Richards character was not. This difference was not enough to pull viewers by itself, but the MTM creative staff determined to make changes in structure and cast to strengthen *Mary's* appeal.

The contributions of Grant Tinker – as legatee and architect both of the MTM quality trademarks – can be inferred through discussions of programming improvements in TV's larger picture in the 1980s, as well as the turn-around of his network, NBC, during the period.

Cheers, for instance, was a comedy that initially received favorable critical notice but lukewarm audience response. NBC stuck with the show, presumably believing in its quality and appeal – and eventually the comedy garnered a wide viewership. Centered in a Boston pub, a comedy series once again relied on a talented ensemble (and their relationships – in this case the tentative romance between Ted Danson and Shelley Long) and occasional incidental characters. And the formula once again worked. Also in the superb cast: George Wendt; John Ratzenberger; Nick Colasanto and Rhea Perlman. Perlman is the real-life wife of Danny DeVito, whose *Taxi* character Louie DePalma was played in a roughly feminine approximation by her in *Cheers.*

The decade opened with the comedy *Bosom Buddies* seeming like a weak premise (two young

men forced, for economic reasons, to board in a women's rooming house, disguising themselves as females), perhaps a step lower than the pandering silliness of *Three's Company.* But the inspired comic turns of stars Tom Hanks and Peter Scolari made the show a memorable comedy series. *It's a Living,* later *Making a Living,* similarly was built upon the contemporary 'jiggle' formula of overt displays of feminine pulchritude and suggestive material; but clever writing and performances allowed the series to lift itself up by the bra-straps. The program, concerning sexy cocktail waitresses, featured Ann Jillian, Wendy Shaal, Susan Sullivan, Barrie Youngfellow, Louise Lasser and Marian Mercer. After searching for secure audience-acceptance on network TV the series moved to cable. *Best of West* was a brilliant but short-lived parody of Western shows, and, in fact, of all fictional Western clichés. The standard virtues and vices – bravery, forbearance, treachery, cowardice – were all stretched to absurd limits on the show. Starring were Joel Higgins, Carlene Watkins, Leonard Frye, Meeno Peluce, the outlandish Tracey Walter and Tom Ewell.

Police Squad! paid a similar sort of homage to its genre, and was also unfortunately short-lived. Starring Leslie Neilsen and Alan North, the series was fashioned after the popular *Airplane* movie spoofs: every cliché of cop stories and crime mysteries was lampooned. Even the very language of television production itself was fair game. Each episode, for instance, began with that week's guest star murdered, never to be bothered again. The closing credits were run over the actors freezing their motions in mid-air, instead of the traditional stop-action film frame of every other show. Surely ('I told you. Don't call me "Shirley," ' Neilsen would inevitably say) *Police Squad!* was a refreshing point in TV comedy's history.

Family Ties was built on the 'hook' of a stereo-typical 1960s couple, married and with a family in the 1980s, who ironically see their children turning into cultural conservatives. The premise was half-honored; the children, especially Michael J Fox (the surprise teen heart-throb of America after his debut) were quintessential yuppies-in-training. But the parents, played by Meredith Baxter-Birney and Michael Gross, didn't even don the wire-rimmed glasses that most hold-overs from the 1960s retained. The other children were played by Justine Bateman and Tina Yothers. Genuinely humorous situations and scripting were as responsible for the series' success as the juvenile capitalism spouted by popular young Fox.

Night Court was the product of *Barney Miller's*

creator, Rheinhold Weege, and bore the previous comedy a not-too-superficial resemblance. The resemblance was not unwelcome, because the quality humorous writing was also evident. Harry Anderson played a judge in night court, and he was positioned therefore to meet the dregs of society in passing parade before his bench. Complicating his already unconventional life (and supplying the proper lunacy for the series) was the fact that his daily contacts — bailiff, DA, clerk, guard — were as loony as the miscreants. Appearing with Anderson were Richard Moll, John LaRoquette, Ellen Foley (replaced by Markie Post) and Selma Diamond (replaced after her death by Florence Halop; both Diamond and Halop, outstanding comedy characters, were curiously under-utilized).

Kate and Allie proved to be a popular — and quality — vehicle for young veterans Susan St James and Jane Curtin. In the sitcom they played divorced women living together with their children, sort of an Odd Couple with feminine

Below: *Mary Tyler Moore played a reporter on a sleazy Chicago newspaper in* Mary, *and James Farentino played Frank, her editor.*

and feminist complications. By request of the stars, incidentally, it was one of the few remaining shows to be produced in New York. (In a strange example of televisionese, when programs retreated from the exclusive use of canned laughter an announcer would state that his show was filmed, or taped, before a 'live audience.')

As NBC patiently climbed to ratings dominance through the early 1980s, one show that premiered in 1985 seemed symbolic of its success and overall creative quality: *The Cosby Show.* The veteran of nightclub comedy and several sitcoms, variety series, animated cartoons and even an adventure show, Cosby not only brought experience but a sizeable group of devoted fans to the new sitcom. In a further example of the death and burial of 1960s and 1970s trends in TV, Cosby's family was not the sort that shouted insults at each other across the yard of the housing project. Cosby played Dr Cliff Huxstable, a prosperous obstetrician, and his wife Clair (played by Phylicia Ayers-Allen) was a

Right: *Jane Curtin (as Allie Lowell) is being not-too-gently quieted by Susan Saint James (as Kate McArdle) in* Kate and Allie. **Below:** *The Keatons — Steve (Michael Gross, left), Elyse (Meredith Baxter-Birney) and Alex (Michael J Fox) win at black jack in* Family Ties.

Right: *Judge Harry Stone (Harry Anderson, left) in one of his many confrontations with Assistant District Attorney Dan Fielding (John LaRoquette) on* Night Court.
Opposite: *William Katt was Ralph Hinkley (later changed to Hanley), a shy boy who could turn himself into* The Greatest American Hero.
Below: *Bill Cosby plays Dr Heathcliff (Cliff) Huxstable on the top-rated* The Cosby Show.

successful lawyer. Their children underwent normal experiences of adolescence — dating, schoolwork, coping. Underpinned by excellent situational writing and memorable reaction-lines, *The Cosby Show* was a success.

Rather sub-dominant were other comedies of the 1980s, including: *Number 96*, a sex-tinged series set in an adult housing complex; *Private Benjamin*, a spinoff from the Goldie Hawn movie; *Mr Merlin*, with Barnard Hughes and Elaine Joyce; *Love, Sidney*, wherein Tony Randall played a homosexual living with an unmarried young mother; *The Greatest American Hero*, a rather clever hour-long series about an unlikely super-hero (Bill Katt) and his government contact (Robert Culp); *One of the Boys*, with Mickey Rooney; *9 to 5*, based on the popular movie and starring Rita Moreno, Valerie Curtin and Rachel Dennison, who resembled her sister Dolly Parton; *Amanda's*, starring Bea Arthur, which could not duplicate the comedic brilliance or critical success of its model, the British *Fawlty Towers*, even when it appropriated certain episodes' scripts word-for-word; *Mr Smith*, a funny, satiric sitcom about a chimp with genius IQ attached to the US Government, starring Leonard Frye as his attendant; and *The Golden Girls*, a wisecracking irreverent series about aging femininity, created by Susan Harris and starring Betty White, Rue McClanahan, Bea Arthur and Estelle Getty.

Several British comedies became popular, sometimes with loyal cults but sometimes with

Below: *Mariette Hartley was Jennifer Barnes and Bill Bixby was Matt Cassidy the two competing co-anchors on the WYN-Boston evening news show in* Goodnight, Beantown.

larger audiences. Prominent was *Fawlty Towers*, a madcap series created by, and starring, John Cleese and his wife Connie Booth, about life in an English resort hotel — or at least life when the hotel is operated by a henpecked, scheming, put-upon incompetent like Basil Fawlty. Cleese, a *Monty Python* alumnus, played his role in the broadest caricature — and to the broadest laughs. Other British hits included *Butterflies, Good Neighbours,* and *To the Manor Born,* a delightful series — delightful because of the wit and the organic, growing relationship between the main characters — about Lady Forbes-Hamilton, a widow, played by Penelope Keith, forced to sell her estate and live nearby in reduced circumstances. When a transplanted Hungarian, a grocery-chain baron (Richard DeVere, as he has taken his new name, played by Peter Bowles) buys her ancestral manor, she asserts proprietary interest. In the series' last episode the pair marry; viewers could never have been in doubt on the subject, but the posings and deflations along the social and romantic paths over several seasons were inspired.

Other comedies on commercial networks in the early 1980s included: *Freebie and the Bean, Harper Valley PTA, Enos, I'm a Big Girl Now, The Two of Us, Lewis and Clark, Gimme a Break, Open All Night, Maggie, Silver Spoons, Punky Brewster, It Takes Two, The New Odd Couple* (they were black), *AfterMASH, Goodnight, Beantown, Jennifer Slept Here, Empire* and *Filthy Rich* (two spoofs of soaps like *Dallas*), *Buffalo Bill* (starring Dabney Coleman as a character so disagreeable he evidently turned the audience off instead of intriguing them), *The Four Seasons, Who's the Boss?* (with *Taxi*'s Tony Danza as a male house-keeper), *Hail to the Chief* (Patty Duke, as the first female US president, in *Soap*-style iconoclasm), *Mr Belvedere, Charlie & Co., 227, Growing Pains, The George Burns Comedy Week* and *Stir Crazy*.

On cable was *Check It Out*, with Don Adams in a grocery-store setting. Popular in syndication was *Benny Hill*, the British import. Appearing only as 'specials' in England, Hill's burlesque-style skits were compiled into nightly half-hours for the appreciative American market. And *Square Pegs* was a unique show in TV comedy

history. Created by humorist Anne Beatts, it portrayed life in a high school, and may have been the first series ever truly to capture the flavor, albeit humorously fashioned, of adolescents' points of view. The attitudes, language and preoccupations were not false or condescending, which had been standard practice throughout television history, even in well-intentioned portrayals. The series, a modest ratings success, seemed, however, to self-destruct, due to reported creative problems within the company.

In the 15 October 1983, issue of *TV Guide*, Stephen Birmingham posed the question, 'Dallas vs Dynasty: Which Show Is Better?' The question might legitimately have been posited about which of the two assembly-lines of venality, corruption and adultery was worse – but in the meantime another point of comparison was which show inspired the most imitations on program schedules. The previous chapter listed the evening soap-operas into the 1980s, but there were other popular dramatic series, besides the MTM successes, as well as minor trends, through the mid-1980s as well.

Above: *A reunion of old comrades in arms, Father Mulcahy (William Christopher), Colonel Potter (Harry Morgan) and Max Klinger (Jamie Farr) on* AfterMASH.

Left: *Blanche (Rue McClanahan, left), Dorothy (Bea Arthur, center) and Rose (Betty White) are three of the main characters on* The Golden Girls.

197

Right: *Detective Mary Beth Lacey (Tyne Daly, left) and Detective Chris Cagney (Sharon Gless) have a confrontation with their boss, Lieutenant Samuels (Al Waxman), on* Cagney and Lacey.
Opposite: *Angela Lansbury is Jessica Beatrice Fletcher, a mystery writer, in* Murder, She Wrote. *In this episode her guest star is Peter Graves.*
Below right: *Sergeant Bosco 'B A' Baracus (Mr T, left) and Captain H M 'Howling Mad' Murdock (Dwight Schultz) are constantly harassing each other on* The A-Team.

Cagney and Lacey scored a hit with viewers – a fact proven by its return to CBS after the network cancelled it. The cop show featured two women officers (played by Tyne Daly and Sharon Gless, the latter replacing Meg Foster when programmers thought the original team would be perceived as having lesbian undertones) and inevitably involved emotional clashes as dramatic as the street-crime conflicts Mary Beth Lacey and Chris Cagney usually found themselves fighting. *The A-Team* at first seemed superficial, then campy, as an unlikely crew of adventurers, including cigar-chomping George Peppard and jewelry-bedecked Mr T, engaged in daring stunts in exotic locales. Just as unlikely a team was the trio in *Riptide*: investigators living on a houseboat, they used old-fashioned gumshoe techniques and newfangled technology like computers and helicopters. Two – Cody and Nick, played by Perry King and Joe Penny – were hunks, and the third (Boz, played by Thom Bray) was a computer expert but a nerd. *Bay City Blues* was yanked from the schedule almost before it had a chance to flop, but in less than two months MTM determined that this minor-league baseball-team setting *à la Hill Street* and *St Elsewhere* would strike out. Among its fine ensemble were Dennis Franz and Pat Corley.

Murder, She Wrote was inspired by Agatha Christie, and was a surprise hit that prefigured TV's new love affair – a second honeymoon – with older actors once banished during the 1960's youth wave. (In the 1980s, advertisers realized that most kids were watching music videos or renting movies for their home VCRs).

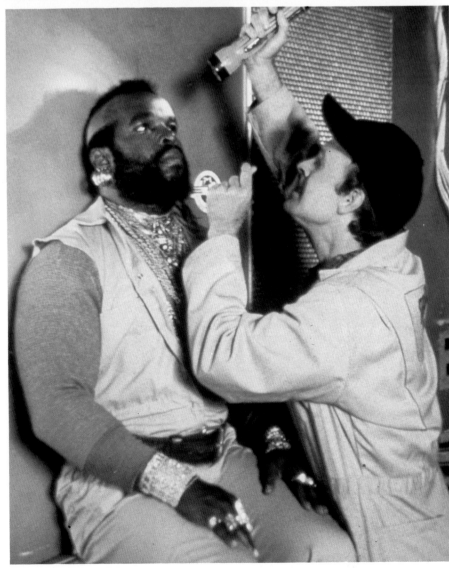

Right: *Nick Ryder and Cody Allen (played by Joe Penny, left, and Perry King) contemplate a replica of the Maltese Falcon on the detective drama series,* Riptide.

Opposite: *One of the most intelligent and adult of the private eye shows is* Moonlighting, *starring Bruce Willis and Cybill Shepherd.*

Angela Lansbury, the superb veteran of stage and screen, moved comfortably to TV as mystery writer Jessica Fletcher who each week solved crimes amid a fulsome array of interesting guest stars. *Crazy Like a Fox* paired an older veteran, Jack Warden, with John Rubenstein; they played a father (unconventional private eye) and son (proper young lawyer) who invariably join forces in solving baffling or dangerous cases. *Call to Glory* was a critically acclaimed series finally mugged by low ratings; it was set in the 1960s and devoted to the lives of characters involved in the space program. Craig T Nelson, Cindy Pickett, and Keenan Wynn starred.

Moonlighting at the very first seemed a clone of *Remington Steele* (its creator, Scott Spenser Gordon, had worked on the latter show), and its self-conscious advertising campaign about being 'the perfect romantic comedy' deserved to raise viewer's barriers of scepticism. But *Moonlighting* proved a notable series, whether by comparison to the excellent *Steele* or judged by its own standards. It starred Cybill Shepherd as Maddie Hayes, owner of a detective agency, and Bruce Willis as David Addison, her unconventional

assistant. Maddie was icy and professional while Addison constantly wisecracked bits of sleuthing and double-entendre — and an ill-concealed but never-consummated romance smoldered beneath their badinage. The program has devised some clever bits, such as having both characters dream about their reactions when set in an unsolved 1940s mystery: we see the same events through different points of view, and the whole episode was broadcast in black and white, lending a period charm.

Other dramatic entries during the 1980s included *Trapper John, MD,* starring Pernell Roberts, nominally a spinoff of *M*A*S*H,* featuring the character many years later in a stateside hospital setting; *The White Shadow,* with Ken Howard as a white coach of a young black basketball team; *Breaking Away,* with Shaun Cassidy and Vincent Gardenia, based on the respected movie; and *Magnum, PI,* starring Tom Selleck and John Hillerman in a show representative of the 1980's genre of humorous crime hours.

Other drama and action programs included the science-fiction *V* (expanded from a mini-

non-dramatic series *Live From the Met, Live From Lincoln Center, Nova,* and *National Geographic,* which moved to cable). British import *Rumpole of the Bailey,* starring Leo McKern, provided several series of first-rate entertainment. The blustery counselor brilliantly charmed opponents and employed stratagems against opponents and judges – and sometimes clients – in this totally engaging series. A complement of characters in chambers as well as Mrs Rumpole ('She who must be obeyed,' quoth Rumpole of Haggard), rounded out the superb cast.

Television drama and 'made-for-TV' movies in the early 1980s included *The Day Christ Died, FDR – The Last Year, Little Lord Fauntleroy* with Ricky Schroeder and Alec Guinness, a TV version of *High Noon, The Bunker* with Anthony Hopkins as Adolf Hitler, *Playing for Time, Haywire, Life on the Mississippi, Living Proof* (the biography of Hank Williams, Jr), *Blood Feud, Mr Halpern and Mr Johnson* with Lawrence Olivier and Jackie Gleason, *The Curious Case of Santa Claus, A Streetcar Named Desire, Ernie Kovacs – Between Laughs, Alice in Wonderland* with a cast of a hundred stars, *Malice in Wonderland,* with Liz Taylor and Jane Alexander as gossip columnists of Hollywood's Golden Era, *Adam,* a moving story starring Daniel J Travanti about missing children, *The Executioner's Song, Bill* with an outstanding performance by Mickey Rooney as a mentally retarded man, and *A Woman Called Golda,* with Ingrid Bergman.

Heartsounds was a sensitive movie starring Mary Tyler Moore and James Garner; and *Still the Beaver* was also surprisingly sensitive as it presented a reunion of the surviving *Leave It to Beaver* cast members, with the halcyon 1950s brought abruptly up to date. *The Burning Bed* was yet another critical surprise, with an effective performance by Farah Fawcett (the former Farah Fawcett-Majors) in a tale of wife-abuse. *Fatal Vision* reconstructed the true story of a military man of exemplary record accused of murdering his wife and daughters.

Among the mini-series were *Disraeli; Tinker, Tailor, Soldier, Spy; Brideshead Revisited; Reilly, Ace of Spies;* and the *Irish RM,* all on PBS. Elsewhere was *Shōgun* and *The Thorn Birds,* two of the genre's most successful, both starring Richard Chamberlain; *The Winds of War; The Acts of Peter and Paul; The Gangster Chronicles; Return to Eden,* an Australian series followed by *Return to Eden: The Story Continues; The Blue and the Gray; North and South; George Washington; Kennedy; Robert Kennedy and His Times; The Last Days of Pompeii; AD; Christopher Columbus; Space; Huckleberry Finn; Hollywood Wives; Peter the Great; Sins; Kane and Abel; Nicholas Nickleby;* and *Forever Amber.*

The Day After was a TV-movie that excited enormous controversy before its airing because it dealt with the effects of a nuclear attack on America. It was expected to turn the viewing public into antiwar activists, but in fact had

series), *Nero Wolfe, Walking Tall, Nurse, King's Crossing, Code Red, The Secrets of Midland Heights, Simon and Simon* and *The Fall Guy* (another pair of light action shows), *Jessica Novak* with Helen Shaver, about a TV newswoman – a case of life imitating art, *T J Hooker, Matt Houston, Hardcastle and McCormick, Scarecrow and Mrs King, Half Nelson, Today's FBI, The Powers of Matthew Star, Father Murphy, Strike Force, McClain's Law, The Devlin Connection, Knight Rider, Eischeid, Mickey Spillane's Mike Hammer, Airwolf, Partners in Crime, Highway to Heaven, Hell Town, Finder of Lost Loves, MacGruder and Loud, MacGyver, The Misfits of Science, Spenser for Hire* and *The Equalizer.*

The 1980s provided a relative wealth of special drama presentation via both one-shot offerings on commercial and public TV, and the frequently utilized mini-series. PBS continued its presentation of the totality of Shakespeare's plays – 37 plays over six years – an extremely significant contribution to at least the potential enrichment of viewers. Public television's regular offerings continued as well in series like *Great Performances, Mystery, American Playhouse* (and

Above: *Jameson Parker (left) and Gerald McRaney play brothers who are also private detectives in* Simon and Simon.

Top: *Stacey Keach played private eye Mike Hammer in the detective drama series* Mickey Spillane's Mike Hammer.

Top right: *Ingrid Bergman in her last role — that of Israeli premier Golda Meir — in* A Woman Called Golda.

virtually no effect on public opinion at all. In a way, the turn of events was a refreshing surprise — the public, contrary to the pessimistic analysis of media scolds, was not yet robotized by television.

Also interesting was the public's reaction to the tragic explosion of the Space Shuttle Challenger in February of 1986: there was widespread and sincere grief in spite of two television-connected factors. Space travel had grown commonplace because of TV coverage, but yet in that frightening instant no one was blasé any longer. And, in spite of hundreds of deaths and explosions simulated every single week on television, the tragedy was searingly real to a public that might reasonably have grown somewhat inured to such imagery.

A continuing dramatic series of cult status was Britain's import, *Dr Who.* In production since 1963 (with a variety of Whos, and more than 75 novels based on the time-travel series) the program inspired not only loyal viewership but newsletters and fan conventions in the US.

Among variety shows, the genre continued to show that it was a television staple, even with new wrinkles. A type of anthology program emerged in the 1980s, the nightly (or daily) entertainment-and-personality report. Some focused on celebrities and media news, like *Entertainment Tonight,* and *We Magazine;* and some featured softer news, talk, and even self-help segments — *PM Magazine, Hour Magazine* and local-oriented variety formats. Major cities developed early-morning talk shows presented before studio audiences (Regis Philbin moved from such a Los Angeles show to ABC's New York City affiliate, and then to Lifetime Cable). *What's Hot, What's Not; All About Us; America;* and *It's a Great Life* were miscellaneous offerings, and Don Lane — born in the Bronx but a star of Australian television — hosted a talk show on American TV for a time. Phil Donahue held Rasputin-like power over America's housewives

as his daytime interview show consistently secured high ratings (a late-night effort in tandem with Gregory Jackson, on ABC, failed). Donahue became a cuddly version of David Susskind, another talented host whose interview programs degenerated into discussions of bizarre sex and radical politics. Jean Shepherd, one of America's great humorists, hosted *Jean Shepherd's America*, and scripted some classic movie-length specials like *Phantom of the Open Hearth* on PBS.

Barbara Mandrell, the perky country-pop singer, fashioned a professional and entertaining variety hour with her two sisters Louise and Irlene. *TV's Bloopers and Practical Jokes* and *Foul-Ups, Bleeps and Blunders* each offered clips of authentic and ersatz embarrassing moments of stars and common folk – updating *Candid Camera*. *Starsearch* was an updated, high-stakes *Amateur Hour*; *Ripley's Believe It or Not* presented interesting facts from around the world, although a few tested the viewers' credulity.

Variety series included *Evening at the Pops*; *Cosmos*, a self-indulgent trip through pop astronomer Carl Sagan's mind via the universe; *The Nashville Palace*, a country-music effort; *River Journeys*, a unique travelogue of the world's major arteries with celebrity narrators; *Doris Day's Best Friends*, a celebrity chat about pets; and *Good Sex With Dr Ruth Westheimer*, who was

a curious gnome of a hostess who discussed sexual techniques and frustrations with her guests and callers.

Among the specials in the early 1980s were those hosted by Ann-Margret, Debby Boone, Larry Gatlin, Mikhail Barishnikov, Johnny Cash, Anne Murray, John Schneider, Luciano Pavarotti, Neil Diamond, Willie Nelson, Billy Crystal and others. Bob Hope was present every season with several specials, and the awards, parades and charity telethons continued, as they are likely to do forever. Country music (on *Austin City Limits*), black music (on *Soul Train*) and pop (on *Solid Gold* and other series) served their specialized audiences. *The People's Court* revived the old *Divorce Court* formula, just as *The New You Asked For It* responded to viewer's requests, or allegedly did, in the fashion of its namesake from the 1950s. Notable specials included the charity *Night of 100 Stars* broadcast from New York's Radio City Music Hall; *Those Fabulous Funnies*, a history of comic strips hosted by Loni Anderson and *Hollywood: The Gift of Laughter*. Alan Thicke, a Canadian, became the latest pretender to the late-night throne worn by talk-show king Johnny Carson — and he became the next flop in a long line of such performers who would have even been content with subservient co-existence. *Thicke of the Night*'s difference was that it was one of the fastest of demises in that situation.

Above left: *In an unusual role for her, Farrah Fawcett starred as Francine Hughes, a battered wife with three children who, after a dozen years of merciless beatings and humiliations, ends up on trial for murdering her ex-husband in* The Burning Bed, *a made-for-TV movie.*

Johnny Carson himself sped toward the quarter-century mark on the *Tonight* Show. The program had become more than a viewing habit: America was comfortable with the Nebraska-born entertainer and his style of mastering the ceremonies night after night. A former magician and veteran of one forgettable motion picture, Carson was a certified TV personality with many shows and many formats to his credit. His own style was a curious pastiche of other comedians' trademarks — Steve Allen's abrupt laugh, some of Jonathan Winters's voices, assorted Jackie Gleason double-takes and Jack Benny's pauses. For years his best laughs came from comments *about* his jokes not being funny (although the *Tonight Show* has boasted a large writing staff), and many of his standup routines were inherited from predecessors like Steve Allen and Jack Paar. The show's announcer, Ed McMahon, relegated himself to the role of buffoon — laughing uncon-

trollably at virtually every remark by Carson; and studio band member Tommy Newsome was the regular butt of humorous insults. Yet Carson achieved a casual atmosphere, masterfully managed; seemingly spontaneous conversations with guests were researched and practically rehearsed with 'talent coordinators' on the staff.

Through the years Carson's time spent on the show has diminished. He vacations more than one-fourth of the year, and the show itself shrank from 90 minutes to an hour. It was, at the time of that adjustment, followed by the *David Letterman Show*, a truly refreshing talk show/comedy hour emanating from New York and produced by Carson's company. Carson's salary at every contract renewal with NBC was the cause of much speculation and awe; it reportedly rose to more than $3 million a year.

The salary game in the TV industry, and the high prices for commercial time, lead many

viewers to endorse the concept of stars deserving what they can get if their popularity is widespread enough. What doesn't occur to many viewers is that when Carson earns millions of dollars a year, when a network prime-time minute costs $400,000, and when mere seconds during Super Bowls and other events cost even more than that, it is not the networks, or advertisers, who ultimately pay. It is the consumer — the viewer. It is a form of tribute to stars and the Entertainment God that rivals the image of Medieval feudalism. In a system of hidden taxation that is more subtle — and possibly more costly — than Value Added Taxes in some countries, Americans blithely pay higher prices for all sorts of consumer products because of celebrities' pay demands and astronomical advertising costs. A major difference between the 1980s and the Middle Ages is that Americans seem to love the system, fawning over the stars' lifestyles in the tabloid press and TV magazines.

When, back in the 1930s, David Sarnoff rejected the possibility of exploring governmental subsidies of the television industry, he was not only being realistic about the free-enterprise traditions of the US; he foresaw a symbiotic relationship of networks, producers, advertisers (and, to him at the time, manufacturers), that would guarantee an ongoing, and expanding, industry. Many varieties of commercial products depend on TV for their exposure, and some simply can't be made to seem more irresistible anywhere better than television. As an illustration of the symbiosis between the broadcast and

Above: *The terrible devastation of an atomic attack on the United States was documented in the TV movie* The Day After.
Left: *Dr Ruth is the star of* Good Sex with Dr Ruth Westheimer.

advertising colossi, cigarette advertising was banned from TV screens in the late 1960s after the most intense pressure from health groups and citizens lobbies; but the effective date of the ban — 1 January 1970 — was moved back to 2 January so that millions of dollars could change hands for the last time during the spate of highly rated sports events and parades on New Year's Day. The television industry can be very nostalgic for certain traditions.

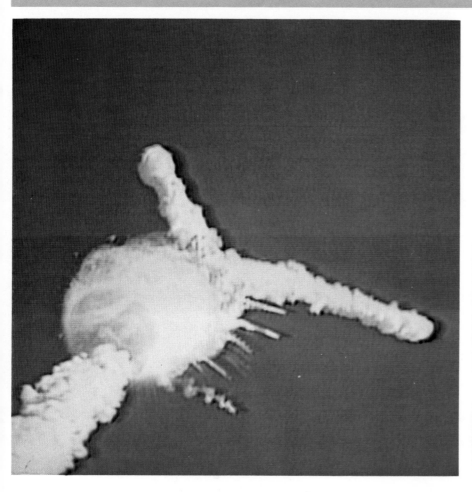

All of which puts viewers in the remarkable position of sitting through dog-food commercials on *The Tonight Show*, being brainwashed or otherwise persuaded that a certain brand is better than one not advertised, and then paying more in the store in order to subsidize those very commercials, and the profits to star and station.

Johnny Carson has also had a wide effect on another industry: his own entertainment industry. Over 25 years he probably launched or revived more performers' careers than all the talent agencies in Beverly Hills. A spot on the Carson show for a struggling comedian is an entree to clubs he or she would never otherwise enter except as a customer; an invitation to return to *Tonight* is a certified Stamp of Approval. Likewise it is accepted that an author's appearance with Carson to hawk his book will result in 10,000 additional sales. Further, Johnny Carson has conferred status on trends and mores. After he has made jests about bondage-sex or marijuana or cocaine they become more acceptable as conversation-pieces through America.

Daytimes in the 1980s continued as before, only more so: old soap-operas continued and new ones were born; several game shows were resurrected and, on cable especially, it seems that entire archives of old black-and-white TV shows belched forth their booty. *Texas, Capitol, Santa Barbara*, and *Loving* all were new entries on network soap schedules. *Rituals* was a syndicated offering that many stations tried in prime-time or late-night. *Another Life* was an attempt by CBN (the Christian Broadcasting Network) to fashion

an episodic soap-opera *with* problems and crises, but *without* the standard drinking, venom and scheming of the traditional models.

CBN also bought up rights for copious numbers of vintage TV series, including many Westerns, family sitcoms and even *The Man From U.N.C.L.E.* A minimum of the cable network's programming was religious as it unveiled its slogan 'The Family Entertainer' in presenting traditional favorites as alternatives to newer shows.

The game show continued to be a staple of daytime fare (although stakes were raised: *The $10,000 Pyramid* was now the *$25,000 Pyramid* on weekdays). There was also *Break the Bank, Headline Chasers, Scrabble*, and the *New Newlywed Game* — the only difference from the old *Newlywed Game* seeming to be the absence of mini-skirts. Richard Simmons and Joannie Gregains were the gurus of the home-exercise crowd, with, undoubtedly, some *voyeurs* tuning in to observe the muscle tone.

Religion on television got to be an issue in the 1980s, just as it was not in the 1940s and 1950s. When early networks started filling their schedules, a complement of religious programming was apportioned to the major faiths. By the 1980s the overwhelming majority of religious programing was bought and paid for by denominations, preachers and religious organizations. There have been criticisms of their presence and stated fears that they are presenting only one side of issues ('On the issue of sin,' one preacher responded, 'I do take one side: I'm agin' it.'). Evangelist Jimmy Swaggart is the most-watched preacher

Above: *Richard and Lindsay Roberts of the Oral Roberts organization.*
Above left: *Many of the shuttle launches including the Challenger's last flight which ended in an explosion on 28 January 1986 were televised live.*

exhortations to 'be saved,' to join, to respond; earlier religious shows on the networks were mostly intellectual discussion forums or homilies.

But as the nature of religious television has changed, so has the response. In 1985 Louis Harris's survey showed that fully one-fifth of all Christians regularly watch TV evangelists, and that such viewership does not diminish but increases or reinforces local church attendance. Other popular religious programs in the 1980s were those of Oral Roberts; Jim Bakker and the *PTL Club*; Kenneth Hagin; Kenneth Copeland; Jerry Falwell (who used his *Old-Time Gospel Hour* as a springboard for becoming a major spokesman on national affairs); James Robison and Billy Graham, perhaps the longest-running TV veteran of the lot.

Pertaining to religion and television, the Rev Donald Wildmon organized in 1977 the National Federation for Decency, with the specific goal of reducing the levels of violence, profanity and sex on family-accessed television. With a support list of 300,000 individuals and churches, Wildmon monitored the incidents of offensive matter and petitioned the advertisers to be aware of what they were, in effect, promoting in addition to their products. He also organized boycotts of sponsors. He has, of course, been accused of everything from book-burning to wanting to establish a theocratic government based in Tupelo, Mississippi; in actuality he is pursuing the same course as civil-rights and feminist groups, or, for instance Action for Children's Television, whose successful pressures have evinced protests from animated-cartoon buffs but few others.

In that realm of children's programming, the ACT ethos continued in the 1980s, even if via camouflage. Superhero cartoons, for instance, seemed to reek with violent acts, but upon examination, the bad guys were invariably stunned unconscious or benumbed with sonic-boom guns instead of merely being shot or punched as in the bad old days. PBS, predictably, provided the most literate and instructional of the fare, their major new programs being *Once Upon a Classic*, *Zoom*, *WonderWorks* and *Reading Rainbow*. CBS presented *30 Minutes* (news), *The New Fat Albert*, *The Dukes*, *Pac Man*, *Tarzan and the Super-Seven*, *The All-New Popeye Hour*, *Jason of Star Command* and *Razzmatazz*. On ABC, besides the continuing quality and variety of the *Afterschool Specials*, there were *The ABC Weekend Special*, *Animals, Animals, Animals*, *The World's Greatest Superfriends* and *Captain Caveman and the Teenangels*. On NBC children had *Main Street*, *Project Peacock* (a continuing, multi-year, children's anthology of drama and advice), *Hot Hero Sandwich*, *Daffy Duck*, *Fred and Barney Meet the Shmoo* and the *Gary Coleman Show*.

Also on Saturday mornings and weekday afternoons were *Inspector Gadget*, *Heathcliff*, *Donkey Kong*, *The Charlie Brown and Snoopy Show*, *Benji*, *Alvin and the Chipmunks*, *Mr T*, *The Littles*,

Above: *Many of the heroes and heroines from the old comic books were animated to entertain children on* Superfriends.

in the world, with 300 stations carrying his weekly services in the US, and many overseas; his tele-production center in Baton Rouge is network-quality. He also produces a daily half-hour of teaching, *A Study in the Word*, and hosts many prime-time specials. The CBN itself *is* a network, and produces the *700 Club* (widely seen around the world), dramatic and charity programming, cartoons and commercials. CBN University continues to offer degrees in television production. Pat Robertson of CBN found himself in the mid-1980s being promoted for a presidential candidacy in 1988.

The very question of religion's role in politics is what gave rise to recommendations for governmental restrictions of religious programs and activities. Most of the TV shows are fundamentalist Protestant; the network-blessed programming of the earlier dispensations were liberal Protestant, Catholic and Jewish. The newer preachers are almost all evangelical, so there are

Above: *Ted Koppel, the mainstay of the* Nightline *news program.*

Some personnel shifts resulted in improved offerings. David Brinkley moved from NBC to ABC and hosted the Sunday-morning *This Week with David Brinkley*, a superior program to ABC's old *Issues and Answers*; Brinkley provides a news reading, correspondents' reports, a focus on one or several issues and a roundtable discussion with an informed group of panelists, including columnist George Will. The venerable *Meet the Press* finally changed its firing-squad format in response to *This Week*, and CBS's *Face the Nation* named Leslie Stahl to be a chatty interviewer of Sunday-morning newsmakers. Bill Moyers, presenting himself as a down-home version of the pontificating Eric Sevareid, shuttled back and forth between PBS and CBS, where he produced occasional *Bill Moyers' Journal* reports, the documentary *Through the Twentieth Century* and provided commentary on evening news.

Enterprise with Milton Friedman, and *Ben Wattenberg at Large* each provided excellent personal views of, respectively, economics and public affairs. Jessica Savitch launched *Frontline*, a series that focused on individual issues. Lloyd Dobbyns revived NBC's *Monitor* news showcase from early radio days, and made it a TV newsmagazine. Roger Mudd was promised (as were viewers who appreciated his objectivity and irony) a weekly news magazine through the 1980s on NBC, and finally received it in the form of *American Digest*. Each of the networks (in response, certainly, to the general competition of cable, and the overnight news on cable in specific) experimented with wee-hours news programs. *NBC News Overnight* had style and bore the interesting personal stamp of anchor Linda Ellerbee, although the show ground an ideological axe more appropriate to George McGovern's era than Ronald Reagan's. Also introduced were pre-breakfast news programs, the most successful being ABC's *World News This Morning* with Steve Bell and Kathleen Sullivan and its NBC counterpart with Connie Chung.

By mid-decade the three network anchors were Tom Brokaw on NBC, Dan Rather (with his tabloid-touted $8 million salary) on CBS and Peter Jennings on ABC, after his network tried a four-anchor format.

The Iranian hostage crisis gave birth on ABC to a nightly update, *America Held Hostage*, hosted by Ted Koppel, which evolved into *Nightline*. This excellent late-night interview program has scored major beats just through Koppel's intense questioning, and utilized satellites and split-screens to make the world its stage. Preceding *Nightline* in format and focus was the equally excellent *MacNeil-Lehrer Report* on PBS. Prior to their informative program, Robert MacNeil was an American who worked for the BBC, and Jim Lehrer was with a Public Television station in Dallas.

Several factors keep reminding viewers — or should — however, that much of TV news is entertainment. Yes, their function is to present

Kidd Video, *Punky Brewster*, *Hulk Hogan's Rock 'n' Wrestling*, *The Berenstain Bears*, *The Wuzzles*, *The Gummi Bears* and the new *Jetsons*. The *Smurfs*, based on the Belgian comic strip *Les Schtroumpfs*, provided a heavy dose of saccharin for youngsters. *He-Man (Masters of the Universe)* was representative of animated cartoons series that were developed first by Japanese toymakers and then made for TV fare as part of a marketing strategy including T-shirts, lunch boxes and mechanical toys. Also in this tradition were *Voltron*, *The Transformers*, *Go Bots*, King Features' *Defenders of the Earth*, Rankin-Bass's *ThunderCats* (written by Leonard Starr, veteran scripter of the *On Stage* and *Annie* comic strips) and *Galaxy Rangers*.

Back on the Sesame side of the street, at least in spirit, were shows on Nickelodeon, the cable channel devoted to kids: *Pinwheel*, *Powerhouse*, *Standby . . . Lights! Camera! Action!* and *Dangermouse*. On the Disney Channel was *Welcome to Pooh Corner*.

In the fields of news and public affairs, some would say that the 1980s brought technological innovation to the images and graphics of presentation, but little of substantive difference. This is not quite true. There have been experimentation shifts and some excellent discussion programs that have put analysis where it can be perceived as such, although major structural changes in TV news were not forthcoming in the early part of the decade. After some talk of expanding the nightly network news to one hour, each of the networks then effected draconian budget cutbacks in their news divisions. Ironically, ABC had the best level of improvement, and maybe the best overall news-presentation quality, after an entertainment man, Roone Arledge, assumed control of the division. The addition of C-SPAN and Cable News Network to home reception clearly increased the level of information provided the American public over television. Even CBN started its own nightly news in 1986, to present another voice.

Above: *Detectives Tubbs (Philip Michael Thomas, left) and Crockett (Don Johnson) plot a new course as they try to run down a band of . Jamaican drug suppliers who have a nasty habit of slaying their business associates, in the 'Cool Runnin'' segment of Miami Vice.*

news, just as the singer's is to sing, and the job is done. But beyond that, the medium is still television, and too often the concern for selling commercials, beating the competition and dazzling the viewer seems paramount. Anchors are still news readers, even if some of them had experience as reporters — and very few did. Tom Brokaw, in spite of his speech defect, was chosen for his presence and appeal, and much was made of the increase in Dan Rather's ratings after he started to wear cozy sweaters — factors that speak as much about the public's powers of discrimination and their demands for substance as about the television industry's commitment to genuine journalism instead of informational sitcoms.

In November of 1985 Peter Jennings asked a Hungarian newsman what the difference was between anchormen in their respective countries. The response was that American news-readers serve commercial interests, whereas the Eastern Europeans serve politics. He was right on both counts, if, in the commercial sense, the Americans are recognized not as subservient to, say, individual corporations, but to ratings, popularity, salaries and profits.

The weakest point, and most revealing aspect, of the television news industry is the phenomenon known as local news. With very few exceptions the local newscast is a presentation light on hard news and investigations, and long on personality pieces and light-weight rehashes masquerading as investigation. Television emits a unique smokescreen when it sends reporters to stand in front of snow-removal equipment on brutally cold evenings, just to 'report' that a city is ready for a storm; it could have been announced in the studio — if it was worth more than a mention in the first place. Perfervid camera crews are always ready to shove microphones in the face of people who have just lost relatives in a disaster: 'How do

you feel at this moment?' Sportcasters invariably shout, and weathermen are evidently hired on some sort of buffoon-scale. 'Happy Talk' news shows have been the norm on American television since the 1970s, but it's not the style that is the problem, it's the substance, or lack of it.

Of all the intellectual insults the television industry has served up through the years (and there has been much, with this book attempting to document the quality programming as well), TV news has consistently been the most insulting. Lowbrow soap-operas and moronic game shows at least never pretend to be what they are not. But the entertainment — and pretty bad entertainment at that — served up as 'news' by networks and, especially, local stations, is supposed to be television's finest face. News and public affairs divisions were charged with ushering in Sarnoff's visions of art galleries in the home. At the best they have brought information and instant news images in rare, memorable moments. But at the worst they have also forced liars and fools on the American public. Unfortunately in television programming, just as in economics, Gresham's Law holds true: The Bad drives out the Good.

But the number three was never set in cement, even when Sarnoff and Paley proved so accurate in other predictions half a century ago. Much of TV history can be related to the three networks because of the personalities that were imbued in their programs. Further, TV shows can be traced according to their production studios or casts, for similar reasons. Entertainment philosophies, political flavor, even basic business-management decisions, have all shaped the course of television history, and have been why the identification of networks and production companies in a historical treatment is appropriate.

But, as we have noted, such control and identification has had a down-side as well. Television in the 1980s has finally learned to look beyond the number three and actually find its commercial continuance and creative salvation.

Finally, one last program — a network series — can provide an apostrophe to the history of television to this point. As it relies on music for its identification, so we may consider it not a recapitulation but a coda before the next movement.

Miami Vice both borrowed from, and inspired, trends in TV programming styles. It reportedly received its impetus from NBC President Brandon Tartikoff's memo: 'MTV cops,' speculating on the popularity of music videos. *Miami Vice* immediately inspired in turn programs like *Hollywood Beat* and *The Insiders*. A police show set in the Florida city, *Vice* centers on vicious drug trafficking and dangerous offenders, and features ultra-hip fashions, set designs and musical scores. Stars Don Johnson (as Sonny Crockett) and Philip Michael Thomas (as Ricardo Tubbs) move through a television world of remarkable integration. Every prop is color-coordinated, both in

1980s shows, and arguably the quintessential TV fare.

If television is personal (the screen is small and intimate, despite its reception by millions) and immediate (despite the modern miracle of VCRs, which create instant libraries of favorites), then *Miami Vice* is an emblem of what TV means in presentation and perception. Even its shortcomings – a tendency to sacrifice plot substance for the flashiness of appearance – is a very symbol of the whole medium's flawed character. When wooden lines are spoken by bit players, or when Edward James Olmos's brooding portrayal of Lieutenant Castillo slips over the line into self-caricature, such events are quickly obliterated by fast music and fast scenery.

Miami Vice is one show that will take critics time to digest, in spite of its visceral demands; in several years it is bound to seem too tied to contemporary *minutiae* and will be passé, but may very well, a generation hence, be viewed as a classic reflection of the times or at least how a talented ensemble of creators and actors responded to the times. Therein may be the ultimate creative use of television, and the criticisms of *Miami Vice*'s hipness, flashiness and obsession with 'superficials' may not be valid criticisms at all. After a half-century of television, critics should finally realize that with a new medium there *should* be a new syntax and vocabulary. Ultimately much of TV's programming to the mid-1980s, even the best of the best, will be seen in a theatrical or stage context. Television has yet to assert its own language and structure.

Music, video techniques, VCR capabilities, the multiplicity of programming opportunities, the ability to 'catch' the world's shows on back-yard satellite dishes, the home-computer tie-ins with the television screen, large-screen sets, stereo sound – and more – mean very literally that the past is prologue in TV's case. That the past has been a very mixed collection of embarrassing material and some quality is, once again, not merely a knock on the commercialism that has invaded the medium. It should perhaps be seen as symptomatic of the American culture. The Greeks gave to the world culture, the Romans law. It has yet to be established whether American culture is the last gasp of Western commerce-oriented expansion, or a unique short burst of technology and invention.

Whatever the case – however the millions of hours of television meld into a larger statement – TV in America has been a precisely perfect mirror. Comics and jazz are America's two native art forms, so there must be no embarrassment that television may be America's theatrical legacy. Constant prodding for higher standards should not be abandoned, but neither should there be any more illusory criticisms of television as a convenient or superficial or illegitimate dramatic medium. The future is just like a TV set: we can change the channels, but the choices are all television.

Above: *Correspondent Peter Jennings in Moscow for ABC's* World News Tonight. **Top:** *Philip Michael Thomas (left) and Don Johnson in a showdown on* Miami Vice.

keeping with style and to whatever is appropriate for the ambiance of the scene. The music is not merely canned or pulled off the shelf to fit routine action or romance requirements; it is specially commissioned, or has been purchased from an established rock star (the score is invariably rock) because its lyrics dovetail with the conceptual rhythm of the episode. Using such an approach – and the very latest editing and video techniques – *Miami Vice* is certainly the most contemporary of

TELEVISION
IN
BRITAIN

The *BBC Yearbook for 1933* includes a photograph of 'a seal being televised.' The seal — Sammy by name — is playing a saxophone, though a serious feature on television, written by John Logie Baird, appears on the opposite page. An interesting juxtaposition, somehow anticipating the history of television, a mixture of technology and trivia. Yet, at its best, the output of the British Broadcasting Corporation (BBC) was destined to make its own history of the medium, touching hearts and minds world-wide. It is perhaps a reflection on our present time that the role of public-service broadcasting is being questioned in the home of Baird. That the BBC is urged to secure income from TV commercials is not itself a new phenomenon. As television began its uncertain life in the 1930s, there were those who thought that sponsorship was the answer to the financing problem. But, until the advent of commercial television in the 1950s, the BBC created the medium on the basis of consumer license fees. So, in Britain, at least, the people made television; it was a public-spirited initiative.

In the 1930s the entertainment millennium seemed imminent in Britain. A new system of regional broadcasting had been introduced by the BBC, replacing the network of city- and town-based low-powered radio stations that had developed in the early 1920s. In those days, the British Broadcasting Company acted as an umbrella organization, but with little promise of necessary expansion. Thus, in 1927, it was restructured as a public corporation — the BBC as we know it today — its guiding light being the truly remarkable Sir John (later Lord) Reith. A man of earnest conviction, who had served his nation well during the first world war, Reith was both aloof and 'homely.' He spoke about the role and shape of radio, as though the instruction had just been handed down from on high. Though it is fashionable, in Britain at least, to deride 'Reithian ethics,' no man did more to shape British broadcasting, and its diversity. With John Logie Baird, John Reith, another Scot, created a great resource for the nation.

A man of rather scholarly appearance, Baird was in his mid-thirties when, in 1923, he developed (with C F Jenkins of the USA) the disc-scanning system which made television possible. John Logie Baird died in the same year that Britain revived its 405 line television service, following the end of World War II, in 1946. It can be said that his niche in television history is that of a popular educator, since he showed a rare flair for triggering consumer interest. Thus, in April 1925, he enlisted the aid of a department

Previous spread: An exterior scene from The Adventures of Sherlock Holmes. *Jeremy Brett (left) was Holmes and David Burke was Dr Watson.* **Below:** *John Logie Baird with the two ventriloquist's dummies he used to test his television transmitter.*

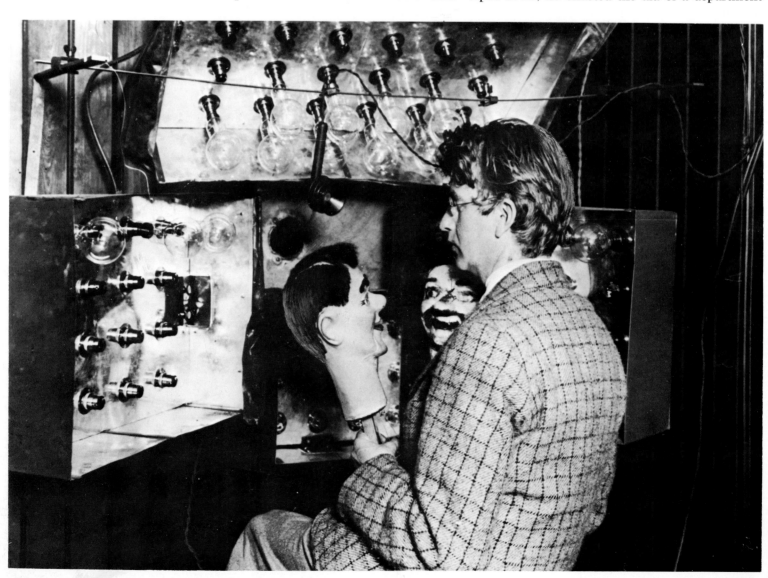

store in London in order to show his equipment to astonished shoppers. His demonstration was simple enough: seemingly no more than a large disc enclosing small segments of glass upon which an image flickered. But, as the inventor explained to anyone who asked as to its potential, television was about to establish itself as a new communication medium beyond anything then known to man. By the beginning of 1926, Baird was ready to demonstrate his system to fellow scientists. Rooms in Soho, in central London, were used, the moving head of a ventriloquist's dummy being the image subject. Baird was certainly a serious scientist, and no man to confuse the issues. But he knew the value of publicity. Whenever he arranged a demonstration of the embryonic equipment, the press usually wanted to know more, and mention the event in large type. Baird called his receiver the televisor, and some examples are today displayed by museums in London, including the collection at the Crystal Palace Museum in south-east London.

The radio manufacturing industry had helped establish the original British Broadcasting Company, it being reasonably argued that people would go out and buy radio sets if they knew that programs were available from a local station. In similar mood, the industry was aware that a television service would create a new market for TV sets, and, with the likelihood of a tail-off in radio sales (as the market achieved near saturation in the later 1930s), this prospect was seen as vital for long-term well-being. Baird took the view that demonstration was at times better than debate. He thought that live transmission of major events would be used in theaters, via large-scale projection television, together with conventional sound movies. Indeed, some experiments of this kind were held, but Baird secured national publicity beyond anything previously enjoyed when he televised Derby Day, 1931. This premiere horse race event in the British racing calendar, held at Epsom in Surrey, would in any case enjoy lead coverage in the sports pages. Baird set up his truck at the winning post, and though his 30-line transmission system hardly gave good pictures, he proved his point: outside broadcasts were entirely possible. His task, that day, was somewhat complicated by interference from nearby telephone cables. In 1932, the event was televised with a new arrangement with the BBC itself.

Prior to Baird's amazing demonstration from Epsom, experimental transmissions had been made from Baird's studios in Long Acre, London, using the London Regional transmitter of the BBC. These had started in the year of the General Strike, 1926, but few people had heard about them. As no receiving equipment was on sale to the general public, reception was limited to those involved in the experiment itself. As Baird himself acknowledged (in the BBC Year Book of 1933) these were 'crude beginnings.' By 1929, however, the experiments were sufficiently advanced

Above: The BBC's television setup for telecasting the 1932 English Derby.

to encourage 'official broadcasts' using the new London Regional facility at Brookmans Park, on the outskirts of London. Although the BBC was naturally interested in the prospect of television – and wanted to make sure that a service developed under its auspices and not under some new commercial upstart – it faced a few problems in the face of growing public interest after 1929's 'official broadcasts' had started.

Although a non-profit organization, funded by consumer license fees, the BBC had retained close associations with the industry, and was involved in the annual showcase, Radiolympia (*i.e.* the radio exhibition at Olympia Exhibition Center in London). It did not want to give the impression that the BBC regarded Baird's system as that approved for long-term investment. No doubt aware of the problem, the Postmaster General, the government official for the administration of communication services, wrote a letter to *The Times*, published on 28 March 1929. He informed the growing number of television-oriented consumers that while no brake would be placed on the Baird Company regarding sale of equipment, 'the purchaser must understand that he buys at his own risk, at a time when the system has not reached a sufficiently advanced stage to warrant its occupying a place in the broadcasting programs.'

That being said, the BBC was able to proceed with a clear lack of definite commitment, though it was generous to Baird. Initially, Baird's company was offered the use of studio facilities close to Waterloo Bridge in south London. This was a further piece of anticipated history, for on the nearby South Bank Site, new techniques in closed-

Above: *Broadcasting House in Portland Place, London, was completed as headquarters of the British Broadcasting Corporation in 1931. Over the entrance are the figures of Prospero and Ariel from Shakespeare's* The Tempest.

circuit television were shown during the Festival of Britain, 1951, at the aptly named Tele-Cinema. Interviews from a small studio in the lobby were shown simultaneously on the large screen in the auditorium, and on national television.

To meet the growing interest from industry and consumers (and no doubt to assert its own growing expertise in the matter) the BBC initiated regular experimental broadcasting, using the Baird system, on 22 August 1932. Earlier in the year, the BBC had taken residence at its new premises in Portland Place, London, W.1 (still the center for national BBC radio services). A subterranean studio had been assigned for Baird's work, and as this had been originally designed for the dance band programs, there is here some indication of the importance with which BBC management regarded the infant medium. Dance bands were among the most popular broadcasters of the time, and were, significantly, signed up by the new commercial stations based on the continent in the later 1930s. Thus, Studio BB became Britain's first true TV studio, and over the following 18 months an astonishing array of performers, players and personalities descended into the limbo beneath Portland Place.

From observations made by those involved, it was almost a self-contained service, able to do much what it wanted, within the BBC strictures on strong language and correct pronunciation. Of course, the equipment was primitive. Singers had to stand close to the camera, which was fixed. A rather penetrating and flickering light was focused on anyone being televised, while the requirements of make-up made participants look like mutants from distant planets. Because faces had to be made up in dead white, the outlines of noses and other features disappeared, therefore having to be subjected to other outline make-up. Lips were made purple to meet the needs of the camera, and eyes shaded blue. As one broadcaster put it, you looked halfway between a ghost and a clown after the make-up had been applied.

Dancers and other acts involving movement had to be carefully coached about their likelihood of going off camera if they went beyond marked lines on the studio floor. Even so, techniques were developed to the point that television's first pantomimist (Dick Whittington) debuted in December 1932.

Even in those early days, the potential of news coverage was clearly recognized. For example, when the celebrated aviators Jim and Amy Mollison returned to Britain following their transAtlantic flight, they were rushed to Studio BB. And, as the BBC had plenty of vaudeville turns in its early days, acts abundant could be secured, including the much-reported seal with the saxophone. Puppets, trick cyclists, people on roller skates and others indicated the kind of television we would be likely to enjoy in the golden age just ahead. This was true of late-night television. Because of technical limitations – including the use of two frequencies, one for sound, the other for vision – it was necessary to start the television transmissions *after* the radio service had closed down for the day, *i.e.* after 11 PM.

For Baird's own team of researchers, the most impressive (and eventually successful) competition came from the major company, Electrical and Music Industries (EMI) based in Hayes, Middlesex, and working with the Marconi Company on a high-definition system. Pressed to make some national statement on the competing systems, the British government set up a committee under Lord Selsdon, charged with making clear recommendations for early action. Set up in May 1934, the committee was a worthy example to similar bodies today, for within six months, it had undertaken considerable research, and produced a clear, concise report – which offered indeed the right choices to the nation. The January 1935 document recommended a high definition system of not less than 240 lines with a minimum of 25 pictures per second, as permitted by ultra short-wave transmission. From the standpoint of our video-minded age, it is interesting to note the Committee's view that sound radio would 'always be the most important factor in broadcasting.' Therefore, television was not to divert resources from radio, as far as the BBC was concerned. Perhaps understandably, some interpreted this as recommendation that a new commercial company should develop a television service, leaving the BBC to handle public service radio. That was *not* the view of the BBC.

So the Committee's proposals were quickly accepted. Two new high definition systems – from Baird (240 line) and Marconi-EMI (405 line) – were chosen for alternate transmissions by the BBC, over a limited period and allowing careful assessment of the end result. Low definition transmissions from Studio BB ended on Wednesday, 11 September 1935. Looking around for a suitable site for the new service, the BBC chose Alexandra Palace, a ghastly-in-appearance center of public entertainments, built in the Victorian

Left: *Jan Bussel and Ann Hogarth with Rufus the Clown and Muffin the Mule. Muffin the Mule was one of the early BBC television programs for children.*

Below: *The huge transmitter at Alexandra Palace.*

era, like the Crystal Palace in which John Logie Baird had now established his research base. 'Ally Pally,' as it was, and is, known, was a good choice from the standpoint of its elevated position several miles north of London. Following leasing of some 55,000 square feet for television purposes, the BBC assigned personnel to make the necessary transformation.

Not since Mr Blandings built his dream house had such energies been displayed. By the fall of 1936, the world's first high-definition service was ready for transmission. Further, the transmitter at Alexandra Palace covered all London and much of the surrounding counties, an impressive audience for television. Following an impressive effort by BBC personnel, the first high-definition program was transmitted on the opening day of Radiolympia, 26 August 1936. This two-week-long trade and consumer fair was truly television-struck, as the quality of both high definition systems became evident to those who had either not seen television or squinted at the tiny screens of the old low definition system. Television viewing facilities at Radiolympia were enjoyed by well over 120,000 visitors, all no doubt returning home to tell their friends and neighbors.

The service itself commenced in November 1936, that is, on a daily basis which could be advertised and promoted by dealers. Program schedules indicated which system was being used that day, but for any perceptive observer, it must have been evident that Baird could not win the contest. His system had a definite disadvantage in that it required an intermediate film processing stage. True, this could be accomplished within a minute, perhaps less, the 17.5 mm film being scanned at six thousand revolutions per minute while still wet. It was a complication that could not be adopted for widespread use. The Marconi-EMI system was in any case the fruit of many years' research, little of it covered in the press. Baird's system was finally abandoned after transmission on Saturday, 13 February 1937. Baird had suffered an earlier blow when a great fire (November 1936) had engulfed his experimental and research facility at the Crystal Palace in south-east London. Built for the Great Exhibition in 1851 at Hyde Park, and moved to its permanent site at Sydenham in 1854, the Crystal Palace had been a great center of culture and recreation. Further, it had been home for Britain's first permanent classical orchestra, under Sir August Manns. Now, it was in ruins, and all Baird's equipment and research with it. Baird was seemingly prepared for the government's announcement as to the acceptance of the Marconi-EMI high definition system. The victory was well deserved, and in one sense timely. One of the fruits of Marconi-EMI research was the creation of the Super Emitron camera tube, which had such sensitivity that outside broadcasts could be made even in poor natural light conditions – as is frequently the case in Britain. The nation's greatest celebration of the 1930s, the Coronation of King George VI, was successfully televised, thanks to the research that Marconi-EMI had put into outside broadcast work. Like that later Coronation (of Queen Elizabeth) in 1953, television proved to be a great sales creator in television receiver business.

John Logie Baird died in 1946. The television service itself had closed abruptly at the end of a Mickey Mouse cartoon, transmitted just after mid-day on 1 September 1939. Two days later, Britain was involved in a great world war, leaving the prewar television schedules a mere memory. During the summer, hopeful estimates had suggested sales of sets reached up to 80,000 by Christmas. At the time that war began, around 23,000 sets were in use. Such was the quality of the Marconi-EMI system though, that it was used for the post-war service — and has only recently ceased operation, as the obsolete but still usable (in mono) service alternative to the 625 line system. Baird is remembered as the man who created television in Britain. Though his designs did not succeed in being adopted as the national standard, Baird awakened the public awareness of a medium soon taken for granted.

In September 1943, some four years after the outbreak of World War II in Europe, the British government set up a committee to consider the re-introduction of a television service at war's end. Post-war reconstruction was very much in the air, and television was certainly part of the better world for the people. The committee conducted more than 30 business sessions under its

chairman, Lord Hankey (hence its description as the Hankey Committee). Representatives of education, business, telecommunications, entertainment and other areas of human activity came along to present their views and experience. Among those offering advice was the pioneer, John Logie Baird.

Although the committee presented its report at the end of December 1944, immediate response from government was not forthcoming. No doubt the government had more on its mind, during those months between invasion of France in June 1944 (D Day) and the end of hostilities. Fortunately, Alexandra Palace remained generally intact. As former television personnel were demobilized from the Armed Forces it became possible for the BBC to top up its production capability, based on a revived television service. Inevitably, the Marconi-EMI system would be used, though as the *BBC Year Book for 1946* pointed out, it gave a picture quality somewhat inferior technically to the definition that might be obtained at the movies. No one worried. It was sufficient cause for joy that television was at last returning to Britain, or at least to London. For the Alexandra Palace transmitter covered London and part of its surrounding counties. True, there were reports of receivers picking up signals well beyond the anticipated 40-mile radius, but these could not be posited as normal reception. Before the war, hobby magazines had not infrequently commented on the Londoners keeping a good thing (*i.e.* television) to themselves. So the re-introduction of television would have to seek early extension beyond the original base.

As the first visits were made to Alexandra Palace, toward the end of 1945, various reminders of 'the old days' were discovered. One writer commented on the almost melancholy reminders of Baird's lost system, left in Ally Pally from the pre-war period. No doubt any television archaeologist would give his eye-teeth for such items today.

Restoration work was no simple matter. Almost everything was in short supply in Britain, possibly even rationed, and in some cases unobtainable. Thus, 'make do and mend,' in the spirit of the clothes-saving campaign of the war, had some relevance to the technical chores. It would be hard to think of any stranger episode in the history of television, in Britain, or for that matter anywhere else.

So BBC Television returned to the screens of Britain – or at least London – on 7 June 1946. The 'welcome back' to the camera was given by one of the medium's most famous presenters, Jasmine Bligh. On a more official and august level, the Postmaster General formally announced the service open. Then, in the spirit that has somehow contributed to British character and eccentricity, the BBC re-ran that same cartoon that had closed the service as war loomed in September 1939. Thus, to Mickey Mouse fell the honor of re-opening the entertainment side of

Above: *The 1946 Victory Day Parade in London was televised. This is the Royal Engineers contingent of the British Army.*
Right: *Mickey Mouse signed off the BBC at the beginning of World War II and signed it on after the victory.*

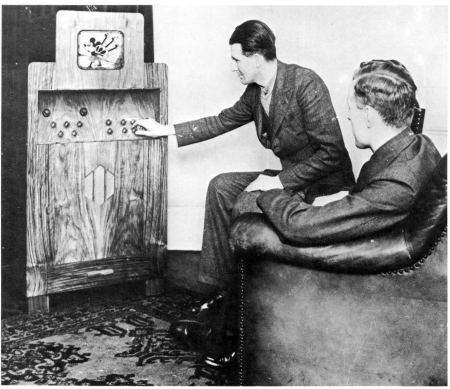

things. On the following day, the Victory Parade in London was transmitted. Despite overcast weather, the picture quality was excellent, thanks to EMI's work on cathode tubes and cameras – plus the redesigned antenna at Alexandra Palace. Despite the perils of the blitzkrieg on London, a very high percentage of television receivers were reported working – after years stored away in attics, cupboards and cellars. One estimate suggests that no less than 20 thousand receivers were working when the television service re-opened. Incidentally, the consumer license fee, per annum, for radio plus television, was then two pounds, around eight dollars at 1946 prices. The flow of new sets onto the market had yet to get into its stride, but a limited number were available, at around £50 (around two hundred dollars at 1946 prices) for a nine- or ten-inch picture tube set. Prices for a similar size portable television set are about the same in UK currency, though transistorized chassis have long since replaced the tube variety that delighted home viewers around 40 years ago.

The public approach to television was a mixture of outright wonder, a desire to be educated via the medium and a sense of theatrical occasion. All that perished after the 1950s, and we will never see such a public appreciation of television again. Output was itself modest. Even by the beginning of the 1950s, there was little more than an hour or so programing in the afternoon (between 3 PM and 4/4:30 PM); an evening segment of about one and a half hours (from 8:30 PM until 10 PM) and perhaps a morning program, though originally weekday mornings were reserved for test cards and demonstration films for the benefit of radio/TV retailers and those installing sets in homes.

Before the war, an afternoon segment might include a 10–15 minute film or information item relating to animals, history or other topic; *British Movietone Newsreel* (repeated in the evening); a weather forecast; a brief excerpt from a theater or ballet performance (but never the complete show; theater management distrusted television, on the whole); or perhaps a cabaret from the studio with carefully selected entertainers.

After close-down at 4 PM, the screen would spring into life once more around 9 PM, with a two-hour program segment including much already shown in the afternoon, but with additional features. Nothing much there to tempt Junior away from his homework, you may think. Probably not, but for anyone reaching for the on/off switch for the first time, it was a magical experience.

Some of the prewar shows were excellent enough to be revived on the return of television to Britain. *Picture Page* — the magazine program devised by Cecil Madden — was a great favorite and triggered other similar formats, like the magazine *Kaleidoscope*. Joan Miller, 'the switchboard girl' (though in fact a very competent actress) opened *Picture Page*, seated at a telephone switchboard connected to a television screen. Miss Miller 'connected' viewers to the subjects of the interview or other items. On the return of the program in 1946, Joan Gilbert was appointed editor. Indeed, a special *Picture Page* was screened to celebrate the issue of 100,000 TV licenses, as a measure of public interest in the medium. During the program, Cecil Madden and the famous newscaster, Leslie Mitchell, talked about the original high-definition program of 1936.

There were many new recruits to the medium, some of them remarkably successful. Fred Streeter, expert gardener and philosopher, was a favorite for many years, while Philip Harben, the television cook, gave a whole generation new insights into the enjoyment of food. By today's standards, the television diet was bland, with an intellectual level that would be considered too high today. Plays, for example, included many

Opposite top: *The Olympic Games held in London in 1948 demonstrated to the world the technical accomplishments of British television. Here a commentator reports on the day's events.*
Above: *Philip Harben in the pantry of the set for his cooking program.*
Opposite bottom: *Jasmine Bligh, the world's first television announcer.*

secure a stock of movies for occasional use but they were aging – pre-war *Hopalong Cassidy* productions, and comedies like the *Topper* series. Ironically, this kind of vintage material has an intrinsic interest to many people today.

John Logie Baird had considered television a likely adjunct to film entertainment – as well as a home entertainment medium. 'Instant news coverage' on the big screen, he thought, would have a wide appeal. Although the Hankey Committee had other matters on their minds, the members also looked for a system which in the future would provide a definition equal to that of the cinema movie, as well as color, and stereoscopic (three dimensional) effect. In the latter regard, one imagines without the need for those green/red plastic lenses required of those enjoying the three dimensional effect.

Attempts to reconcile the movie and television interests were generally unsuccessful, but in the late 1940s discussions were held which proposed some kind of mutual benefit agreement – that is, with television providing some input into cinemas, and film distributors taking a less stringent line on use of films on (British) television. The Cinematograph Exhibitors Association branch of London and the Home Counties (*i.e.* the area receiving television signals, and therefore where the movie versus television conflict was evident) issued a report in 1949, suggesting that 'cinema television can never give a picture comparable to that in definition of a film, and unfortunately the government has given an undertaking to continue the 405 line transmission until 1956.' Toward the end of 1948, a demonstration of large screen television had been presented at a theater in Bromley, Kent. One trade paper, *(Ideal Kinema)*, thought that 'the contrast of the picture was exceedingly good. At best, the picture quality was fully acceptable . . . transmission lines were fully visible, but not noticeably so.'

Britain's know-how in television – much of it derived from war-time research on radar – was demonstrated during the Olympic Games held in London during 1948. Many visitors to London were able to watch major Olympics events on television receivers, and were often impressed by the technical quality. That fortnight in 1948, against a background of a nation still facing many shortages, remains an important feature of television history. For one thing, it made the nation television-conscious in a way that no other event, apart from the Coronations of 1937 and 1953, did. By the end of 1948, the number of licenses held in Britain had reached around 150,000. BBC reporters, covering events embracing some six thousand competitors from around 58 nations, seemed to work almost round the clock. All of the innovations introduced into programing reflected achievements in research and production management. EMI's compact and extremely light sensitive CPS Emitron camera added great potential to outside broadcasts, and

of the classics, by writers from either side of the Atlantic, Eugene O'Neill no less than William Shakespeare. At a time of one-channel television, and that on for a very limited period, the program controllers were perhaps risking public abuse, in the mails and press at least. But on the whole, the output worked surprisingly well, so that casual callers to any home on a Sunday evening would be discouraged from saying anything, steered towards a vacant chair, as if they were late-comers in a live theatrical performance. There were no commercials to make the transition between Acts One and Two, so the BBC devised a series of interval sequences, of five or so minutes duration, showing windmills, potters' wheels and other restful sequences on film.

A main problem – one experienced before the war – was the reluctance of theatrical interests to assist the BBC. It was generally felt that television was likely to diminish theater audiences, that people would stay at home instead of paying decent money for a seat in the auditorium. In vain did the BBC point out that its educational role could help stimulate a wider interest in the theater. There were similar if more understandable objections from the film-making fraternity. In the early post-war era, the BBC managed to

Above: *Lighting the Olympic torch at Wembley at the 1948 Olympic Games in London — one of the biggest television events for the BBC.* **Opposite top:** *The Coronation of Queen Elizabeth II in 1953 was given extensive television coverage. Here, Dr Fisher, The Archbishop of Canterbury, is about to place St Edward's Crown upon Her Majesty's head.*

sports-on-TV. Another innovation was the direct taping of television programs. The BBC, as a non-commercial organization, was able to experiment with innovation, without any problem of offending a sponsor careful of his advertising. Thus transmission of a full-length musical, *No, No, Nanette*, went smoothly, again reinforcing the possibilities of a medium that did not have to be careful of matching the production to time segments between commercials.

The first post-war Radiolympia in 1947 had coincided with the development of the television newsreel. Actors and actresses were offering themselves for work on television, without fear of compromising their standing in the movie business. First use of the television telescope, for amateur interest astronomy programs, came in September 1949. Everywhere, there was a mood of expansion and innovation. In all this, there was due regard for US experience and ideas. Some of the programs from US television were indeed bought for transmission in Britain, these including Joan Davis and Jim Backus in *I Married Joan*, and the documentary series *Victory at Sea*. More were to follow. Occasionally, popular television papers carried reports of the bewildering choice of channels on US systems, as if Britons should be grateful for their one channel and very limited choice. Production resources were in any case stretched at the BBC, though much needed accommodation became available when the BBC purchased the former Rank Film Studios at Lime Grove, Shepherds Bush, in west London. Few seemed to realize that one outcome of the expansion of television, beyond London, was a call for

greater choice, for programing that reflected working-class life and humor. Ironically, that very expansion necessitated a new structure in television, which in effect ensured the introduction of commercial television — that phenomenon considered so unsuited to the British emotional climate, by unperceptive 1930s writers.

On one memorable June day in 1953, the streets of Britain were deserted. Humanity had been spirited away, from all appearances. Few stores seemed to be doing any business; some had closed, and the store clerks gone home to watch television. On that day in England the power of television came into its own. For the first time, the Coronation of a monarch could be seen on television in the most densely populated parts of the United Kingdom. Main transmitters operating at that time were the Alexandra Palace, Sutton Coldfield, Holme Moss, and the recently opened Kirk o' Shotts (Scotland) and Wenvoe (South Wales) transmitters. The latter, on an elevation a few miles outside of Cardiff, provided a signal for south Wales and much of the west of England.

Despite a plethora of splendid occasions on television since that time, nothing has approached the 1953 Coronation in terms of impact on the nation, or for that matter, on sales of television sets. The weekly program and information magazine of the BBC, *The Radio Times*, included a five-page Order of Service — that is, the Service that was to be conducted in appropriate grandeur at Westminster Abbey. Within its pages, too, there was a detailed map of the Coronation Procession route, from Buckingham Palace to Westminster

Abbey, with indications of camera sites and commentators who would be capturing the essence of the day.

The general absence of the population from normal, everyday activity was explained by *The Radio Times*. BBC transmissions on Coronation Day began at 10:15 AM and continued until 11:30 PM, a stretch of available viewing that was itself a novelty. There was a brief interval between 6:20 PM and 8 PM (in the sense that consumers were used to longer delays between program segments).

Right: *Richard Dimbleby, one of the earliest of all television reporters began his career as a journalist.*

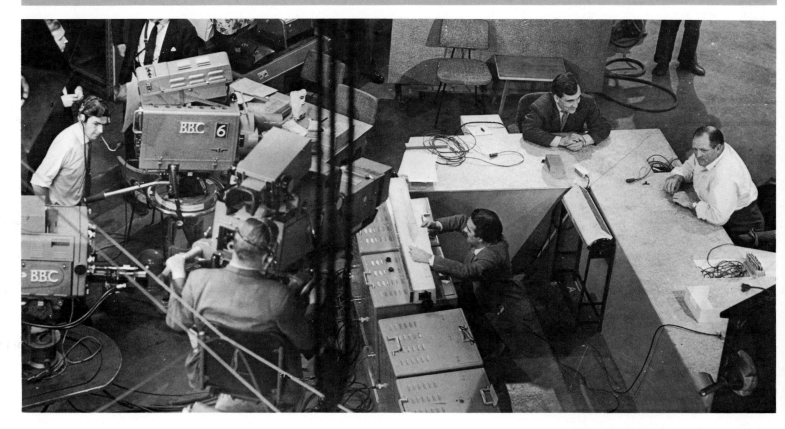

Telerecordings of the event were flown to Canada by the RAF and RCAF, US networks also securing copies for their own transmissions. Using cross-Channel links, the signal also went to Western Europe, stations in France, The Netherlands and West Germany carrying edited versions of the great event. As the output was still in monochrome, cinemas were able to capture useful business by offering color feature films, about the Coronation (*A Queen is Crowned*), one of the few examples of television and film working to mutual advantage.

Coronation apart, the British took television in their stride, and did not let its influence dominate the home. From the Festival of Britain Year 1951, there had been impressive progress, with exchange of programing from European networks. New formats were developed, most of a documentary nature, like the *Special Enquiry* series which examined major national issues (housing and employment were two topics – hardly ever out of the television news reportage in Britain during the 1980s).

Panorama – the Monday evening investigative program – was introduced to the viewing public in 1952, and is one of the longest-running programs in British television. When commercial television shaped its schedules, some counterweight was offered in the Thursday evening *This Week* – but *Panorama* remained the heavyweight in this field of documentary. With Britain's long tradition of documentary film-making, it was hardly surprising that television developed this form of public information.

Most people thought of the BBC as a public educator rather than entertainer, though it must be said that the Light Entertainment Department was producing around four hundred programs

per year by the mid 1950s. Benny Hill, destined to become one of Britain's most popular comedians, began his television career with the BBC (in *Showcase*) while Bob Monkhouse, still highly regarded as a talk show host and television quizmaster, was involved in BBC light entertainment output (in *Fast and Loose*). Some of the formats were adapted from radio. *Music Hall*, a Saturday night sequence of celebrated music hall or vaudeville stars, was apparently based on the long-running radio program of the same name. Vic Oliver, who had worked during the war with Bebe Daniels and Ben Lyon in *Hi Gang* (on BBC radio) returned to his first love, music, for a presentation of light classics, *This is Show Business*.

Music would seem to have been a natural choice for the television producers, though they were aware of the limitations imposed by receiver electronics. Small elliptical loudspeakers, fitted into the run-of-the-mill television chassis, hardly permitted anything approaching a high-fidelity performance. Some of the best work in music presentation occurred where explanation could be allied to performance, a style that is still offered in various productions today. In the early 1950s, the BBC was fortunate enough to secure the talents of three marvelous men of music for the series *The Conductor Speaks*. The trio – Sir Malcolm Sargent, Sir Thomas Beecham and Sir John Barbirolli – were all *characters*, in the best sense of the word, able to project their ideas through the camera lens and microphone into thousands of homes. Such talents were not commonplace and seemed to come naturally.

Another discovery was that of Dr Glyn Daniel, chairman of an unusual quiz game, *Animal, Vegetable or Mineral*, in which a team was called upon to identify a range of artifacts, often of historic significance. Making history come alive was a self-imposed ordinance at the BBC, and the output seemed popular enough, indicated by increasing sales of television sets. Encouraged by Coronation Year coverage, sales reached a total of one million new receivers making a total of more than three million licensed receivers by 1954.

Television could create its own sensations, too. When a television production of *1984* was presented in 1952, the comment that 'Big Brother is watching you' became almost a catch-phrase at home and work. Peter Cushing portrayed Winston Smith, and so excelled in the role that a new interest in Orwell's work was created — resulting in a movie production of *1984* (with Edmund O'Brien as Winston Smith) from a US studio. That television could excel in science fiction, too, was shown in 1953's *Quatermass Experiment*, which was later re-made as a movie.

No one doubted that the BBC could produce quality; the problem increasingly was that of quantity. As television moved increasingly across the nation, regional requirements and a greater

variety (and quantity) of output was required. Learned gentlemen, not much into television themselves, would sternly advise the public that the medium was like a bottle of good wine, to be taken in small quantities and carefully savored. An indication of Saturday night programing may be taken from *The Radio Times* published for the week of the Coronation in 1953. On the Saturday (6 June 1953) you could enjoy an hour-long vintage Adolphe Menjou movie at 3:15 PM, a popular children's program, *Whirligig*, at 5 PM, and then wait the 'decent interval' until the screen offered a compilation of the week's news-reels, followed by a half-hour feature about the making of cricket bats (8:30 PM to 9 PM); the first episode of a detective serial (9 to 9:30 PM) and finally a showcase of Commonwealth musical and artistic talent (9:30 PM to 11 PM).

Under the circumstances, it is a little surprising that the theaters were so fearful of the inroads of television. With its limited hours of transmission, and repeats, the BBC seemed sometimes eager to encourage people to go to the movies. This is meant in no spirit of criticism. Rather, the attitude of the BBC was that of allowing television to grow, rather more gradually than people were ready to permit. In any case, the Corporation had to work within the confines of financial para-meters, which were not so stringent in the matter of commercial television. If any unanswered question may be stated in reference to the new competition, it is rather why the BBC did not itself become the contractor, through new types

of regional organizations. But that subject of debate goes back to pre-television days.

Sponsored programing was not new to Britain. The origins of radio — known more popularly as 'the wireless' — lay in business enterprise, not a state corporation. *The Daily Mail* — having done much to encourage the cause of aviation — turned its attention to infant radio, and in 1920, sponsored a program by Dame Nellie Melba, from Marconi's experimental radio station at Writtle, near Chelmsford in Essex. Commercial companies and publishers helped keep the embryonic British Broadcasting Company afloat during the early 1920s. Even in times nearer the television age, commercial radio companies based in Luxembourg, Normandy and Paris had captured large audiences in Britain from 1934 to the outbreak of World War II. While many reasons might be advanced for prohibiting com-mercial broadcasting in Britain, there seemed to be no evidence of public distaste for it. Such evidence as there was seemed to suggest that British consumers liked an alternative to BBC fare — though they would wish to see the BBC maintained as the main provider on the airwaves.

The post-war Labour Government under Clement Attlee was unsympathetic to the idea. In 1949, The Beveridge Committee, enquiring into the future of the BBC, reinforced the govern-ment's view. However, there was a significant minority report, as the report had been itself approved by 11 votes to four. Selwyn Lloyd, later to become a most effective Speaker of the House of Commons, submitted the minority report which argued that the influence of broadcasting should not be vested in any monopoly, whether that was a private or public monopoly. Among much else, the report proposed that a British television organization should be created as soon as possible, charged with the development of what was then called 'sponsored broadcasting.' Later, more companies could be invited to offer alternative sources of television. Indeed, the report indicated that similar competition might be introduced into radio itself.

In retrospect, it is interesting to see how well Selwyn Lloyd anticipated events that occurred after the mid 1950s. Public opinion polls seemed to suggest public approval of a plan for commercial television. As might be expected, those who had bought television sets were most in favor of an additional service. The *News Chronicle* – a London daily – commissioned a Gallup Poll in August 1952, showing that some 50 percent of television owners favored the introduction of independent, *i.e.* commercial television. By that time, the Labour Government had fallen, and a Conservative Government elected in its place. Television was a live issue, not least because the BBC Charter expired at the end of December 1951 – the year of the change of government. Questions of its continuing status as a monopoly were widely discussed. It looked as though the government would, in effect, continue the policy of the Labour government – which had been strongly opposed (as Lord Jowett, the Labour Lord Chancellor, had indicated) to any plan for sponsored broadcasting.

The government White Paper on Broadcasting, debated in the House of Commons on 11 July 1952, looked for some competition in due course. For the time being, however, the BBC had first claim on such resources as were available. Later in the month, a new license was approved for the BBC's continuation, though now modifying its monopoly position. In effect, the door had been left well open for pressure groups to press for early action. An organization called the National Television Council – formed to resist plans for commercial television – tried to stem the tide moving in favor of this new medium, but, launched in June 1953, the Council had little chance of success. A group of Conservative MPs formed a Radio and Television Group in the same month; in little more than a year, the Television Bill permitting commercial television was given the Royal Assent, after passing through both Houses of Parliament.

Some of those involved in commercial television had been working toward that end for no little time. No man did more to shape these developments than Norman Collins, a former Controller of BBC Television. Norman Collins left the BBC in 1950 in order to devote his considerable expertise and talent to the cause of commercial television. In an article published in *TV News* (29 May 1953) he is described as 'the man

Above: *The ITA Commercial Television Aerial at Beulah Hill, Croydon.*

behind commercial TV.' In the period following his departure from the BBC, noted the reporter, 'he began to organize and negotiate and eventually succeeded in launching a new company which will promote commercial television just as soon as the green light shines. This company, the Associated Broadcasting Development Co., of which Mr Collins is the Chairman, is already engaged in making low cost high definition programs. They will be the key to future TV when programs can be put up for sale.'

Above: *Robin Day became the moderator of the television program Panorama.*

Mr Collins' company, as the newly-named ATV, was one of the first appointed under the Independent Television Act. Following its formation in August 1954, the Independent Television Authority planned a network of television stations, and considered a choice of companies for franchises. There was no shortage of applications. Some 98 had been received by the Independent Television Authority. That criteria for selection were stringent may be measured by the fact that most of those applications were subsequently withdrawn.

Twenty-eight applications were received for the first licenses, for franchises in London, the Midlands and the north of England. This number was dramatically reduced in the light of ITA criteria, only six being considered sufficiently financed and experienced to open a new commercial television service. The first four applicants were thus chosen:

> Granada Television (Northern Region, weekdays);
> Associated Rediffusion (London, weekdays);
> Associated British Cinemas Television (Midlands and Northern Region, weekends);
> Associated Broadcasting Development Company (as ATV, London weekends and Midlands weekdays).

Transmitter installation was quickly begun, so that the first transmitter, at Croydon in Surrey, opened on 22 September 1955, for Associated Rediffusion and Associated Television (ATV) programs. Thereafter a consistent development of commercial television continued, all but completed by the end of 1962, though there have been some changes in franchise holders since that time.

One result of commercial television was an increasing use of US originated material. Little of this had been evident in the single-channel BBC days. Now, with increased transmission hours (and the abandoning of the silent interval between tea-time children's viewing and evening family entertainment) there was more interest in acceptable US material. This was not so surprising. During the war, American servicemen had been stationed in Britain, often generous with their magazines and paperbacks at a time of severe paper shortages in Britain. Hollywood's influence in British movie-going was impressive too, so that programs with film stars in their cast or title had a good start in attracting viewer attention. Thus *Douglas Fairbanks Presents* and *The Errol Flynn Theater* found a likely rapport with British audiences. Further, the more intelligent programs, like *The Dick Powell Theater* attracted their own loyal clientele. *Perry Mason*, like *Charlie Chan*, needed little introduction to Britain. Similarly, detective programs like *77 Sunset Strip*, shown on Sunday evenings, seemed to fit in well with viewers' preferences. US comedy often traveled well, too, from gentle heroes like *Hiram Holliday* to the permanently popular *Sergeant Bilko*; *The Phil Silvers Show* has had re-runs on British television since the original mid- to late-1950s screenings. Indeed, a series was running at the time of Phil Silvers' death in 1985. From the US, too, came the impact of the rock 'n' roll revolution, prompting the BBC to produce a show that featured pop and rock stars, *6.5 Special*. This 1957 initiative has recently been enjoying a renaissance on Channel Four in Britain, perhaps showing that one generation's time past is another generation's research material.

Certainly, the BBC did not have the income enjoyed by the independent television companies. Although still maintaining its spread of balanced programing, the BBC concentrated on those activities in which it excelled, including television drama.

Of course, no one really knew if the attraction of commercial television would endure. Discussions by politicians and other opinion leaders had referred to sponsored programing, as if programs were to be sponsored on the US pattern. The pattern adopted in Britain was that of divorcing promotion from programs, and of including straight-forward sales messages — the commercials — in so-called natural breaks. These natural breaks were strictly controlled by the ITA, in terms of minutes per hour, though in recent times there have been calls for some relaxation of these rules. 'Natural breaks' were frequent cause of comment, as Members of Parliament, for example, drew attention to the inappropriate nature of some commercials in respect of programing within which they appeared.

Even during the great debates of 1954, 'natural breaks' had been thought of as outside programs, *i.e.* that the natural breaks would come either at the commencement or conclusion of programs, but not within them. In light entertainment, they come every quarter hour or so, though some documentary programs are completed without any natural breaks since it is thought damaging for the programs' impact to include them. Advertising agencies had been enthusiastic about commercial television, as one might expect, but booking transmission weeks or even months in advance, on behalf of clients, they could not be aware of the odd way in which the flavor of the program would relate to the message of the commercial.

But the British public liked the programs, and many of the commercials were strong on humor, family sentiment and intrinsic product interest. Thus, a television entrepreneur was moved to remark that a franchise was in effect a license to print money. No doubt he was making a light-hearted comment, but there is no doubt of it: the first five years of commercial television represented a golden era for the medium. Nevertheless, some commercials were clearly exaggerated, like the product that claimed to kill *all* known germs. Innocent as the exaggeration was, it became necessary to institute some industry self-policing

Above: *A scene from 6.5 Special with Lonnie Donegan. This rock 'n' roll show was Britain's answer to American Bandstand.*

of commercials. So in 1964 the Independent Television Companies Association (ITCA) set up a committee to study the script of each television commercial planned for transmission. With its increasing emphasis on drama production and news documentary, the independent network paid the BBC its own compliment, by trying to match the best in BBC output. On the whole, it has been a competition in excellence though no one would deny the flow of trivia – seals playing saxophones and all – that is sometimes evident on both channels.

The commercial companies had at least one other advantage – money apart – in relation to the BBC. Their regional roots permitted them an insight into local and regional interests and possible program formats. The BBC has had a regional radio and television organization for decades, but has tended to assign specific functions and specialities to regions. Thus, the Natural History Unit is based in Bristol, responsible for some of the best programs on television. Granada Television, based in Manchester, had its roots in a great industrial city, which like other cities in Britain, faces the consequences of the decline of traditional industry.

Innovative in many respects, Granada created Britain's most popular long-running serial, the twice-weekly *Coronation Street*. So popular is the program that a retrospective has recently been issued on home video, reminding viewers of the changes that have occurred in *Coronation Street* during the past quarter century. Set in a street of terraced houses in a traditional working class area, the program has the character of North Country life that might be hard to achieve with a London-based production team. Granada Television, from the outset, developed discussion formats, including *What The Papers Say* (which continues to run, but on Channel Four, all these years later). Another successful innovation was *Under Fire*, a two-way televised discussion between an audience in Manchester and 'experts in London.'

Commercial television did not of itself create the so-called consumer society, though it is sometimes so accused. At the time of the introduction of commercial television, food rationing (introduced during World War II) had been belatedly abandoned. People generally wanted to forget the shortages imposed by the war and the wearying decade of shortages and austerity. Earnings were increasing, and with full employment, the 1950s seem now a natural prelude to the swinging sixties — over-rated as that phenomenon was, and is. Teachers remained to be convinced. In

Opposite top: *The original 20 members of the first broadcast of* Coronation Street, *which began in December, 1960, and is still running – surely a record for a soap opera.*

Opposite bottom: *Margot Bryant (Minnie Caldwell), Violet Carson (Ena Sharples) and Lynne Carol (Martha Longhurst) in a scene from Granada Television's* Coronation Street – The First Twenty-Five Years, *telecast in 1985.*

Below: *Brian Inglis appeared on* What the Papers Say.

terms of television's effects on literacy, research may be inconclusive, but as a school-teacher remarked at a conference to general assent, 'the children don't sing nursery rhymes any more . . . they sing the TV jingles.'

By the end of the 1950s, some 93 percent of the nation's population could receive an ITV signal, with suitable antenna. Accessibility of signal off-air was a major reason for the relative failure of cable-supplied television beyond a small percentage of the population.

The impact of television was ultimately that of removing the magic and awe hitherto associated with the great institutions of state. 'Over exposure' is a familiar problem to leaders of any nation; Britain, with its blend of monarchy, democracy, unwritten constitution and dependence upon convention, was perhaps changed more than is generally appreciated, as a result of television. Conventional attitudes of respect toward those in authority, for example, known to those in school in a pre-television age, could not survive the impact of the searching television interviewer. It has been well said that television

'tore away the veil of mystery' surrounding leaders of the nation, including members of the Royal Family (who would nevertheless be highly regarded for other reasons). What, one might ask, would be the impact of a new Coronation on a blasé viewing public? Would the population retire to their living rooms and kitchens to stare at the pomp and ceremony, moved deeply as were another generation in 1953? It seems doubtful. Television has reduced much of contemporary leadership roles to the level of soap opera.

Yet, on a more positive level, television in Britain encouraged a world view, a concern for issues and people far away. Larger screen models were increasingly popular, so that the merchandise that promised '1000 percent improvement' through an enlarging lens fitted to small screen sets, disappeared from the advertising pages. A range of merchandise had been promoted in the earlier 1950s, including the Telemunized Screen which, clipped to a television set, would provide '60 percent clearer, sharper, no-glare pictures; complete freedom from eye fatigue; a revelation

Right: *Peter Cook (left) and Dudley Moore (right) listen to their guest, Peter Sellers on Not Only But Also – March 1965.*

Below: *Harry H Corbett and Wilfrid Brambell in a scene from Steptoe and Son – 1962.*

of detail and picture beauty.' At rather less expense, TeleVizor spectacles were especially designed to ensure restful viewing without distortion or flicker. Another product, basically a tinted sheet, offered an impression of color to monochrome sets.

Color television was on the way, but that was a matter of rather more expense than attaching a plastic frame to the 405-line set.

The success of television, in its public service and commercial aspects, meant lean times for many general-interest magazines. Many disappeared, leaving a gap that has never been filled. Broadcasters, on the other hand, seemed all set for a great era of expansion. On 29 June 1960, the BBC celebrated the opening of the new Television Center in White City, in west London, a showplace of technology, obviously oriented towards color television. Demonstrations of color television were held at the London Radio Show in 1962, and even at that time, Britain's television manufacturing companies would have been able to set up a production line quite quickly. It was an inspired guess that a 625 line system would be adopted, as it was; but the government had to make the decisions – as usual. Consumers, however, said little against the now obsolescent 405 line system, and, as transmission hours now amounted to some 55 hours a week, consumer choice was increasing all the time. Light entertainment was transmitted from the BBC Television Theater in Shepherds Bush, a short distance from the awe-inspiring new Television

Above: *Sid James (right) and Tony Hancock in the BBC's series* Hancock's Half-Hour.

Center, which also acted as the London base for Eurovision, the organization planning for pan-European services.

With commercial television, generally described as ITV (Independent Television), the BBC initiated new formats, some of them controversial. None was more headline-catching than *That Was The Week That Was*, in which a young David Frost acted as presenter. The BBC had always been innovative in humor, and the radio show, *It's That Man Again* (with North country comic Tommy Handley) anticipated some of the 'hell-zapoppin' style of broadcasting in Britain. However, BBC-TV's *That Was The Week That Was* brought new outspoken comment and satire to television, triggering a style that was developed elsewhere and in later programs, like *Not Only . . . But Also* on BBC2. The show soon acquired a late Saturday night audience of 14 million, as it lampooned British institutions, politicians and a great deal more. Some wrote it off as mere 'college humor,' but the program certainly demonstrated the BBC's openness to changing times. *Till Death Us Do Part* was in some ways a close relative, though basically a sitcom based on a London household dominated by a quaint and not too well informed cynic. Lord Reith must have turned in his grave at all these outspoken attacks on the establishment, but these, after all, were the 'swinging sixties,' allegedly the cause of many of the problems Britain has inherited in the 1980s.

Some of the BBC's comedy output had a touch of sheer genius, none more so than the *Hancock's Half-Hour* series which starred Tony Hancock, as a somewhat lugubrious bachelor marooned in a household of people who never appreciated his sensitive nature. Hancock's aspirations to art and the aristocratic life were ever frustrated, and in some ways he was a representative figure of a nation which was itself in industrial decline (disguised as that was from most people). The program enjoyed sales to overseas broadcasting companies, and Tony Hancock enjoyed a wide following in Australia. He is commemorated now on disc, and on a series of BBC Videos issued in 1985, including selected TV programs. *Steptoe and Son* was based on the life and times of a junk dealer and his son, another fellow with hopes of social status (and marriage). Here, too, high hopes were generally frustrated, but the series marvelously captured the affection, and tension, between the widower father and his son. Some 22 million people watched the program, at high points in the series' career, and *Steptoe and Son* passed into television folklore. The sets – showing a junk-filled house – were unlike any known to most television programs!

As already indicated, US programs continued to enjoy a high reputation in Britain, and coincidentally with *Steptoe and Son*, the US series *Wagon Train* reached an audience of around 14 millions. American programs scored in the areas of Westerns and 'cops and robbers,' so that shows like *Bonanza* and *Hawaii Five-O* have themselves enjoyed re-runs over the years. British producers developed the 'cops and robbers' format, but

early attempts were, in modern parlance, 'laid back' in the sense that they focused on the issues that triggered crime, and were about foot-patrol policemen. One of the earliest, and best remembered, was *Dixon of Dock Green*, set in a suburb of London, but not far from the city (hence the docks). Police Constable George Dixon, finely portrayed by a veteran actor and music-hall star, Jack Warner, was developed from a character in a popular British movie, *The Blue Lamp*. Ted (now Lord) Willis wrote the series, which in a way had more in common with a soap opera of the 1980s, than a contemporary crime-busting show like *Starsky and Hutch* (also popular in Britain).

Dixon of Dock Green included much practical advice to the general public, given in a sign-off by the lead actor. In face of the fast moving material coming from the US, however, new formats were clearly needed. So the BBC developed a highly popular program based on mobile patrols, *Z Cars*. Gritty feelings were evident, together with the everyday tensions of police work.

The 1960s is remembered as the decade of space exploration. Daytime television, still a much neglected aspect of the schedules, enjoyed a great boost when the largest-ever (daytime) television audience watched the lift-off from Cape

Canaveral on 5 May 1961. Telstar and its following relations reminded viewers that world-wide broadcasting was just around the corner, beginning with greater links with Europe via the Eurovision concept. Certainly, some fine work was done via Eurovision, and the December 1962 project, *Greatest Theater in the World*, is merely one example. Nine European nation-members of Eurovision carried the BBC-originated play by Terence Rattigan, *Heart to Heart*, using their own simultaneous translation of the script in sound. Strangely, the Eurovision idea never developed to the extent that it might have done. True, there were superb cultural programs like those featuring continental orchestras, and carried on the new BBC2. But for most people, the word Eurovision referred to the annual and sometimes mind-boggling Eurovision Song Contest, in which panels of juries in participating nations judged the merits of pop songs performed by national competitors. For many reasons, including the trans-Atlantic satellite link, British viewers tended to look toward the US for programing made outside Britain itself (though in due course, Australian programing appeared, popularly, in the schedules). President John F Kennedy's visit to Britain and Western Europe in May 1963 was reported to the US by the satellite link.

PREVIOUS SETS   M.SANTANA   SETS GAMES POINTS
C.M.PASARELL   SERVER
1 2 3 4

Above: *Tennis coverage of the All-England Championships at Wimbledon using the new color cameras.*

All of these initiatives could seem peripheral to the main issue of a new line system, and the advent of color. In 1960, the government invited Sir Harry Pilkington (later Lord Pilkington) to consider the future shape of broadcasting in Britain, in relation to the BBC Charter. Reporting in 1962, the Pilkington Committee recommended that the BBC should provide a new 625-line service (while still continuing the 405-line service for a long period, allowing for the slow change-over by consumers). Color should be added to this service as soon as possible. This new UHF service was not long in coming, and was offered in color from mid-1967, in part at least. BBC2 (625-line) as distinct from BBC1 (405-line) was opened on 20 April 1964, covering the London area, the south-east of England and the Midlands. Advance publicity and long-anticipated euphoria was somewhat muted by a breakdown in electricity on the opening night. However that was not recognized as any kind of omen, and BBC2 went from strength to strength. BBC2, though, was considered the thinking man's — and woman's — channel. It carried little light entertainment, but concentrated on documentaries, arts and education programs.

This allowed BBC2 to be marketed to a fairly well defined audience, those most likely to invest in a new set, even though the now obsolescent 405-line only model was still in good working order. *Festivals of Europe* used the Eurovision link to report on great music events, while celebrated actors appeared in *Great Acting*, a series that was in some respects a background to the flow of high quality, and often classic drama on BBC2. Much of this BBC2 television drama was welcomed in overseas markets, so that the BBC was able to create its own program marketing organization — an important aspect of its operations today.

Britain at last secured BBC2 in color, the first regularly-scheduled color TV service in Europe.

The full color service commenced at the beginning of December 1967; transmissions had been included in the BBC2 output since July, primarily the Wimbledon Lawn Tennis Championships. Although the new color service was properly heralded as a great victory for British know-how, it also opened the door to Japanese color television receivers, soon to take a large segment of the market and necessitating the close-down of the British plant. Although Japanese products were originally restricted to small screen sizes, models like the Sony 13-inch tube size Trinitron were highly regarded. In due time, some of the major Japanese countries were to open production in Britain itself, like Sony — which now makes color television sets at Bridgend, south Wales.

World events remained a main theme of television, and never more so than in coverage of the Apollo 11 expedition. The BBC set up a Space Unit to cover space exploration and linked events. Britain's own history of world exploration may have had something to do with the immense popularity of the television coverage of Neil Armstrong's small step onto the lunar surface. Throughout that period, and continuing to our own time, Patrick Moore's *The Sky at Night* and programs on space exploration have remained popular, and prompted a flow of BBC publications linked to the *Sky at Night* programs.

Commercial television still received occasional brickbats relating to trivia in the commercials or programing. As far back as 1959, there had been a flow of mail to the papers, complaining about the 'loudness' of television commercials, while scare stories about subliminal advertising had been raised by consumer activists. But commercial television excelled in many respects, not least in its news coverage, where it might have expected to become second to the BBC's own services.

Yet when the Independent Television News (ITN) transmitters broadcast the thousandth weeknight edition of *News at Ten* in 1971, it had already secured a consistent audience of around 15 million, making it the most popular single news program in Britain. There was no doubt a friendly rivalry between the BBC and ITV in news and outside broadcasts. Granada Television described the work of its *Travelling Eye* teams in its first annual report in 1958, but the outside broadcast *par excellence* might be attributed to the BBC in relation to the 1970 Munich Olympics. In 170 hours of transmission, a small army of commentators, camera crews, technical personnel and back-up staff were used, together with 160 cameras, 23 mobile transmission units, seven color studios, and some 50 video recorders. Sadly, the Munich Olympics was to be remembered as much by a terrorist attack upon a team of participating athletes; in some ways that was symbol of the time. Increased, more effective news coverage did not always make for confidence in the state of the world.

The less-than-idealistic nature of man was

reflected in drama, too. Among the most popular series coming from commercial television during this period were *The Main Chance* (about the life of a somewhat aggressive solicitor, David Main) and *The Plane Makers* (management in-fighting in the aircraft industry).

Children's programing continued to occupy a high priority in the BBC output – and as the Corporation had built up expertise in this field from the earliest days of radio, that is hardly surprising. *Blue Peter*, the mid-week tea-time (5 PM) magazine and knowledge program, had a consistent audience of around nine million,

triggering a flow of good works and good deeds among viewers who have raised great sums for good causes over the years. *Jackanory* utilized the style and talents of actors, actresses, writers and, in a few cases, non-professionals (including children) in reading stories to the camera, together with drawings and other art work illustration. This quarter-hour program introduced children to books that they might otherwise have missed. *Blue Peter* and *Jackanory*, like *News at Ten*, show no sign of losing their popularity in the mid-1980s.

Major series like Dr Kenneth Clark's *Civilisation*

Above: *On the first program, the crew of BBC's* Breakfast TV *was joined by NBC's* Today *show host, Jane Pauley (left).*
Right: *The TV-am presenters relax after their first broadcast — Left to right: Robert Kee, Angela Rippon, David Frost, Anna Ford and Michael Parkinson.*

and Dr Jacob Bronowski's *Ascent of Man* have shown the possibilities of television as a cultural medium, BBC2 having been most active in promotion of this kind of material. BBC2 has also carried Open University programs (*i.e.* for correspondence courses linked to Open University degree and other courses) but the use of the medium for formal educational purposes is limited. After some 40 years of post-war television, tastes seem to change little, though more violence is certainly screened, in drama as well as news coverage of real events. Viewing habits have considerably changed, to the extent that some homes rarely have a meal around the table as in previous generations, but snatch snacks while watching television. Research during the 1970s suggested that, as an average, the British watched television (*i.e.* per head of population)

some $18\frac{1}{2}$ hours a week, around $9\frac{3}{4}$ hours of BBC, and $8\frac{3}{4}$ hours of commercial television (ITV).

Daytime viewing has never been a major aspect of television in Britain, though women's programing in afternoon segments has attempted to build up an audience. It is believed, in the industry itself, that British housewives generally like to be active around the house, and feel somewhat guilty at 'just sitting and watching television.'

Problems in creating new television habits were encountered as both the BBC and a new commercial company, TV-am, introduced breakfast television a few years ago. Beginning with the worthy object of offering early morning news and serious interest short segment material (plus commercials) TV-am ran into considerable

problems, requiring a re-orientation of its planning and new management before moving into a profit-making potential. Today, TV-am is reckoned to have some two-thirds of the total breakfast television audience, around 21 million. The BBC has been urged to abandon its breakfast television service, since it seems likely to remain a minority interest.

Cable television, too, has shown itself hardly likely to be profitable, to any marked extent in the short term. The Hunt Report on Cable in 1982 recommended an opening up of cable television possibilities, suggesting that an adult education channel might be allowed, with appropriate safeguards. The Conservative government, considering the Report, did not approve of any adult educational channel, but quickly moved to make local cable television services possible. However, subsequent legislation on taxation relating to capital allowances added to a discouraging environment, and although cable operations have started in various parts of the country, results in terms of consumer take-up have often been disappointing. With the excellent off-air availability of BBC/ITV signals in most parts of Britain, consumers have tended to find their television interests fulfilled by the existing four channels, plus, perhaps, home video. Similarly, Britain's hopes for DBS (direct broadcast by satellite) have

run into difficulties, relating to initial investment cost, and the uncertainty about their recovery in DBS operations. Original aspirations for a two channel service by the BBC by 1976 were abandoned, together with a later 'Consortium of 21' plan. At the close of 1985, discussions on other DBS possibilities were begun. In television today, nothing is certain except uncertainty. The BBC – having had its request for a £68 per annum consumer license modified by the government to £58 – is planning its own economies, yet at the same time plans to extend daytime transmission, using high quality archive material and original programing.

Many of the original ideas of John Logie Baird came to nothing. Few will recall now his experiments with stereoscopic television in the 1930s. First, he used signals transmitted from the Crystal Palace for a demonstration to a London cinema audience in 1936. Later, he attempted similar three-dimensional experiments with high definition color, but at the time (1942) the government had more pressing matters on its mind. Movie theaters have hardly succeeded with three dimensional presentations, and they have more facilities than that available to the home viewer.

With all the interest in video techniques today, so-called '3-D' is still rated as something of a gimmick. Baird's view that television could help

Above: The Morecambe and Wise Christmas Show. *Ernie Wise is kissing the hand of guest Sir Ralph Richardson, while Eric Morecambe (wearing mustache) and Robert Hardy look on.*

the movies has hardly been developed, apart from large screen transmissions of major sports events by satellite to selected sites. True, British cinemas benefited from television series which triggered feature films with the same characters. *Dad's Army*, a highly successful British television series, based on the adventures of volunteers in the Home Guard (during World War II), was used to generate a full length feature film for theater distribution, while the commercial television series *On The Buses* produced *two* movies. *Till Death Us Do Part* was also adapted for films, with an original script, but using the familiar television characters.

British television secured a flow of full length feature films following the initial breaching of the distributor log-jam in the early days of commercial television. Some of the excellent prewar productions by Sir Alexander Korda were secured for transmission on commercial television, and thereafter feature films offered a welcome alternative to more recent television production. Channel Four, set up to offer a viable alternative to the first commercial network, commissioned films and has in other ways encouraged independent producers. In future times, it will be seen that Channel Four was an important catalyst in the history of British television, moving, in part at least, the production of programing outside the older management structures and into a diversity of independent production units, of varying size, interests and experience.

Among top performers in the history of British television were Eric Morecambe and Ernie Wise, who appeared in their own shows on both channels. Although Eric died from a heart attack earlier in the 1980s, selections from the programs have been released on BBC Video, and re-runs are included in the schedules. Brought up in the music hall tradition, the two comics admitted their original inspiration as coming from Hollywood greats like Abbott and Costello, Laurel and Hardy, but they clearly had their own original style. Among the delights of their shows were the playlets presented with great aplomb but coupled with well-planned disaster. Ernie Wise, who is still busy in show business, allegedly wrote several plays in the course of a single afternoon. Benny Hill is also enjoying a consistent popularity with his *Benny Hill Show* which has, among other matters, an abundance of pretty girls. Benny Hill represents the robust stream of British humor, in some respects reminiscent of music hall.

A great deal of comedy was based on literature, as in the case of the several programs based on the works of P G Wodehouse. First of these was *The World of Wooster* on BBC2 in 1964. Later, *Wodehouse Playhouse* provided a great showcase for miscellaneous pieces. BBC2 found another winner in the 1960s, with *The World of Beachcomber* based on a long-running newspaper comment column and books by 'Beachcomber' (J B Morton). Humor was sometimes based on a

Above: *BBC's* What's My Line? *On the panel, left to right: Lady Barnett, Michael Denison, Barbara Kelly and Gilbert Harding.*

Left: *A revival of Eamonn Andrews' (left) popular program,* This Is Your Life *in 1980. The guest (on right) is Derek Jameson.*

Above: *British television's most popular host — Terry Wogan.*

241

group of characters, as in *All Gas and Gaiters*, a lively series about a group of Anglican clergymen in a cloistered retreat – or in social comment, *The Likely Lads*, also on BBC, being the on-going record of two young men out to make good in modern Britain (a theme later developed in *The Liver Birds*, about two young women sharing a flat in Liverpool).

MGM Television's *Dr Kildare* series was popular in Britain, and as one of the early home-made soap operas had a hospital theme (*Emergency Ward Ten*) that was only to be expected. Medical interest programs developed in the 1960s, with well-informed presentations relating to hospital life and surgery. On a fictional level, one of the most popular programs was *Dr Finlay's Casebook*, written by A J Cronin, and based on the life of a reforming young doctor, Dr Finlay, working with an older colleague, Dr Cameron, in Scotland during the 1920s. Period backgrounds have always attracted large audiences in Britain, one reason why television drama (based on classic works by Shakespeare, Tolstoy, Shaw and other great writers) proved so successful.

One of the most successful TV series in Britain was *The Forsyte Saga*, which gave a great impetus to early BBC2 color transmissions. Shown on Sunday evenings, it occasionally required clergymen to close their evensong services promptly in order to allow the congregation to reach home in time for the opening credits at 7:15 PM. *The Forsyte Saga* won the Silver Medal of the Royal Television Society, and was certainly faithful to the Galsworthy text.

Several attempts to involve the viewing public have been included in 'vox populi' programing, though with relatively little success. In 1972, the BBC introduced *Talkback*, which gave members of a TV audience opportunity to express their views. Only in relatively recent years has anything approaching an effective format been devised – on Channel Four, where a half-hour *Right to Reply* program invites viewers into the studio, to discuss programs with producers. In addition, two booths are provided, one in London and the other in Glasgow, to permit people to come in off the street and videotape their views in private (some of these being selected for broadcast).

Consumer-information programing has developed in recent years, too, and again Channel Four has shown a pioneering spirit with its investigative *4 What It's Worth*. Reporters track down the wayward, and handle complaints from consumers who have failed to secure aid through other initiatives. Like other programs, *4 What It's Worth* offers a free monthly information sheet, relating to information given on the program. Many programs now offer fact sheets, free (though requiring postage) and covering various self-help activities. The increase in books, videotapes and teaching kits is one of the more interesting aspects of television. Most important series, of a documentary or educational nature, now offer an optional publication, often on sale at newsstands.

Television programs of former years may fade away, but in Britain only on a temporary basis. Re-runs of 'comedy classics' are included in peak time scheduling, especially on BBC channels; the BBC Video Catalogue also reveals some of yesteryear's best-loved shows.

Among television legends recently released on home video are programs from *Hancock's Half-Hour* (BBC), which had already established itself as one of the most popular sitcoms on BBC radio when it moved to television in 1956. Written by two of television's most prolific playwrights, Ray Galton and Alan Simpson, the series starred Tony Hancock, an erstwhile though usually unsuccessful social climber living in Railway Cuttings, East Cheam. A bachelor approaching middle age, Tony Hancock was portrayed as a lugubrious man with high hopes of artistic success and perhaps even fame. However, in this regard, his attempts at self-assertion were frustrated by a

Above: *Basil Fawlty (John Cleese), observed by his wife Sybil (Prunella Scales) attempts to serve a gourmet meal at* Fawlty Towers.
Top: Monty Python's Flying Circus: *Michael Palin, Graham Chapman, John Cleese, Eric Idle and Terry Jones.*
Opposite: *Four different actors have played* Dr Who, *among them Peter Davison (top) and Tom Baker (below).*

get-rich-quick fellow played by Sid James — a gravel-voiced actor from South Africa whose flair in movie comedy contributed to the enormous success of the *Carry On* movies. Tony Hancock decided against making further TV shows in 1961, perhaps feeling that the somewhat claustrophobic format had exhausted the possibilities. In fact the shows remained legendary, and represent the actor's best work. Ray Galton and Alan Simpson moved on to create another winner, *Steptoe and Son* (BBC) which focused on the domestic disasters of a junk-man and his son, the younger man not unlike Hancock in his search for artistic satisfaction — and a wife who could cook.

The Hancock show had appeared on TV in the year of the Suez Crisis, when Britain discovered that its international power was now severely restricted, at least by way of military adventures. In the aftermath of Suez, Britons took a more jaundiced view of themselves and their institutions. Among the more evident examples of a less respectful society was Johnny Speight's series *Till Death Us Do Part* (BBC) starring Warren Mitchell as Alf Garnett, an aging Londoner ready to inflict his family with torrents of ill-informed comment about anything that came to mind. The program worked partly on the basis of its innovative character, and the writer had certainly lively insight into the kind of conversation one might overhear on the bus or in the pub. Casting was also good, with Dandy Nichols as Alf's long-suffering wife, Una Stubbs as his daughter and Anthony Booth as the Liverpudlian 'layabout' son-in-law. During a second series of the popular show in 1967, audiences reached around 18 million.

Humor of a somewhat abrasive variety found a large public during the 1970s in the satiric show, *Monty Python's Flying Circus* (BBC), which lampooned many institutions and characters. The British preoccupation with establishing organizations to solve social problems, for example, was target of an item, 'The Ministry of Silly Walks,' showing how the art of silly walking was now being organized by a new government department. John Cleese, one of the stars of the show, went on to write, with his wife and co-star, Connie Booth, a series which satirized the worst examples of British hotel life, *Fawlty Towers*. Cleese was a hotel proprietor Basil Fawlty, who possessed a combination of dull wit and fast temper. Here, as in many other comedy shows on both BBC and ITV, the script was noted for its inherent wit; and this, indeed, may be one of the keys to success on British television. Nat Hiken's work on *Sergeant Bilko* (*The Phil Silvers Show*) has been long appreciated in Britain, partly because of its pace.

Nostalgia and the search for a good life have combined in rural program formats, like *The Good Life* in Britain (shown in the US as *Good Neighbors*) and *Green Acres* in the USA. *The Good Life* (BBC) starred Richard Briers and Felicity

Kendal as a former advertising man and his wife, who opt for self-sufficiency, *Mother Earth News* style, but in a respectable commuter suburb of London. The foils for their adventures are their affluent neighbors, played by Penelope Keith and Paul Eddington.

Dad's Army (BBC) starred Arthur Lowe as bank manager turned part-time platoon commander of a Home Guard unit during World War II. The Home Guard consisted of men over army call-up age (plus the occasional teenager) who were required to defend the country in the event of invasion. Among the many veteran actors in the series were Arnold Ridley (who wrote the famous comedy play, *The Ghost Train*), John le Mesurier, and Clive Dunn as the local town butcher Lance-Corporal Jones, a quizzical character who reportedly fought in the Boer War. Jimmy Perry, with David Croft, also wrote another nostalgic series, *Hi-De-Hi!* (BBC) set in a holiday camp during the 1950s, before Britons went abroad for their holidays. The somewhat regimented and occasionally disaster-strewn life of holiday camp entertainment was beautifully captured in the series, which has enjoyed re-runs. Although there have been small variations in casting, *Hi De Hi*, like *Dad's Army*, is almost a television repertory company, with many characters present throughout the series.

Dick Clement and Ian la Frenais — two of Britain's top writers — created a different style of nostalgia with *The Likely Lads* (BBC), starring James Bolam and Rodney Bewes as two young men growing up in the north of England. James Bolam, a somewhat abrasive character, exhibited working class mores while Rodney Bewes played the 'business game' and at the same time tried to channel the energies of his friend into 'normal ambitions.' Bolam, as Terry, wound up in the army, and with a broken marriage, while Bewes, as Bob, seemed set for the affluent lifestyle thought to be a main purpose in life in modern Britain. In some respects, the program attacked the attitudes of modern Britain: the lack of any vision beyond the merely material.

This critique was excellently presented in *The Fall and Rise of Reginald Perrin*, which will no doubt prove to be as great a legend as the Hancock shows. Written by David Nobbs, the show included one of Britain's most competent and popular actors, Leonard Rossiter, as Reginald Perrin, executive in a food novelty company. As a member of middle management, Perrin was called upon once to oversee advertising for a new range of exotic flavor desserts, in spite of his imminent mental breakdown. At other times an episode would reveal the general frivolity of his life. Superb casting included John Barron as the head of Sunshine Desserts, a man with almost as much eccentricity as Perrin himself. Such programs fall into a light-entertainment category in terms of definition, but represent a form of social comment.

In similar vein, *Porridge* (BBC), written by

Clement and la Frenais, was set in one of Britain's long out-dated and crumbling Victorian prisons, with Ronnie Barker as Fletch, a somewhat habitual thief who was determined that this would be his last stretch. His cell-mate, the youthful first offender Godber (played by Richard Beckinsale) looked to Fletch for occasional help, and the series was thus about relationships inside prison. There were many fine cameo performances in this series, including Peter Vaughan as Harry Grout, the prison 'baron.' Ronnie Barker is one of British television's best-known actors, and his other work has included *Open All Hours* (BBC) about the ups and downs of a retail store proprietor, Arkwright, who has an eye on the district nurse across the street. Incidentally, the role of the district nurse brought well-earned compliments to actress Linda Baron.

Roy Clarke, another of Britain's top writers, was responsible for *Last of The Summer Wine* (BBC) which, among much else, put the North Country town of Carnforth onto the tourist map. The series, set in Carnforth, followed the adventures of three old-timers: Compo (Bill Owen), Clegg (Peter Sallis) and Foggy (Brian Wilde). Characters were well-drawn with fine contrast, Compo being a somewhat untidy character who liked a good laugh, while Foggy was a self-respecting fellow who talked of his important work in the armed services (he was in fact, a sign-writer). Brian Wilde had also starred in *Porridge* as a somewhat ineffectual prison officer, and has an impressive list of television credits. Bill Owen has been a film actor over many years, and Peter

Above: *Kynaston Reeves (as Mr Quelch, the Form Master) on the ground after bumping into Gerald Campion as Billy Bunter.*
Opposite top: Love Thy Neighbour *with Keith Marsh, Rudolph Walker, Nina Baden-Semper, Kate Williams, Jack Smethurst and Tommy Godfrey.*
Opposite bottom: *Jimmy Edwards with some of his pupils in the comedy* Whack-O.

Sallis is well-known for stage and screen roles. Another 'star' of the show is the scenery around Carnforth, the hills and lanes of north England — plus the occasional old car and local eccentric. Compo's high regard for a respectable married lady, Nora is one of the sub-themes in the series.

Commercial television (ITV) also presented many fine comedy programs, including *Love Thy Neighbour*, which looked at the relationship between two families — one white, the other black. Tackling a serious problem — that of harmony between ethnic groups in Britain — the series was noteworthy for its acting. The white couple, played by Kate Williams and Jack Smethurst, managed to get along, after various misunderstandings, with their recent arrivals in the next house up the street. Both performers were Joint ITV Personalities in the 1973 Variety Club Awards, and Nina Baden-Semper, the black wife, was named as Outstanding New Female Personality in the same year.

Please Sir (ITV) followed the career of a somewhat idealistic but rather dim school-teacher in a modern comprehensive school. School comedies are not new in British entertainment. In the early days of television, the best-selling *Billy Bunter* stories, written by Frank Richards, were adapted for British television, Gerald Campion playing the part of the 'fat boy of the Remove.' According to reports of the time, city gentlemen left work early in order to reach home in time for transmissions on the Children's Output on BBC (then the only channel). Later, well-known television comic Jimmy Edwards starred in *Whack-O*, a

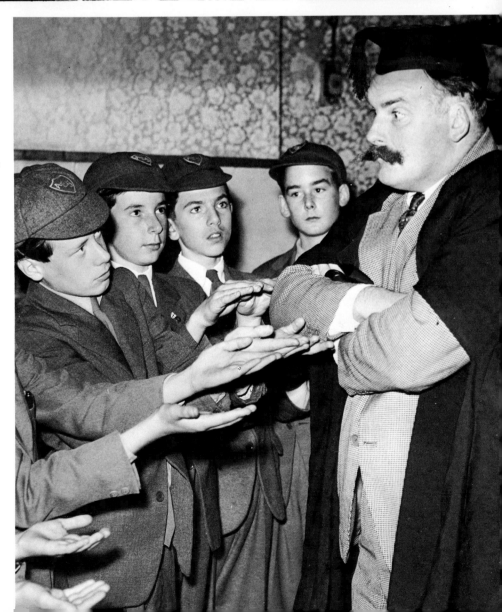

series set in a seedy public school, Chistlehurst (no relation to any real-life academy or institution) with veteran Arthur Howard as his somewhat timid assistant. It was good knock-about comedy. More recently, BBC's *Grange Hill* proved a popular early evening serial, based on life in a large comprehensive school. With teenage actors, the series achieved a high degree of realism, with humor and real life situations.

ITV captured the attention of film and TV buffs, as well as collectors, with shows like *Movie Memories*, presented by Roy Hudd. This half-hour program in front of a studio audience recalled the movie-going pleasures of yesteryear including real-life experiences of movie projectionists and usherettes, and movie clips and interviews with famous old-time stars. Hudd became noted for his work in music-hall research and presentations. One of television's most successful shows was *Those Were The Days*, only recently brought to a final conclusion. Reviving the classic period of British music hall, the show came from the handsome setting of The City Varieties, Leeds, Yorkshire, with re-creations of famous music-hall acts, plus some contemporary stars in speciality routines. The audience for this BBC program dressed in period costume, thereby achieving further realism for a singularly merry show.

Looks Familiar (ITV) also proved a lively format for the recollection of great works in movies, radio, song-writing and other media. A trio of guest panelists (usually stars from radio, television or films) were invited to identify memorabilia, film clips, songs and so on. The delight of the program was the memories provided by guests, relating to their own careers and friendships with well-known stars. Devised by Denis Gifford – a well-known writer on comic books, radio and TV of yesteryear . . . *Looks Familiar* was hosted by Dennis Norden who, with Frank Muir, wrote many highly successful radio and TV series.

Quiz shows and panel games have long flourished on television on both national channels, but few seem destined for immortality in Television's Hall of Fame. *What's My Line?* was one of the longest-running shows, and a similar trans-Atlantic show (in terms of origins) *This Is Your Life* (ITV), was one of Britain's most popular programs. *Call My Bluff* (BBC), devised by Mark Goodson, was a contest between two panels, relating to definitions of unusual words; *My Music* (BBC) had two celebrity teams involved in identifying music, instruments, ephemera and other items.

Pop music has been featured in many shows, from *Juke Box Jury* in the 1950s, to the latest format, *The Tube*, created by Tyne Tees Television for Channel Four – a 90-minute program featuring both new groups and well-established artists.

Above: *Two of the satirical puppets on* Spitting Image – *Norman Tebbitt and Margaret Thatcher.*
Opposite top: *A typical number on* The Benny Hill Show.
Opposite bottom: *A variety act from* The Tube.

BBC's *Old Grey Whistle Test* was an hour-long program looking at current work in popular music, and *Top of The Pops*, the chart-oriented show on BBC, was probably the most popular of any pop program ever on British television.

Well-known comedians like Benny Hill created formats that proved popular throughout the world. The late Eric Morecambe, with his partner, Ernie Wise, was highly esteemed in Britain, *The Morecambe and Wise Show* attracting large audiences in both BBC and ITV presentations.

Drama should need little introduction, seeing that BBC productions were world-acknowledged in the early days of television. ITV, too, secured world markets for programs like *Upstairs, Downstairs,* the story of a middle-class family during changing times earlier this century.

With perhaps an innate feel for historic interest subjects, television producers excelled in tackling classic works. *The Age of Kings,* a 13-part serial based on Shakespeare's plays, created a new sense of television's possibilities in the early 1960s. Later, Keith Michell was to portray another monarch, in *The Six Wives of Henry VIII* (BBC, 1971). Truly a legend almost before the cathode-ray tube faded was the 1960s' production of *The Forsyte Saga* (BBC), Donald Wilson's adaptation of John Galsworthy's epic work. So popular was the series that it had to be repeated on BBC1 (405 line) following its premiere on

Above: *Reginald Bosanquet of the* News at Ten *on ITV.*
Above right: *Television was at the Munich Olympics in 1972 when the Israeli athletes were being held hostage by hooded figures.*
Opposite: *Stephanie Beecham starred in Central TV's serial* Connie.

BBC2 (625 line). In the cast were Kenneth More, a highly acclaimed British movie actor, who played Jolyon; Nyree Dawn Porter and Eric Porter also starred. Beautiful to behold, this was also the first major drama series to be presented in color. Production standards were high, and according to reports, church congregations ended their meetings precisely on time in order to reach home in time for opening credits — Sunday evenings at 7:15.

War and Peace (BBC) was adapted by Jack Pullman in 1972 as a 26-part series based on Tolstoy's masterful work. Commercial television also showed a flair for period drama, though this was sometimes under-rated. *Inheritance*, based on the books by Phyllis Bentley, superbly captured the spirit of industrial Britain struggling towards a wider democracy.

A sense of period has been evident in less ambitious work, too. Many popular series such as the original *Stories from Kipling* with Joss Ackland (BBC), showed an imaginative approach to small-screen presentation. Sherlock Holmes, for example, was well portrayed by Douglas Wilmer in a BBC series, the worthy Dr Watson played by Nigel Stock. ITV offered another series of Victorian detective work with its *Sergeant Cluff* series. The works of Charles Dickens have also been often serialized, with excellent portrayals of hard times during the great days of the British Empire.

Although US programs like *77 Sunset Strip* and *Perry Mason* set a standard of slickness and style

not always seen in British productions, in the late 1950s/early 1960s some British series achieved noteworthy quality. *Maigret*, the series of French detective mysteries based on the books of Georges Simenon, was one of the most popular programs of the early 1960s, with Rupert Davies playing the French detective. Another BBC series followed the life and deeds of mobile patrolmen in *Z Cars*, which in 1962 brought a new realism to the concept of police work to British viewers. Set in the dockland area of Liverpool, the series showed policemen as fallible, hard-working human beings . . . not saints. Controversial at the time, *Z Cars* would perhaps be considered routine material today, but casting was excellent, and the backgrounds authentic.

From its inception, television gave playwrights opportunity to explore the new electronic medium, and among the excellent initiatives was commercial television's *Armchair Theatre*. A Midlands regional (ATV) series encouraged major writers like Harold Pinter and Alun Owen to write for the new medium.

During the 1980s, major series like *Brideshead Revisited* and *The Jewel in the Crown* made by Granada (ITV) have shown that quality can still be the name of the game in a medium sometimes described as 'the least worst television in the world.' Wit and reality are combined in series like *Rumpole of the Bailey* (ITV) written by barrister-turned-playwright John Mortimer. That television is able to produce this kind of work is itself indication of dedication among much trivia.

News and documentary programs continue to play an important role in the schedules. The longest running and most prestigious program in this field is the BBC Monday evening *Panorama*, a style of investigative journalism that has maintained very high standards of reportage. *News At Ten* was launched on commercial television stations on 3 July 1967, and represented a breakthrough in news coverage. Use of satellite links and other innovations has made this 'a landmark in independent broadcasting,' as it was described in a retrospective article in *Airwaves: The Quarterly Journal of the Independent Broadcasting Authority* (Autumn 1985). Magazine-type programs, including background to news as well as current-affairs material of a lighter nature, go back to the prewar days. In post-war Britain, the BBC introduced the early evening *Tonight* when the early evening 'quiet time' (when screens went dark

while the children were put to bed) was abandoned. This magazine program was in its way one of the most successful approaches to handling early-evening television, and some who worked on the program have gone on to distinguished television careers; Alan Whicker, well known for his *Whicker's World* series (ITV) began his globe-trotting work for television reportage, during the great days of *Tonight* as a young foreign correspondent.

In educational and historic-interest programing, there were major series like *The World At War* (ITV), which followed the course of World War II, and innovative programs like *Timewatch* (BBC), which transported viewers back in time — the television set as a time machine — enabling examination of issues in history, in Britain and elsewhere. Programs for ethnic minorities, unknown in Britain in the 1960s, are now a regular aspect of schedules, while Channel Four (the second commercial channel) in Wales has a large component of Welsh language output. Values and traditions are much questioned in television, and no one would deny that times have changed since the days of John Logie Baird's experiments. Abandoning of some social mores has hardly helped the cohesiveness of the family or of the nation, but it would be amiss merely to blame television for that. In any case, religious programing, in terms of broadcast services, discussion programs and features like *Jesus of Nazareth* (ITV), which featured Robert Powell as Jesus, have brought major issues of belief to the forefront.

Television in Britain reflects the truth of the old saying, 'Nothing is constant except change.' At the same time, it also attempts to confirm that Nothing is better than excellence.

Acknowledgments

The author and publisher would like to thank the following people who helped in the preparation of this book: Mike Rose, who designed it; Thomas G Aylesworth, who edited it; Mary R Raho and Donna Cornell who did the picture research; and Ron Watson who compiled the index.

BBC Hulton Picture Library: 14, 16 (top), 42, 214, 216, 219 (bottom), 220 (bottom), 226, 229
Marcello Bertinetti: 181 (bottom).
Bettmann Archive: 136 (bottom left), 137 (bottom).
Bison Picture Library: 5, 10 (bottom), 11 (bottom), 17, 23 (bottom), 32–33, 39, 46, 48, 52–53, 56, 57, 58–59, 60, 63 (bottom), 64, 65, 77, 81, 84, 85 (bottom), 90, 91, 96, 97 (top and bottom), 98, 100 (bottom), 101, 103, 104, 105 (top and bottom right), 106–107, 108, 109 (bottom), 111 (bottom), 115 (bottom), 120, 121, 124 (top), 140, 141, 144 (left), 145, 146, 147 (top left), 149 (bottom), 150, 151 (bottom), 153, 154 (bottom), 157, 158 (top), 159, 165 (top), 167, 169, 170 (top), 178, 180, 183, 184–185, 187, 189, 190, 191, 195 (top), 196, 198, 202, 203 (top right), 248 (left).
CBS: 35 (top).
Central Independent Television: 246, 249.
Channel 4 Television: 247 (bottom).
Foto Fantasies: 2 (left bottom and center top) 2–3, 4 (right), 25, 30 (left), 34, 35 (bottom), 38 (bottom), 51, 60, 62, 63 (top), 69 (bottom), 71, 72, 73, 74, 75, 76, 78, 79 (top), 80, 85 (top), 86, 88, 97 (center), 99, 100 (top), 102, 105 (bottom left), 109 (left), 110, 111 (top), 112, 113, 114, 115 (top), 116 (bottom), 117, 118, 119, 124, 125 (top), 127, 128, 129, 142, 143, 144 (right), 146 (top and bottom right), 147 (top right and bottom), 148, 149 (top), 151 (top), 152 (top), 154 (top), 154, 155, 156, 158 (bottom), 160, 161, 162, 163, 164, 165 (bottom), 166, 168, 170, 171 (top), 173 (bottom), 174, 175 (top), 176, 179 (all three), 182, 186, 188, 193, 195 (bottom), 197 (top), 199, 200, 201, 203 (top and bottom left), 204, 205, 206, 208, 210, 211 (top), 242, 243 (bottom).
Granada Television: 212–213, 230, 231, 250–251.
Lyndon Baines Johnson Library: 135.
John F Kennedy Library: 130 (top).
Rick Marschall: 18, 126 (bottom), 174, 194, 243 (top).
Museum of Modern Art Film Stills Archives: 15 (top), 45 (right).
National Baseball Library, Cooperstown, New York: 130 (bottom left).
NBC: 7, 12, 13, 15 (bottom), 19, 33 (top), 47 (bottom).
Peter Newark's Historical Pictures: 8, 9, 10 (top), 31, 131 (top), 215.
Phototèque: 20, 21, 22, 23 (top left), 26, 27, 28–29, 30 (right), 33 (bottom), 36, 37, 38 (top), 40–41, 43, 44, 45 (left), 47 (top), 49, 50, 54, 55, 68, 69 (top), 70, 79 (bottom), 87, 89, 92, 127 (bottom right and left), 130 (bottom right), 131 (bottom), 134, 136, 137 (top), 152 (bottom), 170 (bottom), 172, 173 (top), 176 (bottom), 181, 192, 197 (bottom), 209, 211 (bottom).
RCA: 7.
Oral Roberts Evangelistic Association, Incorporated: 207 (top right).
S & G Press Agency Ltd.: 11 (top), 16 (bottom), 116 (top), 217 (top), 220 (top), 223 (bottom), 224, 225, 227 (bottom), 232, 233, 234, 235, 236, 237, 238, 239, 240, 241, 244, 245 (bottom).
Thames Television: 2 (right bottom), 3 (center), 4 (left), 240–241, 245 (top), 247 (top), 250.
TPS/Central Press: 219 (top), 222.
TPS/Fox: 94–5, 223 (top), 227 (top).
TPS/Keystone: 217 (bottom), 221, 248 (right).
UPI/Bettmann Newsphotos: 3 (top right), 207 (top left).